WHELDON'S
COSTING SIMPLIFIED

WHELDON'S
COSTING SIMPLIFIED

L. W. J. OWLER
FCIS, ACMA, FSS

and

J. L. BROWN
MSc, FCMA, FCCA, FBIM

SIXTH EDITION

Pitman

PITMAN PUBLISHING
128 Long Acre, London WC2E 9AN

A Division of Longman Group UK Limited

© Macdonald & Evans Ltd 1985

Sixth edition first published in Great Britain 1985
Reprinted 1987, 1989

British Library Cataloguing in Publication Data
Wheldon, Harold J
Wheldon's costing simplified — 6th ed.
1. Cost accounting
I. Title   II. Owler, L. W. J.   III Brown, J. L.
657'.42   HF5686.C8
ISBN 0 273 02765 4
ISBN 0 273 02766 2 (ISE)

Typeset by Anneset, Weston-super-Mare, Avon
Produced by Longman Group (FE) Ltd
Printed in Hong Kong

Preface to the Sixth Edition

THIS book was rewritten for the third edition in order to provide an introduction to the subject of cost accounting for those who are preparing for the preparatory examinations of the professional bodies, and those of the Royal Society of Arts, London Chamber of Commerce and other bodies, in which cost accounting is included as part of the normal accounting course.

It is gratifying to find that these aims appear to have been achieved. The authors are particularly pleased that many readers are engaged in industry, but not necessarily in the cost accounting field. The pressure of "cost-consciousness" in all sections of industry makes executives aware of the necessity of some knowledge of the subject, and this book gives them what they require.

In the sixth edition the opportunity has been taken to bring the text up to date and to provide a number of recent questions. In response to many requests from readers, suggested answers have been provided for all numerical questions. It is hoped that these will be useful to all examination candidates.

All the professional bodies approached have readily given their consent to the use of their examination papers—*see* the code below.

ACA	Chartered Association of Certified Accountants.
AIA	Association of International Accountants.
BIM	British Institute of Management.
ICAEW	Institute of Chartered Accountants of England and Wales.
ICAS	Institute of Chartered Accountants in Scotland.
ICSA	Institute of Chartered Secretaries and Administrators.
SCCA	Society of Company and Commercial Accountants.
IAADP	Institute of Book-keepers and Related Data Processing (now The Institute of Administrative Accounting and Data Processing).
ICMA	Chartered Institute of Management Accountants.
LCCI	London Chamber of Commerce.
RSA	Royal Society of Arts.

1984

LWJO
JLB

v

Contents

vii

List of Illustrations

Chapter 1

Introduction

Definition of Cost Accounting

WHEN cost accountants speak of cost accounting they have in mind the ascertainment of:

(a) the cost of manufacturing a product; or
(b) the cost of giving a service; or
(c) the way in which costs can be controlled.

In elementary book-keeping we begin by considering the books kept by a single trader who purchases goods and then resells them at a profit. In such cases the balance sheet, together with the trading and profit and loss account, are quite sufficient to reveal the financial position of the trader.

Later on, however, we reach the stage of preparing manufacturing accounts, and from these accounts we are able to discover the cost of manufacture of the finished goods. However, if several classes of goods are manufactured we must have an analysed manufacturing account, and this will demand much greater attention to detail.

It is this detailed analysis of expenditure and sales which constitutes the subject of cost accounting in the sense of (a) above.

The Cost Accounts

From what has been said, it will be seen that cost accounting is an extension of ordinary financial accounting, and uses the same principles of debit and credit. Indeed, it is by no means necessary to have a separate set of cost accounting books, and the growing practice is to have only one system of accounts, which may be so designed as to give the necessary information:

(a) to draw up normal financial accounts; and
(b) to compile the cost statements and cost data required.

1

Such a scheme is illustrated in regard to materials in Figure 1. It will be seen that we have all the necessary information about materials to begin the preparation of a manufacturing account:

(*a*) opening stock (if any);
(*b*) *Add* purchases;
(*c*) *Less* closing stock;

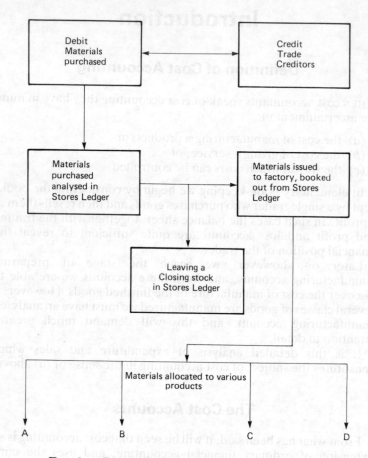

FIG. 1.—*Diagram to illustrate flow of materials*

and we also are building up the cost of the materials used in the products made.

Cost and Prices

One of the reasons why manufacturers introduce a cost accounting system into their businesses is the hope that it will help them in fixing the selling prices. Thus, if they find that the cost of manufacture of an article is £3.00 and they want to make a profit of 25% on sales, they will reason that the £3.00 is 75% of the sales value, and that the profit is equal to the addition of £1.00 to the cost (since 25% is one-third of 75%). The selling price would thus be

$$£3.00 \text{ plus } £1.00 = £4.00$$

However, a manufacturer nowadays has often no power to dictate his price to the market. There are others in competition with him, and he has to accept the market price.

Cost accounting now really begins to be of service, for it will enable the manufacturer to see more clearly how he may reduce his costs to meet the conditions with which he is faced.

Costs and Profits

The maintenance and improvement of profit margins will be one of the main concerns of the manufacturer. He will use his cost accounting system to reveal not only the directions in which he may reduce his usage of labour and materials, but also the degree to which wastage and inefficiencies are causing excessive costs.

Example

Costs may show that a product has required

5 units of material at £3   £15
30 hours labour at £1   £30

If this is considered too high, a cheaper material at £2.50 may be tried instead, and reorganisation of methods may allow the product to be made in 25 hours.

Continuous comparison of costs, period with period, may ultimately go to prove that only 4½ units of material are really required, and that the elimination of lost time through stoppages of the machinery will save another 5 hours from the time taken.

The maintenance of profits depends partly on the stability of selling prices, but it also depends on the maintenance of steady costs. In times of prosperity, when business is brisk, it is not difficult to make a profit, but the less-prudent businessman often then fails to realise the benefit of continuing to exercise a strict control over his costs, and this may easily lead to smaller profits being obtained than could have been secured.

Purposes of Cost Accounts

The main purposes of cost accounts may now be summarised.

(a) To arrive at the cost of production of every unit, job, process, operation, or department, by close analysis of all expenditure.

(b) To indicate to management any inefficiencies and waste which are thereby revealed.

(c) To serve as a guide to price fixing.

(d) To provide comparative statements of costs in which the costs of the current period are compared with the costs of a previous period or, more helpfully, with the budgeted costs.

(e) To take action in respect of significant variations of the costs from the budgeted figures, and thus to control costs.

Desirable Conditions for a Cost Accounting System

A cost accounting system is not an arrangement which should be imposed on a business: rather should it be developed from a careful consideration of the business itself, and its special needs. It should therefore arise out of the business and be adapted to it.

The aim should be to make the cost accounting system as simple as possible, and acceptable to the accountancy staff; obviously, to be of any value it must produce helpful results promptly.

Certain conditions are essential to success.

(a) There must be an efficient system of stores and stock control.

(b) There must be a well-designed wages procedure, including the method of charging up labour costs to production.

(c) There must be a sound plan for the collection of all indirect expense (overhead) under suitable headings, and for its absorption to products or service departments on a predetermined basis.

(d) The cost and financial accounts should preferably be one integrated system. If not, the separate systems must allow for ease of reconciliation.

(e) Standardised printed forms should be introduced wherever possible, giving the name of the form, and containing instructions as to what use is to be made of it.

(f) The status of the cost accountant should be defined, and his responsibilities and duties made clear: authority should be given for him to have access to all works records.

Examination Questions

1. The proprietor of a medium-sized factory asks you to perform an investigation with a view to installing a costing system. What are the main considerations that would govern the form of costing system you would recommend? (*CAA*)

2. A manufacturer has been recommended to have an efficient costing system installed, but it is doubtful whether the results will justify the expense incurred. Submit your Report to the manufacturer and indicate the benefits which will accrue if a proper system is installed, and state what further information should be available to the manufacturer.

3. Costing systems are classified according to the requirements they are designed to meet. Enumerate them and give an example of a business to which each is applicable.

4. Detail the particular aims and purposes sought to be gained by the installation of a cost accounting system in a business manufacturing products for sale to the public through retail stockists. (*LCCI*)

5. Costing has been described as "a tool of industrial management". Comment on and expand this description. (*BIM*)

6. A small business with fifty employees and three main sections, cutting, machining and finishing, manufactures four products. The management has relied on a financial accounting system created and developed to meet statutory obligations but it is now considering the installation of a costing system.

You are required to prepare a report for management listing nine benefits you would expect to follow from the introduction of a cost accounting system. (*ICMA*)

Chapter 2

Elements of Cost

The Analysis and Classification of Expenditure

IN Chapter 1 we saw that the subject of cost accounting was intimately concerned with analysing the expenditure of a business in great detail.

The main classifications are:

(a) materials;
(b) wages;
(c) expenses.

Each of these will be considered more fully in subsequent chapters, but in arriving at the cost of production it is necessary to realise at the outset that:

(a) not all materials purchased become part of the product;
(b) not all wages incurred relate to actual manufacturing operations;
(c) very few expenses indeed can be regarded as being directly part of the product cost.

There are, therefore, two broad divisions to be noted:

Direct expenditure	*Indirect expenditure*
Materials	Materials
Wages	Wages
Expenses	Expenses

The terms direct and indirect are to be understood as follows.

Direct materials means the cost of materials which enter into and become part of the product, e.g. the flour in bread, the clay in bricks, the leather in shoes and the wood in furniture. In some cases, however, it is not so easy to determine whether a material is to be regarded as direct or not, and the custom of the trade has to be taken

6

into account or a decision which appears fair and reasonable in the circumstances has to be made.

Direct wages means the cost of wages paid to operatives who are immediately concerned with the manufacture of a product, that is to say, who "do" something to the raw material. If the concern is not a manufacturing business, but instead renders a service, then the term is related to those employees who directly carry out that service. Examples of direct wages would be those paid to bakers, clay getters, shoemakers, cabinet-makers, and in the second category, to bus drivers and conductors, and to postmen.

Direct expenses means those expenses incurred which without doubt are as much a cost of the product as are direct materials. Such might be the provision of special drawings, or the cost of a special pattern. The amount of such expenses is likely to be relatively small, and the heading is often ignored with no great disadvantage.

The sum of direct materials, direct wages, and direct expenses is known as the *prime cost*.

Indirect materials, wages, and expenses. These may be simply defined as all expenditure other than that regarded as direct. Although in accountancy the term "indirect expenses" is a common one, and is used in a general sense, cost accountants have sought for a term which would definitely be understood to be embracive of indirect materials, wages, and expenses. This they have found in the word "overhead", and it is this expression which will be used in the subsequent pages of this book. In the United States the word "burden" is used to convey the same idea. So difficult and thorny are some of the problems relating to overhead and its treatment in cost accounts that one may perhaps be pardoned for saying that the cost accountant's "burden" is "overhead".

Subdivision of Overhead

For the sake of classifying overhead suitably, it is subdivided into:

(a) production overhead;
(b) administrative overhead;
(c) selling overhead;
(d) distribution overhead.

The cost accounting organisation for the collection of data under these headings will be more fully dealt with in Chapters 9–11, and at present it is sufficient for the student to understand the general nature of the terms.

Production Overhead

This refers to the indirect works expenditure incurred, and consists of the three elements noted above.

(a) Indirect materials. Any materials used in the course of manufacture which either cannot be traced as part of the product or which are too small in value to be conveniently measured. Examples of indirect materials are:

> brooms, brushes;
> dustbins;
> soap;
> oils and grease.

In the category of direct materials of minor value which are treated as indirect, we may instance:

> thread used in shoe manufacture;
> glue used in the furniture trade.

(b) Indirect labour. The cost of labour employed in the works or factory which is ancillary to production. Examples are:

> inspectors;
> supervisors;
> workshop cleaners;
> internal transport staff.

(c) Indirect expenses. Expenses incurred by the undertaking which may be either allocated to the factory or partially apportioned to it. Examples are:

> power, lighting, and heating;
> rent and rates;
> water;
> insurance;
> depreciation.

It will also include services such as:

> works canteen;
> industrial nurse;
> fire precautions;
> research.

Administration Overhead

This refers to the expense incurred in the direction, control, and administration of an undertaking. The same elements of material, labour, and expenses permeate the headings under this and the remaining two classifications, but it is not usually necessary to consider them in those separate categories. Examples of administration overhead are:

> salaries and wages of executives and clerks on the administrative staff;
> rent and rates;
> lighting and heating;
> insurance;
> office printing and stationery.

Selling Overhead

This classification comprises the costs incurred in securing orders from customers for the products dealt in by the concern. Examples are:

> salaries and commissions paid to the sales manager, representatives, or sales staff;
> advertising;
> sales department expenses;
> samples and displays;
> catalogues.

Distribution Overhead

This consists of all expenditure incurred in handling the product from the time it is completed in the works until it reaches its destination. Examples of such expenditure are:

> warehouse wages and salaries;
> packing cases;
> loading expenses;
> upkeep and running charges of delivery vans.

Specimen Question

A firm's manufacturing, trading, and profit and loss account for the year ended December 31 was as follows:

Manufacturing Account

	£		£
Raw material used	10,000	Manufacturing cost of	
Wages	15,000	11,000 units of product	
Factory expenses	8,000	transferred to stock	33,000
Work-in-progress			
January 1	— —		
December 31	— —		
	£33,000		£33,000

Finished Goods Stock Account

	£		£
Balance January 1 5,000		Transfer to trading	
units £3	15,000	account	30,000
Transfer from manufac-		Balance in stock c/f	
turing account	33,000	6,000 units £3	18,000
	£48,000		£48,000

Trading Account

	£		£
Manufacturing cost of		Sales—10,000 units £5	50,000
goods sold	30,000		
Gross profit c/d	20,000		
	£50,000		£50,000

Profit and Loss Account

	£		£
Administration expenses		Gross profit b/d	20,000
(detailed)	5,000		
Selling expenses			
(detailed)	3,000		

Distribution expenses (detailed)	2,000	
Net profit	10,000	
	£20,000	£20,000

You are asked to show the same figures, but using the layout and nomenclature commonly adopted by cost accountants.

Answer

Production Cost Statement

Year ended December 31		*Production 11,000 units*	
		Total cost	*Cost per unit*
Prime cost			
Direct material	£10,000		
Direct wages	£15,000		
Direct expenses	—	£25,000	£2·27
Production overhead			
Indirect material			
Indirect wages			
Indirect expenses		£8,000	£0·73
Total production cost		£33,000	£3·00

Cost of Sales

Year ended December 31	*Sales 10,000 units*
	£
Production cost of sales	30,000
Administration overhead	5,000
Selling overhead	3,000
Distribution overhead	2,000
Total cost of sales	£40,000

Cost Accounting Profit and Loss Account

	£		£
Cost of sales	40,000	Sales	50,000
Profit	10,000		
	£50,000		£50,000

Examination Questions

1. Divide "Total Cost" into its main elements, name them and give one example of each. (*SCCA*)

2. Give the meaning of "Cost unit" and say what you consider the "Cost unit" would be in the following industries:

Iron foundry   Collieries
Weaving textiles   Electricity generation

(*SCCA*)

3. (*a*) What do you understand by the term "unit of cost"?

(*b*) State the units of cost which you consider are most applicable to any three industries known to you. (*ICAEW*)

4. State how you would allocate the following items under their headings of (*a*) Works Expenses; (*b*) Administration Expenses; (*c*) Selling Expenses; and (*d*) Distribution Expenses:

Depreciation of offices   Directors' fees
Salaries to Sales Managers   Loss of weight in transit to
Costing Department   customers
Patent fees   Advertising
Transport   Postage and stationery
Bill discount   Dividend on investments
Rents   received
            Interest paid on bank overdraft

(*ICMA*)

5. Assuming that cost accounting methods are used in the several departments of the Rosalind Dress Company, state how you would deal with the following items in the cost accounts:

(*a*) Bad debts   (*c*) Trade discounts on sales
(*b*) Losses due to theft   (*d*) Trade discounts on purchases

(*ICMA*)

Chapter 3

The Methods of Cost Accounting

THE general principles of cost accounting are the same in every system, but the methods of collating and presenting the costs may vary with the type of production to be costed.

Basically there are two types of cost accounting methods:

(a) job cost or production order cost;
(b) process cost or unit cost.

The first method is suitable for plants manufacturing products for different customers according to different specifications, or for one customer whose specifications are subject to frequent changes. The second method is suitable where a product is manufactured in a continuous process, and it is not necessary to know the actual cost of each unit produced.

The job cost method necessitates a very detailed cost analysis, but the resulting cost information is relatively accurate. On the other hand, the process cost method is not nearly so detailed, the cost per unit being ascertained by averaging the actual costs incurred over the period in question. However each method plays its part in cost accounting, the nature of the product manufactured determining which method should be adopted.

Methods of Ascertaining Actual Costs

From these two basic types of cost accounting methods, eight methods of ascertaining *actual* costs may be identified; these methods have emerged because peculiarities of certain kinds of production have resulted in the adoption of variations in procedure. They are briefly defined below, but the more important methods will be described more fully in succeeding chapters.

1. Job Costing

This is sometimes referred to as terminal costing. It also includes contract costing. This method is used to cost jobs or contracts that

13

are kept separate during manufacture or construction. It is applicable, for instance, to job order work in factories and work by contractors, builders, constructional engineers, shipbuilders, printers, municipal engineers, garages, film studios, etc. The unit of cost is the job, order, or contract, and the accounts show the cost of each order. This is discussed further in Chapter 14.

2. Batch Costing

This is a form of job costing, a convenient batch of production being treated as a job. Each batch is separately costed, from which unit costs are determined for the units produced. It is useful for biscuit factories, bakeries, etc.

3. Unit Costing

This was formerly known as output or single costing. It is a method of costing by the unit of production where manufacture is continuous and the units are identical, or may be made so by means of ratios. It may be employed in conjunction with batch, operation, or process costing, and is suitable for such undertakings as collieries, quarries, flour-mills, steel-works, paper-mills, breweries, etc., in all of which there is a standard or natural unit of production. It is also used in municipal costing.

Examples of suggested units of cost in certain industries are as follows.

Industry	Unit of cost	Industry	Unit of cost
Steel-works	Tonne of steel	Copper-mines	Tonne of copper
Quarries	Tonne of stone	Paper-mill	Tonne (or per kilogram)
Collieries	Tonne of coal	Textile factory	Metre of material
Milling	Sack of flour	Brick-making	Thousand bricks
Breweries	Barrel of beer	Spinning-mill	Kilogram of yarn

In effect, when all the units produced are identical the cost per unit is ascertained by finding the total expenditure and dividing by the number of units produced in a given period. This is discussed further in Chapter 15.

4. Operating Costing

This is unit costing as applied to the costing of services, such as those afforded by railways, motor-coaches, carriers, electricity supply and water undertakings. For example, in the case of the transport services mentioned, it may be desired to know the cost per kilometre, per tonne, per passenger, or the cost per tonne/km, per passenger/km, per parcel/km etc.; or in the case of the undertakings mentioned it may be desired to know the cost per kilowatt/hour, per litre, etc. This is discussed further in Chapter 16.

5. Operation Costing

This is a method of unit costing by operations in connection with mass production and repetitive production. It is particularly useful where the production is put in hand in large quantities of standardised units, as is usually necessary to ensure working at minimum cost. There is usually an uninterrupted flow of production, and the work is divided up into as many operations as are convenient, thus obtaining the fullest advantage of division of labour to ensure maximum output at each operation. Usually, also, machine tools specially designed for each operation are employed.

In this method the cost per unit is found for each operation and also for the finished unit. It is used in industries such as those mentioned below in connection with multiple costing.

6. Process Costing

This is sometimes referred to as continuous or average costing. This is a method of costing production by processes in which:

(a) the product of the process becomes the material of a subsequent process; or

(b) the different products and by-products (if any) are produced simultaneously at the same process; or

(c) the products, differing only in shape or form on completion, are not separately distinguishable from one another during one or more processes of manufacture.

Typical industries for which the method is suitable are concerned with chemicals, textiles, foods, paints and varnishes, etc. The cost of each process, and the cost per unit at each stage, are usually shown by the accounts. In simple process accounts the finding of the cost per unit at each process is similar to the procedure used in unit costing referred to above. This is discussed further in Chapter 17.

7. Multiple Costing

This is sometimes referred to as composite costing. It is used when there are a variety of component parts separately produced and subsequently assembled in a complex organisation, separate costs being compiled for each of the many parts manufactured. This method is used in factories manufacturing cycles, motor-cars, engines, radios, aeroplanes, and other complex products.

8. Departmental Costing

This is a method of ascertaining the cost of operating a department or cost centre. This is frequently necessary because of the need of control of expenditure in a department, e.g. the cost of running a research department, or because of the desire to allocate the costs of a department to another department or cost unit, e.g. the allocation of the inspection department costs to production departments or the allocation of costs of the stores to various contracts.

Special Systems

The nature of the product will determine which of the eight methods will be adopted in any business. However, in addition to these methods, mention should be made of three other systems which are not alternatives to those discussed already, but are techniques which may be adopted for special purposes of control and policy.

1. Uniform Costing

This term refers to the use of a common method of costing for different undertakings or producers in the same industry. When used in a number of factories operated under a central control, detailed costs can be compared and considered with the assurance that the figures under each heading have been built up on the same basis.

A uniform system may also be adopted by an association or federation of manufacturers in an industry, not usually for purposes of cost comparisons, but for guidance of the members and sometimes for joint action for the benefit of the industry. Chapter 19 is devoted to this subject.

2. Marginal Costing

This is concerned particularly with the effect which fixed overhead has on the running of a business. It is a method of interpreting costs of a product at given volumes of output. It will be apparent that certain items of cost are, within limits, fixed or constant for each unit produced, whatever the quantity, but other costs vary according to the output quantity. A marginal cost is the amount of change in aggregate cost resulting from an increase or decrease in the volume of output by one unit of production. This method is discussed further in Chapter 18.

3. Standard Costing

This includes the term predetermined costing. Under this method the actual performance is compared with the predetermined performance, thus revealing any variance between the two. These variances can then be investigated, so that, where necessary, management can take the required action. This valuable aid in cost control is discussed in more detail in Chapter 21.

"Cost Plus" Costing

Reference may now be made to a method of cost accounting which is very infrequently used in industry in modern times, except, perhaps, in the building trade and in firms engaged on Government contracts during war-time. However, this method was used widely before the introduction of the more modern techniques which have been outlined above. Such contracts originated in the building trade, and were costed by what is known as the cost plus method of costing.

This is a form of costing in connection with contracts placed with manufacturers or builders on the basis of cost plus an agreed percentage of profits. The cost refers to direct material, direct labour, and admissible direct expenses, such as plant hire, transport of plant and materials, etc. To the cost is added an agreed sum or percentage to cover overhead expenses and profit.

The method was much used before and during the First World War and to a lesser extent during the Second World War. Surprisingly enough, it is still used frequently in the building trade even in the U.S.A. It is normally used only when there is need for rapid execution of contracts without waiting for the fixing of definite contract prices. The method is not regarded as satisfactory in normal circumstances owing to the possibility of abuse. When the method is used, the accounts are scrutinised by accountants appointed by the authority which placed the contracts. The reason for avoiding the use of this system whenever possible will be obvious after considering the following points.

(*a*) It is in the contractor's interest to run the cost as high as possible, so that the percentage profit which is calculated on the total cost will be high.

(*b*) There is a great possibility of collusion between the contractors and any sub-contractors or merchants supplying materials or services.

(*c*) Inefficiency may be encouraged, resulting in overtime being necessary to complete the contract in time. This is beneficial to the employees, who receive larger pay packets, and to the employers, who receive larger profit. Ironically, the contractee may even be happy because the job is completed in time.

However expedient this method may be, and in some circumstances it may be the only possible method, it cannot be considered scientific costing.

Examination Questions

1. Explain the distinction between Process, Single, and Job Costing; state the industries to which each is suitable.   (*LCCI*)

2. What would you take as the unit of cost in the following cases:

(*a*) Iron foundry   (*e*) Building contractors
(*b*) Electricity undertaking   (*f*) Stevedore
(*c*) Machine toolmakers   (*g*) Railway company
(*d*) Brewery   (*RSA*)

3. Describe briefly the different methods of costing known to you and the type of product to which they are respectively applicable.
(*RSA*)

4. Assume three methods of costing: Job method, Process method, and Unit method. What method would you apply in the following industries: motor-car manufacturing; tanning; electricity supply; coal-mining; weaving; iron founding; boot manufacturing; sugar refinery; shipbuilding? State your reasons for the application.
(*ICMA*)

5. State which system of costing will be most suitable in *three* of the following concerns:

(*a*) Brickworks   (*d*) Road haulage contractor
(*b*) Motor-car manufacturer   (*e*) Practising accountant
(*c*) Builder and contractor

Give reasons for your answer in each case.   (*AIA*)

6. A client with a small factory, employing twenty workers, including clerical staff, asks you to undertake an investigation with a

view to installing a costing system. What are the main considerations that would govern the form of costing system you would recommend? (*AIA*)

7. What do you understand by:

(*a*) Fixed Expenses; Variable Expenses; Semi-Variable Expenses
(*b*) Direct Expenses; Indirect Expenses
(*c*) Job Costing; Process Costing? (*BIM*)

Chapter 4

Purchasing Procedure

IN practically all business organisations large sums of money are invested in raw materials, parts, supplies, finished goods, and equipment. In many large companies the cost of materials is more than 50% of the sales value. It follows, therefore, that the profitability of a company may be determined to a considerable extent by the efficient operation of the purchasing department. By the introduction of proved purchasing procedures, the high cost of investment in purchases can be reduced and savings effected in such items as obsolescence, pilfering and stock shortages.

Briefly the objectives of the purchasing department are to procure goods and services of the right quality, in the right quantity, at the right time, in the right place, and at the right price.

Organisation in the Purchasing Department

In each industry and in different works within an industry the detailed organisation will vary according to particular conditions and ideas, but the general procedure and principles outlined in this chapter may be regarded as typical, although particularly suitable for an engineering or similar factory. The forms used as illustrations are based on some actually in use, but again will vary in ruling and wording to suit particular needs.

A large engineering firm will require an efficient purchasing department, while, on the other hand, a small concern may have all functions, including purchasing, carried out by the owner. However, it is essential that in any company, whether large or small, only one person or one department should be authorised to place orders with suppliers, otherwise purchase orders may be duplicated.

The head of the department is usually designated as chief buyer or purchasing agent. In a large manufacturing business he has considerable responsibility, because much money can be lost or saved by his department. He requires a good technical knowledge of the industry and a large measure of administrative and organising ability; he must keep in constant touch with market prices, reports, and market tendencies, and have a working knowledge of contract law and procedure, together with a practical understanding of the principles of economic laws.

In some large businesses buying has been decentralised; in other words, each department is responsible for its own purchasing. However, most businesses operate one buying department, which is usually a very satisfactory arrangement.

Centralised Buying

The advantages of centralised buying are:

(a) a firm policy can be initiated with regard to conditions of purchasing, e.g. terms of payment;

(b) standardisation of articles is facilitated;

(c) expert buying staff is concentrated in one department;

(d) the number of people authorised to make purchase commitments is reduced;

(e) combined purchasing power may result in reduced prices of commodities.

The disadvantages are:

(a) the creation of a special department may lead to high administration costs;

(b) the purchasing procedure is much less flexible than that geared to special departments.

Procedure in the Purchasing Department

The buyer should be provided with a schedule of technical specifications of the materials usually required, each item having a code number which will be quoted by those issuing purchase requisitions.

The department should keep files suitably indexed, both under the names of suppliers and materials. Records of prices and quantities for all materials should be kept in schedule form, arranged to show the seasonal and other movements of prices.

No purchases should be permitted except on receipt of duly authorised purchase requisitions, but in the case of materials largely and regularly used, forward contracts may be made after consultation with management. Where purchase contracts are placed, a record of orders issued against them and deliveries made should be kept.

The Purchase of Materials

The buyer acts upon requisitions received from the storekeeper for all stores materials and, in some instances, other requisitions may come from the engineer, drawing office, or other responsible sources for new kinds of material not previously stocked, e.g. special materials for a particular order or new design. Consideration must be given to factors other than price, viz. to specifications, conditions of delivery, various charges, times of delivery, terms of payment, and discount.

The purchase requisition (Fig. 2) may be routed as follows:

(a) to the purchasing department;
(b) to the production control department;
(c) retained in the issuing department.

After the buyer has decided which quotation is most acceptable, a purchase order (Fig. 3) is prepared, which is evidence of the contract between the buyer and the supplier. The number of copies of the purchase order which is prepared depends on the organisation of the business: a large concern may use five copies while a small concern may use only three copies. These may be routed as follows:

(a) to the supplier;
(b) to the receiving department;
(c) to the accounting department;
(d) to the department which initiated the purchase requisition;
(e) retained in the purchasing department.

PURCHASE REQUISITION				
Date 23rd Feb. 19...		**No.:** 3208		
Date Required: 1st March 19...		**Department:** CENTRAL STORES		
Quantity	Description	Stock Code No.	Purchase Order No.	Supplier
3,000	50 mm × 10 mm Steel Carriage Bolts	S.B.23	9790	Universal Supply
Requisitioned by: P. J. Dillon		**Approved by:** C. G. Hardy		

FIG. 2.—*Purchase requisition*

Requisitions for materials regularly kept in stock might be initiated by the storekeeper; for other types of material by the department requiring them.

Note—The last two columns are completed by the buyer.

The important work of following up deliveries by due date is the duty of the buyer. For this purpose the copy purchase order, which is retained in the department, may be filed in delivery date order as stated on each copy by the buyer, so that probable daily deliveries may be checked. Any delays must be followed up by writing to the supplier.

PURCHASE ORDER

From: **No.** 9790

M. Stuart
Goforth, Northumbria

To: Universal Supply   **Our Ref:** 3208
       London SW17   **Date:** 24th Feb. 19...

Please supply, in accordance with the instructions herein, the following:

Quantity	Description	Price	Unit	Delivery
3,000	50 mm × 10 mm Steel Carriage Bolts	£0·10	each	28th Feb. 19...

Delivery:	Ship to:	Terms:	Account	Signed by:
Free	Central Stores	5% Monthly Account	**No.:** 57	C. Graeme Buyer

FIG. 3.—*Purchase order*

Care should be taken to ensure that the purchase order specifies the date and terms of delivery, and the cash discount available if payment is made within the stipulated period.

Use of Code Numbers for Materials

The use of code numbers for identifying each item carried in the stores is an advantage, not only to the purchasing department and production control department but also to the stores ledger clerk, in that ambiguity in description of articles is eliminated and much time and writing is saved. The code may consist of symbols and numbers, or numbers only. For example, the symbols B and S could be given to represent brass and steel; the number following the symbol to

identify the size, quality, etc.: thus B.0640 for brass screws 06 mm ×
40 mm; S.0640 for steel screws of the same size.

All standard articles will have identifying symbols and numbers,
so the system will require careful compilation. In practice,
storemen, clerks and draughtsmen find these codes easy to work
with, since the code numbers of the more frequently used materials
are readily memorised. In the cost department the pricing of issued
material is facilitated, and uncertainty as to size and kind of material
is avoided.

Procedure on Receipt of Materials

Delivery notes or advices of despatch usually accompany
deliveries from suppliers, so these should be directed to the
receiving clerk or storekeeper. Invoices received are passed direct
to the accounts department to be checked for payment.

Materials entering the factory should be unloaded at special receiving centres. These should be situated as near to the road, railway
siding, canal, or wharf as possible, yet at the same time be accessible
from any part of the factory, so as to minimise handling charges.

The receiving department should receive a copy of the purchase
order, so that, if necessary, arrangements can be made to unload the
materials—special apparatus may be necessary to handle heavy or
bulky materials. However, it is often advisable that this copy should
not show quantities ordered, but only indicate that a shipment of
certain materials is expected; this results in the receiving clerk being
obliged to check the goods physically rather than to rely on data
shown on the purchase order as a guide to quantities received.

Goods should be inspected for quality to ensure that they comply
with any specification which may have been stated on the purchase
order. In many large firms an inspection department is attached to
the receiving department, while in small firms the storekeeper is
responsible for inspection. If any goods are rejected the inspector
will enter the reason for rejection on a special rejection report, so
that the buyer is immediately informed and can contact the supplier.

The Goods Received Note

Full particulars of goods received are entered on a goods received
note (Fig. 4). Routing of the goods received note will depend on the
organisation.

A suggested routing is:

(a) to the purchasing department;

(*b*) to the accounts department;
(*c*) to the department which initiated the purchase requisition;
(*d*) to the stores;
(*e*) retained in the receiving department.

The completed goods received note is then passed to the official responsible for approving the goods, who signs the notes and sends them, with the goods, to the storekeeper. Where the storekeeper is responsible for receiving and approving goods, he will prepare the goods received note.

When the purchasing department receives a copy of the goods received note, together with the receiving clerk's copy of the purchase order, the order can be marked off in the order book.

GOODS RECEIVED NOTE						
From: Smith, Jones & Co., Birmingham					**G.R. No.** 59 **Date:** 5 Mar. 19...	
Goods	Quantity	Packages	Order No.	For Office Use		
				Rate	£	
			4721			
Carrier BR	**Received by** P. Martin	**Goods Inspection Report** Correct. J. Graeme				
Purchase Requisition No. 284	**Noted on Progress Chart** 5/621	**Bin No.** 72	**Stores Ledger** 212	**Invoice No.** 360	**A/cs. Ref.** P.J. 84	

FIG. 4.—*Goods received note*

This note is made out by the receiving department when goods are received, and is priced by the cost department from copy orders. It forms the basis of entries in the stores ledger made in advance of receipt of invoices, with which they are later agreed.

Checking Inward Invoices

Invoices received are numbered consecutively on entry into the invoice register. The purchasing department clerk enters on it the order number, goods received note number, and signs for the accuracy of the particulars ascertained from the copy order and the goods received note. The copy order retained should be marked with the invoice number and goods received note number, to preclude the passing of a possible duplicate invoice.

If the invoice is in order the buyer will sign and pass it to the accounts department for payment. There it will be checked to ensure that any calculations are correct. The invoice is entered in the purchases day book, from which the supplier's account is credited in the creditors ledger. The total of the purchases day book is debited to purchases account in the general ledger and credited to creditors control account. The accounting entries are discussed further in Chapter 12.

Examination questions on Chapters 4–6 are given at the end of Chapter 6.

Chapter 5

Stores Routine

Importance and Location of the Stores

Importance of the Stores

IN most manufacturing companies a large part of money invested is represented by stocks. Serious losses may be suffered in companies with inefficient stores techniques. Insufficient stocks may result in costly production hold-ups, or rush shipments may mean increased costs of production. On the other hand, stocks which are too large result in capital being tied up unnecessarily, and increased costs of storage and obsolescence.

The stores in many small firms is often neglected, and it is not realised that materials represent an equivalent amount of cash. Material pilferage, deterioration of materials, and careless handling of stores lead to reduced profits, or even losses, so it is essential that to obtain the maximum advantage of a cost accounting system an efficient, well-equipped stores be maintained.

Location of the Stores

The organisation of the stores will depend on the type of industry, size of the firm, and policy of the management. However, in general, we can define two types of stores organisation: central stores and sub-stores.

The location of the stores should be carefully planned so as to ensure maximum efficiency. It should be as near to the receiving department as possible, so that haulage charges are at a minimum. At the same time there should be easy access to all departments, especially to those in which heavy or bulky materials are to be delivered.

In large factories where there are many departments it is possible that the stores cannot be situated where it is convenient to deliver to all departments and at the same time be near to the receiving department, so it is often necessary to set up sub-stores to serve a particular part of the organisation. The central stores will then issue to the sub-stores the materials specially required for the department or departments serviced by the sub-store. It is strongly recommended that the storekeeper of each sub-store should be responsible to the chief storekeeper. This will ensure that a uniform policy of buying, storing, and issuing is followed.

Centralised Storage

The advantages of operating central stores as compared with sub-stores are as follows:

(*a*) economy in staff and concentration of experts in one department;
(*b*) reduced clerical costs and economy in records and stationery;
(*c*) better supervision is possible;
(*d*) staff become acquainted with different types of stores, which is very useful if anyone is absent from work;
(*e*) better layout of stores;
(*f*) inventory checks facilitated;
(*g*) stocks are kept to a minimum, thus reducing storage space;
(*h*) fewer obsolete articles;
(*i*) the amount of capital invested in stock is minimised.

The disadvantages are likely to be:

(*a*) increased transportation costs;
(*b*) the stores may be situated at some distance from many departments, thus causing inconvenience and delay;
(*c*) breakdowns in transport or hold-ups in central stores may cause production stoppages in departments.

Organisation Within the Stores

Layout of the Stores

Shelves, racks, bins, etc., should be situated in clearly defined lanes, so that easy access is possible. In many cases it may be necessary to allow enough room for the passage of trucks, so white lines should be painted on the floor, determining the position of storage containers.

The Imprest System

It is sometimes the practice of large organisations to use the imprest system of stores control, which operates in rather a similar way to a petty-cash system. For each item in stock a quantity will be determined, which represents the number of articles which should be on hand at the beginning of any period. At the end of a period the storekeeper of each sub-store will requisition from the central stores the number of articles required to bring the stock up to the predetermined quantity.

For example, let us assume that the imprest amount which has been set for a material is 1,000 units. During the week ending 28th July, issues of the material have reduced the stock to 280 units. The sub-storekeeper would issue a requisition from the central storekeeper for 720 units to ensure that at the beginning of the next week 1,000 units are in stock.

The Storekeeper

The stores should be under the control of one person, who may be known as the storekeeper, chief storekeeper, or stores superintendent. He should be a man of wide experience in stores routine, able to organise the operation of the stores, of undoubted integrity, and capable of controlling men under his authority.

His duties and responsibilities may be as follows:

(*a*) maintaining the stores in a tidy manner;
(*b*) accepting materials into the stores, after having ascertained that the delivery complies with specifications detailed on the purchase order, goods received note, or stores debit note;
(*c*) correct positioning of all materials in store;
(*d*) checking the bin card balances with the physical quantities in the bins;
(*e*) requisitioning further supplies from the purchasing department when the reorder level is reached on any material;
(*f*) preventing unauthorised persons entering the stores;
(*g*) issuing materials against authorised stores requisition notes;
(*h*) advising management of obsolete or slow-moving stocks.

Requisitioning for Stores

The storekeeper is guided when requisitioning for stores—this was outlined briefly on p. 22—by the maximum and minimum quantity which he is authorised to store in respect of each kind of material, and the reorder level. These items are shown on the bin card (Fig. 8).

The maximum stock is fixed by taking into account such aspects as:

(*a*) rate of consumption of the material;

(b) time necessary to obtain new supplies;

(c) finance—if stocks are unnecessarily high, capital is locked up which could probably be otherwise employed;

(d) storage space—the provision of, and cost of, maintaining the necessary storage room must be considered;

(e) possibility of loss by evaporation, deterioration, etc.;

(f) extent to which price fluctuation may be important;

(g) risks of changing specifications and obsolescence;

(h) seasonal considerations as to both price and availability of supplies, e.g. market shortages;

(i) economic ordering quantities.

The minimum stock is fixed by taking into account:

(a) rate of consumption of the material;

(b) time necessary to obtain delivery of supplies.

The reordering level is the quantity fixed between the maximum and minimum stock figures, at which time it is essential to initiate purchase requisitions for new supplies of the material. This level will usually be slightly higher than the minimum stock figure, so as to cover such emergencies as abnormal usage of the material or unexpected delay in delivery of new supplies.

It is fixed by taking into account:

(a) rate of consumption of the material;

(b) time necessary to obtain new supplies.

Example of the Calculation of Stock Levels

The materials analyst has forecast the following data in respect of material MS6:

Maximum consumption of material per week:	400 units
Normal consumption of material per week:	300 units
Minimum consumption of material per week:	200 units
Reorder quantity:	2,000 units
Reorder period:	4-6 weeks

Reorder level

$$\text{Max. C} \times \text{Max. RP}$$
$$400 \text{ units} \times 6 \text{ weeks} \qquad \textit{2,400 units}$$

This level is calculated first, because the maximum and minimum stock levels both include the reorder level in their formulae. It considers the longest period of time and the maximum usage of materials which could be expected.

Minimum stock level

$$RL - (NC \times NRP)$$
$$2,400 - (300 \text{ units} \times 5 \text{ weeks}) \qquad \textit{900 units}$$

This level considers the average or normal consumption expected. Stocks should not normally fall below this level, but the buffer stock is maintained in case of emergencies.

Maximum stock level

$$RL - (\text{Min. C} \times \text{Min. RP}) + RQ$$
$$2,400 - (200 \text{ units} \times 4 \text{ weeks}) + 2,000 \ \textit{3,600 units}$$

This level considers the lowest rate of consumption which could be expected if delivery was received in the shortest possible time. The addition of the reorder quantity shows the highest point in inventory which would be allowed. Stocks should never be allowed to rise above this point without special authority.

Average stock level

This measures the average level of stock held during an accounting period. One simple formula which may be used for calculating this level is as follows:

$$\frac{\text{Max. stock} + \text{Min. stock}}{2}$$

If we use the figures given in the previous example, it is found that the average stock level is:

$$\frac{3,600 + 900}{2} \qquad \textit{2,250 units}$$

The average stock level is a useful measurement when considering stores turnover.

Turnover of Stores Materials

It is useful to compare the turnover of different grades and kinds of materials as a means of detecting stock which does not move regularly, thus enabling management to avoid keeping capital locked up in undesirable stocks. It is not an infrequent occurrence for a particular item of stock to be overlooked for long periods unless means are taken to prevent such accumulations. The balance of stores, compared with the total withdrawals, indicates how many times a year the stock is renewed.

The formula is:

$$\frac{\text{Consumption of materials}}{\text{Average stock of materials}}$$

Example

A simple trading account of J. Stuart PLC is as follows:

Trading account for the period ending 31st March

Opening stock	£8,000	Sales	£100,000
Purchases	64,000	Closing stock	12,000
Gross profit	40,000		
	£112,000		£112,000

Stores turnover: $\dfrac{£60,000}{£10,000}$ *6 times pa*

The stores turnover is once every two months, which is quite a satisfactory rate. It is difficult to generalise, but a turnover of once every two to three months would be considered satisfactory in most industries.

NOTE

1. Average stock calculation. In this example, there is no mention of stock levels being maintained, so it is not possible to use the formula given earlier for average stock. It is therefore necessary to use another simple formula which is used in situations such as this:

$$\frac{\text{Opening stock} + \text{Closing stock}}{2}$$
$$\frac{£8,000 + £12,000}{2}$$

2. Consumption of materials: Opening stock + Purchases − Closing stock.

Receipt and Issue of Material

Receipt

Purchased materials are passed into the custody of the storekeeper when they have been examined and approved. Some articles or parts are not purchased from outside suppliers, but are made in the works. These will be inspected in the usual course and then passed into stores; it is desirable that a goods received note be prepared for these articles in order to keep the accounts uniform.

The storekeeper will enter receipt of goods on a bin card (see below). Any goods which are rejected are entered on a goods rejected note, which is sent to the purchasing department. The supplier will be informed and a debit note will be sent to him.

Issue

The cost of materials is frequently the largest element of cost in production, so it is imperative that all stores shall be recorded as promptly and as accurately as possible. In most companies the storekeeper is allowed to issue materials only on presentation of an authorised materials requisition.

Materials requisition

This document (Fig. 5), sometimes termed stores requisition, is an authorisation to the storekeeper to issue raw materials, finished parts, or other types of stock. It is usually signed by the foreman of the department requiring the material, but in special cases when extra-large quantities or very costly materials are needed for production, the manager's signature may be necessary. Frequently the planning or progress department issue these requisitions to the foreman, who presents them to the storekeeper as and when required.

The storekeeper will enter the details of the materials requisition on to the appropriate bin cards and adjust the balances in the stock column. The note will then be routed to the cost department, where it will be evaluated from the stores ledger. The stores ledger will be credited in the appropriate stores account and an entry will be made on the materials abstract for posting to the debit of the appropriate account in the cost ledger.

Stores Record

Two records are usually kept of materials received, issued, or transferred—namely on the bin cards and in the stores ledger. The bin cards are written up in the stores, but the stores ledger is usually kept in the cost department or in the stores office. There are three advantages in this procedure:

(*a*) The storekeeper is required to do the minimum amount of clerical work.

(*b*) The accounting records are maintained more accurately and in a better condition by an experienced stores clerk than by an assistant in the stores.

(*c*) A check is provided, in that the balances on the bin cards in the stores can be compared with the balances in the stores ledger.

MATERIALS REQUISITION							
Department: Assembly Shop No. 2					**No.**: 1234		
Charge to: Job No. P23.					**Date**: 1st March 19...		
Quantity	Details	Stock Code No.	Weight	Rate £	Amount	£	Notes
600	50 mm × 10 mm Steel Carriage Bolts	S.B.23	—	0.10	60	00	—
Signed by: J. Paul		**Bin No.**: 241			**Cost Department**		
Approved by: G. David		**Storeman**: J. Lewis			**Priced by**: O. T. Ball		
		Stores Ledger: 346			**Checked by**: I. A. Smart		

FIG. 5.—*Materials requisition*

This note is made out by the department requiring materials from stores or by the production control department. The stores ledger account concerned is credited and the job or process is debited.

Transfer of Materials

Transfers of materials from one sub-store to another should be recorded by means of a materials transfer note or a materials requisition note marked "transfer". This note can then be used in the cost department for making the necessary debit and credit. Where transfers are numerous it is sometimes the practice to have special columns in the bin cards for recording the details of the transfer.

MATERIALS TRANSFER NOTE

Issuing Department: Assembly Shop No. 2   **No.:** 320

Receiving Department: Assembly Shop No. 4   **Date:** 11th March 19...

Quantity	Details	Stock Code No.	Weight	Rate £	Amount £	Notes
60	50 mm × 10 mm steel carriage bolts	S.B.23	—	0.10	6.00	—

Issued by: G. David
From Job No.: P23

Received by: C. Moore
To Job No.: R78

Cost Department
Priced by: O. T. Ball
Checked by: I. A. Smart

FIG. 6.—*Materials transfer note*

This form is necessary to cover the transfer of material from one job to another and from one department to another.

Note—The cost department is responsible for pricing.

The transfer of materials from one job to another in the factory should be strictly prohibited unless the procedure is adequately recorded on a materials transfer note (Fig. 6).

Materials transfer note

This document records all the necessary data for debiting and crediting the accounts affected in the cost ledger. Transfers may occur when there is not enough material in the stores to meet an urgent order, so materials in another department engaged on less urgent work may be appropriated. In such a case there must be provision for the reissue of material to the job from which the material had been transferred. Failure to record transfers would result in incorrect costs of the jobs concerned.

Material Issued in Excess of Requirements

Frequently bulk material has to be issued in excess of the needs of a particular job. This is the case with sheet iron or steel bars, which in some instances cannot be cut off to the exact size required in the stores, and which can be more advantageously operated upon when full size in the factory. The procedure is to charge out the full quantity issued, and when the excess is returned to store a materials return note is completed, signed by the foreman, and handed to the storekeeper.

MATERIALS RETURN NOTE						
Issuing Dept.: Assembly Shop No. 2				**No.:** 16		
Credit to: Job No. P23				**Date:** 12th March 19...		
Quantity	Details	Stock Code No.	Weight	Rate £	Amount £	Notes
120	50 mm × 10 mm steel carriage bolts	S.B.23	—	0.10	12.00	—
Signed by: J. Paul **Approved by:** G. David	**Bin No.:** 241				**Cost Department** **Priced by:** O. T. Ball	
	Storeman: J. Lewis **Stores Ledger No.** 346				**Checked by:** I. A. Smart	

FIG. 7.—*Materials return note*

When excess material is returned to stores a form such as this is used to ensure that the job concerned receives credit for the material, and that the stores can keep its records correctly.

Materials return note

This document (Fig. 7), sometimes termed a stores debit note, is an authorisation to return to the storekeeper raw material, finished parts, or other stock no longer required by the factory. These notes may be produced in the same design as a materials requisition, but may be printed in red to distinguish them.

On receipt of the note the storekeeper will enter the details on the bin card and place the goods in the appropriate receptacle; the stores ledger clerk will debit the appropriate stores account; the cost ledger clerk will credit the job account for which the goods were returned.

Bin Cards

Materials are stored in appropriate bins, drawers, shelves, or other receptacles; some are stacked, others racked. For each kind of material a separate record is kept on a bin card (Fig. 8), showing in detail all receipts and issues. The bin cards thus assist the storekeeper in controlling the stock position.

BIN CARD

Description: ....
....

Reorder Quantity: ....
Stores Ledger Fo.: ....

Bin No.: ....
Code No.: ....
Maximum Stock level: ....
Minimum Stock level: ....
Reorder level: ....

Receipts			Issues			Balance	Remarks
Date	G.R. No.	Quan-tity	Date	M.R. No.	Quan-tity	Quantity	Goods on Order and Audit Notes

FIG. 8.—*Bin Card*

The storekeeper records the movement in and out of the materials under his control. He should show in the balance column the actual quantity of the particular material in stock at any time.

Note—G.R. No.: goods received note number.

M.R. No.: materials requisition number.

For each material in store the maximum and minimum quantities to be carried are stated on the card. These limits, which are determined by the production control department, were discussed on p. 29. From time to time these maxima and minima will be reviewed and may be altered to suit current requirements.

To facilitate ordering of further supplies, the normal quantity to order is sometimes stated at the head of the card; this quantity will indicate the customary market units to as to avoid requisitions for irregular quantities.

The various receptacles in which materials are stored are numbered, the bin card for each being similarly numbered. Where identifying code numbers are used for materials it is advantageous to attach them to the bin and to quote them on the bin card.

Stores Ledger

The stores ledger is kept in the cost accounting department. In it is recorded the same information as the storekeeper records on the bin cards, but also the money values are shown. Correct stores accounting is as important as accounting for cash, hence the separation of this clerical work from the actual handling of the materials in store. The ledger is usually of the loose-leaf or card type, each account representing an item of material. The ruling of the accounts may be as shown in Fig. 9.

The debit side is prepared from the goods received notes or invoices, also from materials return notes; the credit side either directly from the materials requisitions or from the abstract summary compiled from them. Additional columns may be shown for materials ordered and for materials reserved for special jobs.

Stores Control

The Perpetual Inventory System

This is a method of recording stores balances after every receipt and issue of materials, so that the balance of stock at any time can be ascertained immediately. It is often used in conjunction with a system referred to as "continuous inventory", which is a method of making a physical check on stores balances at frequent, irregular intervals.

The balances of any account in the stores ledger for a particular item of stock should agree with the balance on the bin card, and a frequent checking of these dual records should be made as well as of the actual quantity in stock.

In large stores a system of continuous checking is instituted, a number of items of material being counted daily and compared with the bin cards and stores ledger, by a stores audit clerk. Discrepancies are investigated; many may be clerical errors, which will be corrected. When, however, the stock is incorrect an investigation is made, after which any shortage or surplus is adjusted in the records to make them correspond with the physical stock. This may be done conveniently by making out a credit note or debit note, as the case may be, for the difference and then, after obtaining authority to pass the adjustment through the cost journal, crediting (or debiting) a stock adjustment account. The balance on that account is written off direct to profit and loss account at appropriate times.

STORES LEDGER ACCOUNT

MATERIAL: ....

Code: ....
Reorder Quantity: ....

Maximum Quantity: ....
Minimum Quantity: ....
Reorder Level: ....

Folio: ....
Location: ....

Ordered			Reserved			Received					Issued				Stock			Stock Checked		Remarks
Date	Ref.	Quantity	Date	Ref.	Quantity	Date	G.R. No.	Quantity	Price	Amount	M.R. No.	Quantity	Price	Amount	Quantity	Price	Amount	Date	Initials	

Fig. 9.—*Stores ledger account (1)*

The columns ordered, reserved, and stock checked are memoranda only, and are sometimes excluded from stores ledgers. The first two columns may be very useful, because they show goods ordered and not yet received and also goods which have been reserved for future production. The last column shows when stock was checked and brief details of check.

Note—G.R. No.: goods received note number.
  M.R. No.: materials requisition number.

The common causes of differences are incorrect entries, breakages, pilferage, evaporation, breaking bulk, short or over issues, absorption of moisture, and placing of stores in the wrong bins.

The advantages of the system are as follows.

(*a*) The long and costly work of a stocktaking is avoided, and the value of the stock of materials as shown by the stores ledger can be obtained quickly for the preparation of a profit and loss account and balance sheet.

(*b*) A continual, detailed, reliable check on the stores is obtained.

(*c*) Discrepancies are readily discovered and localised, giving an opportunity for preventing a recurrence in many cases.

(*d*) The moral effect on the staff tends to greater care, and serves as a deterrent to dishonesty.

(*e*) The audit extends to comparison of the actual stock with the authorised maxima and minima, thus ensuring that adequate stocks are maintained within the prescribed limits.

(*f*) The storekeeper's duty of attending to replenishments is facilitated, as he is kept informed of the stock of every kind of material.

(*g*) The stock being kept within the limits decided upon by the management, the working capital sunk in stores materials cannot exceed the amount arranged for.

(*h*) The disadvantages of excessive stocks are avoided, e.g. (*i*) loss of interest on capital locked up in stock; (*ii*) loss through deterioration; (*iii*) danger of depreciation in market values; (*iv*) risks of obsolescence.

(*i*) It is not necessary to stop production so as to carry out a complete physical stocktaking.

(*j*) Experienced men can be employed to check the stock at regular intervals.

Materials Issued at an Inflated Price

Wastage of materials frequently occurs in a store due to evaporation, deterioration in quality, or some similar cause. When this occurs it is necessary to charge materials issued to production at an inflated price to ensure that the true cost is recovered.

If 100 kg of material is bought at £0·54 per kg, and it is known from past experience that the normal wastage of this material is 10%, the charge to production would be $\frac{£54}{90}$ = £0·60.

Recording Material Notes

Goods received notes are priced from orders or invoices, and material requisitions are priced from the stores ledger. Material transfer notes and materials return notes are priced from the cost ledger. A summary of the procedure is shown in Fig. 10.

RECORDING
MATERIALS NOTES

GOODS RECEIVED NOTES ARE PRICED FROM ORDERS OR INVOICES

MATERIALS REQUISITIONS ARE PRICED FROM THE STORES LEDGER

MATERIALS TRANSFER NOTES ARE PRICED FROM THE COST LEDGER

OR COST CARD

BIN CARD	
IN	OUT
GOODS RECEIVED NOTES	MATERIALS REQUISITIONS
MATERIALS RETURN NOTES	

STORES LEDGER	
DR	CR
GOODS RECEIVED NOTES	MATERIALS REQUISITIONS
MATERIALS RETURN NOTES	

COST LEDGER	
DR	CR
MATERIALS REQUISITIONS	MATERIALS RETURN NOTES
MATERIALS TRANSFER NOTES	

FIG. 10.—*Accounting for material*

Categories of Stock

It is usual to keep separate stores for raw materials, finished parts, finished goods, etc. Definitions of the kinds of stock are as follows.

Raw materials

Primary materials purchased or produced either in a natural or manufactured condition. Manufactured materials of one industry are often the raw materials of another, e.g. the finished product of a steel mill may be the raw material of an engineering factory.

Work in progress

This is production that has not yet reached the stage of completion.

Finished parts

These are items or sub-assemblies put into store awaiting final assembly or sale as spares.

Finished stock

This is the completed product awaiting sale or despatch.

Small tools

In a general engineering factory such tools form a large and valuable stock, consisting of drills, dies, etc.

Stores Expenses

The expenses involved in operating a stores in a large company may be very high. Usually the expenses are collected into stores overhead and charged to production overhead. However, if it can be ascertained that expenses have been incurred on a specific order or job, then the expenses may be charged thereto as an addition to the cost of materials. Carriage inwards and handling costs may be treated in a similar way.

Examination Questions on Chapters 4–6 are given at the end of Chapter 6.

Chapter 6

Methods of Valuing Materials Issues

THERE are many methods of valuing materials issues, but it is proposed to examine only a limited number in this book. The choice of method depends largely on the policy and the particular conditions of the business.

To illustrate the system of recording materials issues under some of the important methods the following transactions are recorded:

January	1	Received	1,200	units at	£1·50 per unit.
January	14	Received	300	units at	£1·40 per unit.
January	30	Issued	700	units at	— per unit.
February	21	Received	600	units at	£1·55 per unit.
March	4	Received	500	units at	£1·60 per unit.
March	28	Issued	900	units at	— per unit.
April	15	Issued	400	units at	— per unit.
May	21	Received	800	units at	£1·45 per unit.
June	4	Issued	1,000	units at	— per unit.
June	20	Received	200	units at	£1·60 per unit.

NOTE: For simplicity of illustration, the amounts columns in the following accounts have been calculated to the nearest £1; in practice, calculations would usually show pence also.

1. First in First Out (FIFO) (Fig. 11)

The stores are deemed, for book-keeping purposes, to have been issued from the earliest lot delivered until exhausted, then from the next delivery. In this way the charge in the accounts is the actual cost price of each lot. The stores ledger clerk can ascertain from the accounts when each consignment is completed. Where market fluctuations are frequent and considerable the method sometimes produces curious and unfair results as between one job and another; e.g. materials purchased at £0·75 per unit may be issued to job A, but materials issued to job B may be from a later supply which cost £1·00 each. If transactions are numerous and the price fluctuates considerably the method is very involved, which may increase the possibility of errors.

STORES LEDGER ACCOUNT

Materials: ....   Maximum Quantity: ....   Reorder Level: ....   Folio: ....
Code: ....   Minimum Quantity: ....   Reorder Quantity: ....   Location: ....

Date	G.R. No.	Receipts Quantity	Price £	Amount £	M.R. No.	Issues Quantity	Price £	Amount £	Stock Quantity	Price £	Amount £
Jan. 4		1,200	1·50	1,800					1,200	1·50	1,800
14		300	1·40	420					1,500		2,220
30						700	1·50	1,050	800		1,170
Feb. 21		600	1·55	930					1,400		2,100
Mar. 4		500	1·60	800					1,900		2,900
28						500	1·50	750			
						300	1·40	420			
						100	1·55	155			
						900			1,000		1,575
Apr. 15						400	1·55	620	600		955
May 21		800	1·45	1,160					1,400		2,115
June 4						100	1·55	155			
						500	1·60	800			
						400	1·45	580			
						1,000			400		580
20		200	1·60	320					600		900

FIG. 11.—*Stores Ledger Account* (2) (FIFO)

This account has been entered on the first-in first-out principle, which has the same effect as if materials were issued in strict chronological order.

Note—The closing stock represents:

$$
\begin{array}{lr}
& £ \\
400 \text{ units at } £1·45 \text{ per unit} = & 580 \\
200 \text{ units at } £1·60 \text{ per unit} = & 320 \\
\hline
600 & 900 \\
\hline
\end{array}
$$

A great advantage of FIFO is that in stock valuation, stock is not only at cost but is also as closely representative of current prices as possible. When prices are falling the material charge to production is high, while the cost of stock replacement will be low. Conversely, when prices are rising the charge to production will be low, while the replacement cost will be high.

2. Last in First Out (LIFO) (Fig. 12)

This method operates in reverse to FIFO; material received in the latest delivery is, for book-keeping purposes, deemed to have been issued first. As with FIFO, the charge in the accounts is the actual cost price. However, it suffers from the same disadvantages mentioned under FIFO, namely unfair comparison of job costs and involved calculations. LIFO also suffers from the disadvantage that, although stock is at cost, the price is that of earliest material purchased, so that it does not represent current price levels, as a result of which it may be necessary to write off stock losses during periods of falling prices because the book values of the materials will exceed market value.

A great advantage of LIFO is that the charge to production is as closely related to current price levels as possible. Assuming the purchase of materials was in recent times, it will not be necessary to ascertain market values.

In times of inflation LIFO is considered to be an effective system of pricing because the high-priced purchases are charged to production, while stocks are retained at low prices. However it must be noted that, particularly in the UK, taxation authorities do not favour this system.

3. Simple Average (Fig. 13)

This method may be used advantageously when it is not possible to identify each item separately and when prices of purchases do not fluctuate very much. It is relatively easy to operate.

To calculate the issue price, the total of the prices paid for the material is divided by the number of prices paid in the calculation. This may result in the charge to production not being at actual cost, e.g.

1 unit   purchased at £1·00 per unit
1,000 units purchased at £0·50 per unit

The average price is $\dfrac{(£1·00 + £0·50)}{2} = £0·75$

STORES LEDGER ACCOUNT

| Materials: | Maximum Quantity: | Reorder Level: | Folio: |
| Code: | Minimum Quantity: | Reorder Quantity: | Location: |

Date		Receipts			Issues				Stock		
	G.R. No.	Quantity	Price £	Amount £	M.R. No.	Quantity	Price £	Amount £	Quantity	Price £	Amount £
Jan. 4		1,200	1·50	1,800					1,200	1·50	1,800
14		300	1·40	420					1,500		2,220
30						700	300 1·40 / 400 1·50	420 / 600	800		1,200
Feb. 21		600	1·55	930					1,400		2,130
Mar. 4		500	1·60	800					1,900		2,930
28						900	500 1·60 / 400 1·55	800 / 620	1,000		1,510
Apr. 15						400	200 1·55 / 200 1·50	310 / 300	600		900
May 21		800	1·45	1,160					1,400		2,060
June 4						1,000	800 1·45 / 200 1·50	1,160 / 300	400		600
20		200	1·60	320					600		920

Fig. 12.—*Stores Ledger Account* (3) (LIFO)

This records the same facts as in Fig. 11, but on the last-in first-out principle. This tends to charge current production with current prices.

Note.—The closing stock represents:

£
400 units at £1·50 per unit = 600
200 units at £1·60 per unit = 320
                                600

From this exaggerated example it can readily be seen that the issue price is not the cost price.

It will be noticed that in this illustration (Fig. 13) the design of the account has been changed slightly. Cumulative quantity columns have been introduced so that comparisons, one with another, can be made to ascertain which materials have been fully issued from stock. It is recommended that the cumulative issues column is not entered until after the price has been calculated.

Example

In the first issue:

Cumulative receipts 1,500; Cumulative issues nil, so price is:

$$\frac{(£1 \cdot 50 + £1 \cdot 40)}{2} = £1 \cdot 45$$

In the second issue:

Cumulative receipts 2,600; Cumulative issues 700, so price is:

$$\frac{(£1 \cdot 50 + £1 \cdot 40 + £1 \cdot 55 + £1 \cdot 60)}{4} = £1 \cdot 51$$

In the third issue:

Cumulative receipts 2,600; Cumulative issues 1,600, so price is:

$$\frac{(£1 \cdot 55 + £1 \cdot 60)}{2} = £1 \cdot 57\frac{1}{2}$$

(1,600 exceeds cum. receipts to Jan. 14 (1,500) so stock at £1·50 and £1·40 is exhausted.)

In the fourth issue:

Cumulative receipts 3,400; Cumulative issues 2,000, so price is:

$$\frac{(£1 \cdot 55 + £1 \cdot 60 + £1 \cdot 45)}{3} = £1 \cdot 53\frac{1}{3}$$

4. Standard Price (Fig. 14)

A standard or predetermined issue price is calculated, which takes into consideration a number of factors which may influence the price of materials in a future period; such factors include:

(*a*) the possibility of a rise in prices due to expected wage increases;

STORES LEDGER ACCOUNT

Materials: ....   Maximum Quantity: ....   Reorder Level: ....   Folio: ....

Code: ....   Minimum Quantity: ....   Reorder Quantity: ....   Location: ....

Date	G.R. No.	Receipts				M.R. No.	Issues					Stock		
		Quantity		Price £	Amount £		Quantity		Price £	Amount £		Quantity	Price £	Amount £
		Actual	Cum.				Actual	Cum.						
Jan. 4		1,200	1,200	1·50	1,800							1,200	1·50	1,800
14		300	1,500	1·40	420							1,500		2,220
30							700	700	1·45	1,015		800		1,205
Feb. 21		600	2,100	1·55	930							1,400		2,135
Mar. 4		500	2,600	1·60	800							1,900		2,935
28							900	1,600	1·51	1,359		1,000		1,576
Apr. 15							400	2,000	1·57½	630		600		946
May 21		800	3,400	1·45	1,160							1,400		2,106
June 4							1,000	3,000	1·53⅓	1,533		400		573
20		200	3,600	1·60	320							600		893

FIG. 13.—*Stores ledger account* (4) (*simple average*)

Under the average methods of pricing material, the identity of material in store disappears, so that the closing stock figures cannot be verified as under the previous systems.

(*b*) the likelihood of a rise or fall in prices due to market conditions.

A standard price will be calculated for each item in store, which can then be compared with the actual price paid. If the actual price paid exceeds standard, then a loss will be realised; if the actual price is less than standard a profit will be obtained.

This method is relatively easy to operate, because all issues of an item are calculated at the same price. A great advantage is the opportunity to check the efficiency of purchasing materials, by seeing whether or not the actual price exceeds standard.

It should be noted that this method can be utilised in most industries, even though a system of standard costing is not in operation, although, of course, the greatest benefit will be obtained under a standard costing system. In this illustration it is assumed that the standard price of the material has been calculated to be £1·50 per unit.

It can be seen from Fig. 14 that the value of closing stock is over-valued, due to the fact that production has been charged at the standard price which is lower than the actual price. It should be noted that if the standard price charged to production had been higher than the actual price the value of stock would have been under-valued.

To check the efficiency of purchasing materials: (Actual receipts × Standard price) − Actual amount.

$$(3,600 \times £1·50) = £5,400$$
$$£5,400 - £5,430 = - £30$$

Actual amount paid exceeds standard cost of materials, so there has been a loss of £30 in purchasing. Again if the closing stock is valued at standard price the value would be 600 × £1·50 = £900, while the actual amount shown in the account is £930, giving a difference of £30.

Miscellaneous Systems of Valuing Material Issues

For reference purposes, the following systems are briefly mentioned.

Base stock

This is rather similar to FIFO in operation, with the addition of a fixed minimum stock of the material always being carried at original cost. This minimum stock is never charged to production, so it is rather in the nature of a fixed asset.

STORES LEDGER ACCOUNT

Materials: ....   Maximum Quantity: ....   Folio: ....
Code: ....   Minimum Quantity: ....   Location: ....
Reorder Level: ....
Reorder Quantity: ....

Date	G.R. No.	Receipts Quantity	Receipts Price £	Receipts Amount £	M.R. No.	Issues Quantity	Issues Price £	Issues Amount £	Stock Quantity	Stock Price £	Stock Amount £
Jan.	1	1,200	1·50	1,800					1,200	1·50	1,800
	14	300	1·40	420					1,500		2,220
	30					700	1·50	1,050	800		1,170
Feb.	21	600	1·55	930					1,400		2,100
Mar.	4	500	1·60	800					1,900		2,900
	28					900	1·50	1,350	1,000		1,550
Apr.	15					400	1·50	600	600		950
May	21	800	1·45	1,160					1,400		2,110
June	4					1,000	1·50	1,500	400		610
	20	200	1·60	320					600		930

FIG. 14.—*Stores ledger account* (5) (*standard price*)

Under the standard price method the closing stock figures cannot be verified. This method ensures that production is charged always at the standard price for the material; variances from the actual price paid being transferred to price variance account.

Weighted average price

This is similar to the simple average price, except that whenever a new purchase is made, the cost is added to the value of the balance in hand and the total thus arrived at is averaged by dividing by the new quantity then available.

Current market price

Each issue is charged out at current rates. To maintain proper stores control, differences between cost and prices must be debited or credited to a stores adjustment account.

Highest in first out (HIFO)

Materials issued from stores are charged at the rate of the highest-priced material in stores. This rate continues either until the material at that high price is exhausted, after which the next-highest price is used, or until a new batch of materials is received at a rate which is higher than the previous high price. This method attempts to ensure that materials issued to production absorb the high costs of materials, leaving stocks at relatively low-priced rates. In times of a rising price market, it would be rather similar to the current market price, with the exception that it would use actual prices paid rather than prices which are current in the market.

Next in first out (NIFO)

Materials issued are not charged at a price which has been paid, but rather at a price which has been committed or ordered. Let us assume, for example, that in stock there are two batches of materials, one at £1·20 and one at £1·40, and that there is a further batch of materials on order at £1·50 which has not yet been received. If materials were issued now, they would be priced at £1·50. This method is obviously an attempt to be more realistic than the current market price method; instead of ascertaining the current market price at the time of issue, one uses the latest price at which one has ordered new supplies of the materials.

Stock valuation

It must be observed that the method of valuing stores for the annual balance sheet is quite independent of the system for pricing out materials for cost-accounting purposes. The recognised method of valuing stores for the balance sheet is at the lowest of cost or current replacement price. It should also be noted that the methods discussed in this chapter are methods of pricing out materials, not methods of physically issuing materials. For example, the materials issued may be priced using a LIFO system, but it certainly would not follow that materials were issued by the storekeeper in this way.

The problem which arises from valuing stocks in the cost accounts at one price and the stock in the financial accounts at another price is discussed more fully in Chapter 13.

Examination Questions

Also includes questions on Chapters 4 and 5

1 Enumerate and explain briefly the functions of the books and documents which are normally required for the maintenance of an efficient record of stores. *(SCCA)*

2. Give a description of the essential documents necessary to operate a simple stock control system and a brief description of how these work. *(SCCA)*

3. What factors should be taken into account in determining whether or not to buy increased quantities of materials for stock with discounts given for large quantities? *(SCCA)*

4. Submit a layout for a stores requisition note suitable for use in connection with the issue of varied raw materials and subsequently as a prime record for entry in the costing records. *(AIA)*

5. (*a*) In connection with a material control system, describe the functions of the following documents, stating clearly the essential information they should provide:

(*i*) Purchase requisition.

(*ii*) Bin card.

(*iii*) Materials requisition.

(*iv*) Goods received note.

(*v*) Discrepancy note.

(*b*) "Stock-holdings should be neither too high nor too low." Comment briefly. *(ACA)*

6. Devise a form for recording the receipt of materials and state how the form assists the system of internal control. *(IAADP)*

7. The buyer for a wholesale business wishes to install in his warehouse a system which will give him the following information:

(*a*) the normal rate of consumption of goods carried in stock;

(*b*) rapid information on the delivery position so as to enable him to chase goods on order.

Give your recommendations for dealing with the problems under (*a*) and (*b*) above. *(ICMA)*

8. What are the essential functions in the physical control of raw materials and stores? *(SCA)*

9. Describe a system relating to the purchase of materials which

will ensure that the buying department, the goods inward department, and the cost office will work on the basis of common information and which will ensure the accuracy and authenticity of all payments made.   *(IAADP)*

10. Draft a form of bin or locker card with three specimen entries thereon, and explain the purpose and utility of such cards.   *(IA)*

11. Draw up a specimen bin card for use in a general store, and give your reasoned advice as to whether it should be kept in the stores office or alongside the goods to which it relates.   *(RSA)*

12. Name the essential documents for stores stock control and briefly define the function of each document.   *(SCA)*

13. Outline the matters to which consideration should be given when planning the location and layout of a factory stores.
(IAADP)

14. It is found that systematic thefts have taken place from the stores of a large company manufacturing small machine parts. Beyond the entry of purchase invoices in the bought journal, no records of stores have been kept. You are desired to recommend an adequate system for the supervision of the stores in future, including the rulings of any books or forms you consider necessary. Prepare therefore whatever instructions or explanations you consider it advisable to issue to the persons who will keep the future stores records, and append your proposed rulings.   *(LCCI)*

15. It is found that material in excess of actual requirements has been drawn out of store by one department, but that it is required for use in another department; what are the cost accounting records that should be kept?   *(IA)*

16. In the context of materials used in production, what do you understand by the term "stock control"?

Mention briefly some of the considerations which influence the decision as to levels of stocks held.   *(ACA)*

17. At the time of the great American slump of the late 1920s, it was said that "stocks are the graveyard of a business." Give your views on this statement. Is it pertinent now? What steps would you take to avoid a similar situation today?   *(ICMA)*

18. As cost accountant of a complex engineering company where the cost of the stores control system is relatively high when compared with the value of stocks in hand:

(a) submit to management a brief report outlining the major items of cost involved in the stores control system;

(b) discuss briefly two methods by which these costs could be absorbed into product costs.   *(ICMA)*

19. Briefly describe a system of recording the receipt and issue of goods from store to departments in any manufacturing business with which you are familiar.   *(ICSA)*

20. How far is the efficiency of a costing system dependent upon the accuracy of stores recording? *(IA)*

21. Explain the imprest system of stores control and discuss its advantages and disadvantages. *(ICMA)*

22. Define the following and say on which basis each should be determined: (*a*) minimum stock; (*b*) maximum stock; (*c*) ordering level. *(RSA)*

23. Define reordering level and explain its relation to maximum and minimum stock levels. What factors must be considered in fixing reordering levels and quantities? *(ICMA)*

24. As cost accountant of a manufacturing concern of medium size, you have proposed to the directors that the stores control system should be improved. Your proposals are to be discussed by the directors at their next board meeting. To enable them to appreciate the basic requirements of an up-to-date system the directors have asked you to present a report concentrating on certain definite aspects.

Prepare a report to the directors dealing particularly with the following:

(*a*) The steps to be taken to introduce maximum, minimum and reorder stock levels, enumerating the factors to be considered in setting each level and stating the advantages to be gained by their use.

(*b*) The importance of stores turnover as a measure in considering requirements for working capital. *(ICMA)*

25. What factors should be taken into consideration in fixing maximum and minimum stock levels for raw materials? In what circumstances, and at which periods, would you suggest a revision of the levels? How are ordering quantities affected (if at all) by those levels? *(ICMA)*

26. Financial loss can be incurred through carrying excessive or insufficient quantities of stocks and stores.

1. Tabulate, giving examples, the various causes of such financial loss.

2. (*a*) Explain what you understand by the terms—
   (*i*) Minimum stock level.
   (*ii*) Maximum stock level.
   (*iii*) Reorder level.

(*b*) What factors are taken into account in calculating these levels? *(ICAS)*

27. What do you understand by perpetual inventory, and what are the advantages of the system? *(CAA)*

28. In a factory where "continuous stocktaking" is carried out periodically discrepancies are discovered. Suggest possible causes of these discrepancies. *(ACA)*

29. What objects are attained by the adoption of a scheme of "perpetual inventory"? Describe the procedures that become necessary and show how revealed differences either of quantity or of quality are dealt with in the cost accounts.   *(RSA)*

30. "Perpetual inventory methods dispense with the necessity for annual stocktaking." Explain "perpetual inventory" and discuss briefly the circumstances under which the above statement can be regarded as true.   *(ACA)*

31. (a) There may be a danger that stores requisitions do not give a clear description of what is required or that the store-keeper may wrongly identify an item. As a result incorrect materials or parts may be issued, with consequent delay in production. Also there is the danger that the wrong account in the stores ledger may be credited.

Set out the essential features of a stores accounting system which would help to overcome these difficulties.

(b) What is meant by the terms "perpetual inventory" and "continuous stocktaking"?   *(ACA)*

32. A system of continuous stock-taking is operated in a large engineering company. Stock-takers frequently discover discrepancies when checking stocks of raw materials.

As cost accountant of the company, you are required to submit a report to the board of directors, in which you should suggest possible causes for these discrepancies. Outline the cost accounting treatment required for normal and abnormal losses in stores.

(ICMA)

33. The company in which you are accountant maintains perpetual inventory records. At a recent stock check the records for a certain item gave a stock balance of fifty units while the actual physical stock was only thirty-five units.

1. Give possible reasons for this discrepancy between book and physical stock.

2. Suggest rules which will result in the perpetual inventory records being accurate and the system working effectively.

3. What are the benefits to be expected from maintaining perpetual inventory records?   *(ICAS)*

34. Describe briefly how you would conduct the audit of a system of continuous stocktaking and what procedure you would adopt to deal with the differences.   *(ICMA)*

35. What methods of pricing issues from stores are in common use? Explain the steps which must be taken under each method to ensure the balancing of the stores ledger account.   *(RSA)*

36. State the various methods of pricing stores requisitions with which you are familiar, and discuss their respective merits.   *(RSA)*

37. State in tabular form the effects upon production costs and

stock values of using each of the three methods of pricing issues from stocks known as: (*a*) First in first out; (*b*) Average cost; (*c*) Last in first out. *(SCA)*

38. In periods of (*a*) steadily rising prices and (*b*) steadily falling prices, state what principles you would follow in pricing materials:

1. issued to production orders (which may be in process for up to 6 months);
2. in preparing estimates for quotations;
3. in valuing stocks at the end of an accounting period.

Give brief reasons. *(ICMA)*

39. Explain the various circumstances under which the issue price of a stores material may be higher than the last purchase price. *(ICMA)*

40. During periods of rapid increase or decrease in prices of materials used in production, which of the following methods of pricing stores issues results in the most accurate costing of goods manufactured and sold: (*a*) FIFO; (*b*) Actual cost method; (*c*) Average cost method; (*d*) LIFO; (*e*) Standard cost method? Give reasons in support of your answer. *(ICMA)*

41. Discuss the factors to be considered when establishing reorder levels and economic order quantities for the materials purchased by a manufacturing company. *(AIA)*

42. (*a*) State why it is often necessary for a manufacturing business to hold stocks of:

(*i*) raw materials;
(*ii*) finished goods.

(*b*) Discuss the effect in times of inflation on valuation of stocks and on product costs of using for the pricing of issues of raw materials:

(*i*) last-in first-out (LIFO) method;
(*ii*) first-in first-out (FIFO) method;
(*iii*) weighted average method.

(*c*) Explain why it is frequently found useful in the control of finished stocks to establish:

(*i*) maximum stock levels;
(*ii*) reorder stock levels; and
(*iii*) minimum stock levels. *(RSA)*

43. What added costs become involved in both excessive and obsolete stocks? What procedures can be instituted to ensure that these items are under regular review? *(RSA)*

44. At stock-taking it is required to know how many months' consumption of each important material is on hand. How would you present such figures? What action would you recommend to avoid undue amounts of unactive stocks? *(LCCI)*

45. What action would you advise to prevent capital lying idle in obsolete and slow-moving stocks of materials? *(IAADP)*

46. You are asked to advise a manufacturing company regarding the installation of a stores ledger. Draft a report to the directors, stating:

(*a*) The advantages of keeping a stores ledger.

(*b*) The documents from which the entries therein will be made.

(*c*) The various methods available for pricing issues.

(*d*) The effect of (*c*) upon the balances on hand. *(IAADP)*

47. Differences between the book balance of materials on hand and the physical stock can be divided into two groups:

(*a*) differences caused by errors in the records and posting;

(*b*) differences caused by the treatment of the material itself.

Set out the classes of differences arising in each group, and the methods by which such differences can be controlled. *(LCCI)*

48. (*a*) Explain fully what you understand by the following terms used in connection with stock control.

Reorder level.

Minimum stock level

Maximum stock level.

Average stock level.

(*b*) Use the following figures to calculate each of the levels mentioned in (*a*).

Normal usage	60 per week
Minimum usage	20 per week
Maximum usage	100 per week
Reorder quantity	400 per week
Reorder period	3–7 weeks *(AIA)*

49. Two components, A and B, are used as follows:

Normal usage	50 per week each
Minimum usage	25 per week each
Maximum usage	75 per week each
Reorder quantity	A: 300; B: 500
Reorder period	A: 4 to 6 weeks: B: 2 to 4 weeks

Calculate for each component:

(*a*) reorder level;

(*b*) minimum level;

(*c*) maximum level;

(*d*) average stock level.

Comment briefly on the difference in levels for the two components. *(ICMA)*

50. A company uses raw material A in the manufacture of its products. There is given below information extracted from the company's raw material stores ledger.

| March | Received | | Issued |
	Quantity in units	Total value	Quantity in units
		£	
1	180	720	
4			120
8	120	552	
11			90
14	90	432	
17			72
21			48
24	120	624	
28			46

You are required for raw material A to:

(a) prepare a ruling of a stores ledger account and to record in it the transactions for the month given above using the weighted average method of pricing;

(b) state:

(i) in units and value the stock loss if the physical stock in hand at 31 March was 130 units;

(ii) the value of the physical stock in hand at 31 March, using the last in first out method of pricing.   (RSA)

51. Consideration is being given to the method to be used for the pricing of issues from a raw material stores ledger. The account for a certain material for the month of April has been used for this. A comparison of the results achieved by two different pricing methods has been commenced and partially completed. These results are:

Date	Receipts		Issues		
				First	Second
	Quantity	Value	Quantity	method	method
April	in units	£	in units	value £	value £
1	600	750			
3	200	240			
8			400	500	490
9	500	575			

| Date | Receipts | | Issues | | |
	Quantity in units	Value £	Quantity in units	First method value £	Second method value £
April					
10			400	490	460
11	600	660			
14			400	460	440
16	500	600			
18			400	445	480
21			300	330	
22	500	575			
24			600	715	
25	400	480			
28			300	345	

There was no opening stock.
Stock in hand at April 30 was 480 units.
You are required to:

(a) identify and state both the first and second methods of pricing used;

(b) complete the account for the second pricing method;

(c) list briefly the merits and demerits of the second pricing method.   (ICMA)

52. The stores ledger account for a certain material for the month of October, includes the data given below.

You are to assume the following alternative methods are being considered and are required to calculate the values of:

(a) the stores loss at 31 October, using first-in first-out system;

(b) issues of five of the following:

(i)   27 October using last in first out system;
(ii)   22 October using highest in first out system;
(iii)   14 October using next in first out system;
(iv)   27 October using simple average system;
(v)   9 October using weighted average system;
(vi)   19 October using periodic simple average system;
(vii)   5 October using periodic weighted average system.

Date	Ordered			Received			Issued			Balance in stock		
	Q.	P.	A.	Q.	P.	A.	Q.	P.	A.	Q.	P.	A.
October		£	£		£	£		£	£		£	£
1										420	1·20	
2	500	1·25										
5							200					
7				300	1·25							
9							400					
10				200	1·25							
12	500	1·20										
14							200					
15	500	1·30										
16				400	1·20							
19							300					
20				100	1·20							
21				200	1·30							
22							300					
23	500	1·35										
24				300	1·30							
26				200	1·35							
27							400					
28				300	1·35							
29	500	1·25										
30							200					
31	Actual stock in hand									380		

Key Q = Quantity
P = Price
A = Amount   *(ICMA)*

Chapter 7

Organisation for Wages Control

Introduction

WAGES paid to employees in the factory and offices constitute one of the heaviest items of expenditure in any business, and, as a great deal of it is usually paid out in cash, the organisation needs to be well designed to suit the particular circumstances, and simple and fool-proof in operation.

Wages control consists of five main divisions of responsibility, as follows.

(*a*) Personnel recording.
(*b*) Recording gate times.
(*c*) Preparation of payroll.
(*d*) Allocation of wages to jobs or processes.
(*e*) Making up and paying out wages.

Personnel Records

When a worker is engaged, the personnel officer asks him to complete a record sheet, which is filed for subsequent reference. He is then given an identifying "clock number" which will be used each week on his "clock card".

Recording Gate Times

It is considered important to record the "in" and "out" times of workers entering and leaving the factory because, generally speaking, these times become the basis on which payment is made at a stated rate per hour. Even if workers are not paid by the hour, but by piece-work rates, that is to say at so much per piece satisfactorily completed, it is still very useful to know for other purposes how many hours they have been at work, and "clocking on" is therefore to be recommended. Only in cases of workers being paid by the week, and whose absence can be reported by other means, can the rule be relaxed.

The methods of recording which are employed vary considerably according to the outlook and prosperity of the concern. Old-fashioned methods, such as the use of brass checks or discs, and dial recorders still function satisfactorily for their purpose and tend to be retained. However, the modern time recorder represents such an advance in this field that more and more firms are making use of them. It will be sufficient for the purpose of this book to describe such a system.

No. 525 NO. .... NAME .... WEEK ENDING .... 19 .. Harlow | IN	OUT	IN	OUT	Total | (blank grid) ORDINARY TIME / OVERTIME / LESS NAT. INS. / OTHER DEDUC'NS — Hours Rate £ p NET WAGES	**NO.** .... **NAME** .... **WEEK ENDING** HOURS WORKED — HRS. HRS. OVERTIME ALLOWANCE — HRS. HRS. TOTAL — HRS. HRS. DAY / IN / OUT / IN / OUT / Total M Tu W Th F S Su (AM/PM grid) NET AMOUNT PAYABLE .... RECEIVED THE NET AMOUNT PAYABLE AS STATED Signed ....

FIG. 15—*Clock Card— usual type*

This shows the normal type of clock card for use with a card time recorder. It provides sufficient space for the calculation of the wages due, prior to entry on the wages sheets.

FIG. 16—*Clock Card— alternative type*

This type of card provides a means of differentiating between "straight time" and overtime premium. This is most valuable in the proper apportionment of wages.

Illustrations of clock cards for use in these machines are given in Figs. 15 and 16, and the machine itself is illustrated in Fig. 17.

The clock cards are ruled so that an employee's time is recorded in a special column. The machine is pre-set each day to allow for the card to be inserted in the slot of the machine up to the required depth. As soon as the card reaches the stop position the machine automatically and immediately stamps the time on it, changing from a blue marking to a red one at the appropriate time to indicate lateness and overtime working.

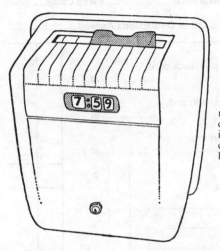

FIG. 17—*Card time recorder*

In this type of card recorder it is only necessary for the worker to insert his clock card into the machine. The time is then automatically stamped in the correct position, and in red ink if he is late.

On the reverse side of the card it is easy to have printed rulings to facilitate calculation of the wages due, but many firms prefer to have a specially ruled form for the purpose. They find that the space on the typical clock card is too cramped to do the job clearly. An illustration of such a ruling is given in Fig. 18.

Special arrangements have to be made, of course, for the calculation of the wages due to piece-workers, and this may be explained by taking an example, as follows.

Example

Workers are employed in packing peaches into display cases. They are paid at the rate of £0·10 per case packed and passing inspection.

Each worker will stack the filled cases on to a pallet—that is a raised platform which can afterwards be moved by means of a fork lift truck—and when the requisite number has been stacked will be given a signed chit entitling him or her to payment for so many cases at £0·10 each.

On presentation of these chits at the end of the week a summary is made and this summary forms the basis of payment.

X Y Z PLC—WAGES CALCULATION SHEET

Name............................. Department.................................. Clock No................

Rate of Pay..................... National Insurance...................... PAYE Code............

Holiday Savings................................. Other Deductions Agreed.....................

		£	p
Hours worked—Ordinary time per clock card	.... at		
Overtime per clock card	.... at		
Overtime premium	.... at		
	£ p		
Bonus, 10% on total earnings			
Less: PAYE			
National Insurance			
Holiday savings			
Net amount payable		£	
Employer's National Insurance..............			

CALCULATION OF PAYE

Total pay to last week

Total pay this week

Less Tax free pay to date

Taxable pay per coding

Tax this week   £

FIG. 18—*Wages calculation sheet*

A specimen form for the calculation of the wages due to a piece-worker in a machine shop is shown in Fig. 19.

PIECE-WORK ORDER

No.: ....

Employee's Name: ....   Date: ....

Clock No.: ....   Time Taken: ....

Part: ....   Price: ....

Operation: ....   Quantity: ....

No. Made	Passed	Rejected	Rate	£

Signed Employee: Signed Inspection:

Foreman:

FIG. 19.—*Piece-work order*

These orders are the employee's entitlement to be paid for the quantity of pieces he has completed which satisfactorily pass inspection. The agreed piece-work price is stated, as well as details of the work to be done.

Preparation of Payroll

As soon as the wages for an individual have been calculated and checked they are entered on the payroll or wages sheet. This will be done department by department, so that the total wages incurred by each may be ascertained. An illustration of a payroll is given in Fig. 20.

In many large firms the name of each employee, his clock number, his income-tax coding, his rate of pay, and the standard deductions for national insurance, etc., are recorded on "addressograph" plates. A straight list may be run off to help in the completion of the clock cards, and the payroll may be initially prepared in the same way. If, as has been suggested, separate wage

PAYROLL

No.	Name	Total hours worked	Rate	Basic pay	Over-time premium	Gross pay	Free pay	Taxable pay to date	Tax due to date	Tax refunds	Total Deductions	Net pay	Net pay	Em-ployer Nat. Ins.
				£	£	£	£	£	£	£	£	£		£

Fig. 20.—*Payroll*

This specimen of a payroll allows for an additional wages column to be used for a particular purpose such as overtime premium. Most firms have them specially printed to suit their own requirements.

calculation forms are used, these may be started by the plates, which need not then be used on the payroll.

The payroll columns may be completed by handwritten figures, using one of the advertised systems, which at one and the same operation will produce the payroll, the personal earnings card for each employee, and the employee's pay slip. Alternatively, a front-feed accounting machine may be used for neat, speedy, and accurate results. Such machines will also automatically produce the totals of the columns. Such a machine is illustrated in Fig. 21.

In many firms microcomputers have taken over this part of the accounting system. Even relatively small firms can now afford to operate a microcomputer which can be programmed to undertake effectively the tasks referred to above.

Allocation of Wages to Jobs and Processes

The allocation of wages to departments is done from the payroll itself. In the case of some concerns the production departments may correspond to processes, and the direct labour cost incurred for a process is obtained at once from the payroll.

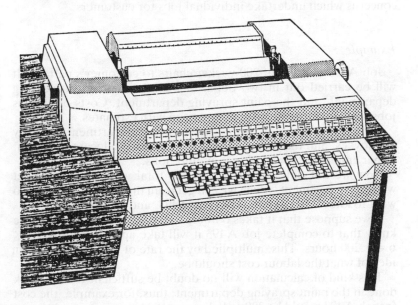

FIG. 21.—*Full-text full-keyboard accounting machine*

Example

A sweet manufacturer has the following production departments:
                      boiling
                      rolling
                      wrapping
The gross wages incurred in these departments for the month of November were: boiling, £1,600; rolling, £1,550; and wrapping, £1,500. These figures are those shown in the payroll.

This means that the payroll will be sectionalised into boiling, rolling and wrapping departments. If we imagine that the specimen payroll shown in Fig. 20 refers to the boiling department, then the total of the gross pay column will show the figure of £1,600.

In addition to production departments, most concerns have a number of ancillary departments known as service departments. These are so named because they render services to the concern as a whole. Examples of such departments are the boiler-house, the works canteen, and the tool-room. The wages of such departments will also be obtained from sections of the payroll.

However, there is a special wages problem involved in the case of concerns which undertake individual jobs for customers.

Example

Job A493 consists of 200 wicker chairs to customer's pattern. It will be carried out in two departments, viz. the basket weaving department, and the paint spraying department. Costs of various jobs are kept separately for comparison with estimates.

Let us suppose that the basket weaving department has fifty employees, and that ten of them have job A493 allocated to them. Other employees are working on other jobs.

Now we not only want to know the total wages of the basket weaving department, which we can get from the payroll, but we also want to know the labour cost of job A493, and of other jobs.

If we suppose that it takes 6 hours to fabricate a wicker chair we know that to complete job A493 it will take approximately 200 × 6 = 1,200 hours. This, multiplied by the rate of pay, will give us an idea of what the labour cost should be.

This kind of calculation will no doubt be sufficient for the work done in the paint spraying department; thus, for example, the cost for job A493 would be 200 × ½ hour = 100 hours × rate of pay.

However, with regard to the basket weaving department, we want greater accuracy, so therefore we make use of one of the methods, usually applied to engineering workshops, illustrated in Figs. 22 and 23.

In such undertakings as this a system has to be devised to ensure that the wages of each production department are correctly charged up to the various jobs done by that department.

Early methods of doing this were by handwritten weekly or daily time sheets. These methods still persist in connection with the building and civil engineering industry, for the jobs done are on scattered sites and remote from organised control.

In factory work, however, electric time recorders can be easily adapted to the purpose.

Figure 22 shows a time card issued to F. Smith, an employee in an engineering department. As he begins work on a job, and again as he finishes his work on a job, he has his card stamped with the time. The job no. on which he works is given in the left-hand column. Thus he began to work on job 67 at 6.02 on 7 July and finished his work on that job at 7.00. The time taken is therefore recorded as 1 hour. In the case of job 108 he began work at 7.00, as soon as he finished on job 67. There was a meal break of half-an-hour, and he finished on that job at 10.01. Allowing for the meal break, the working time is recorded as 2½ hours.

At the end of each day, Smith's wages chargeable to production (time taken × rate of pay) will be calculated and analysed to the jobs on which he has worked, and the total agreed. This will be done for every other employee, and thus the wages cost of each job will be totalled and established.

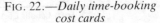

FIG. 22.—*Daily time-booking cost cards*
The time spent on each job by a worker is recorded by a Gledhill–Brook recording clock.

JOB COST CARD   I.T.R. LSF 1228

ORDER No. .4.2.2..... DRAWING No. ...9.0......... PATTERN No. .4.3.1......

Special Instructions ....

....

Date STARTED 2.9/8...
FINISHED 3.0/8..

Workman No	OPERATION		Cost £ p	Rate £ p	Time Taken Hrs	Time Taken Min	
17	Dressing	Off	2·04	3·60	—	34	AUG 29 8:34
		On					AUG 29 8:00
15	Marking Off	Off	7·20	4·80	1	30	AUG 29 10:06
		On					AUG 29 8:36
9	Rough Planing	Off	4·27	4·20	1	01	AUG 29 11:09
		On					AUG 29 10:08
4	Rough Turning	Off	12·74	4·20	3	02	AUG 29 5:02
		On					AUG 29 2:00
3	Turning	Off	17·85	4·50	3	58	AUG 30 11:58
		On					AUG 30 8:00
21	Planing	Off	2·10	4·50	—	28	AUG 30 12:28
		On					AUG 30 12:00
8	Grinding	Off	7·57	5·10	1	29	AUG 30 3:01
		On					AUG 30 1:32
7	Drilling	Off	3·50	4·20	—	50	AUG 30 3:54
		On					AUG 30 3:04
19	Cleaning Off	Off	2·03	3·30	—	37	AUG 30 4:34
		On					AUG 30 3:57
38	Finishing	Off	5·20	4·80	1	05	AUG 30 5:40
		On					AUG 30 4:35
		Off					
		On					
		Off					
		On					

Total Labour Cost , ...£ 64·50 p

ENTER MATERIAL USED ON REVERSE SIDE

FIG. 23.—*Labour Cost Card*

Instead of, or in addition to, a separate job ticket, a cost card sometimes travels with each job as it goes from operation to operation. In this way the times can be worked out and the total labour cost found. It will be noted that the illustration is headed "Job Cost Card" because it provides for materials to be entered on the reverse side. As this is somewhat unusual, the caption has been altered.

In Fig. 23 is shown an example of another method of arriving at the cost of each job. In this case the cost card for a job is issued to the first employee to work on that particular job. It is accompanied by a blueprint of the details of the job, which each employee in turn must read and interpret. The job cost card and blueprint therefore travels with the work, and is clocked "on" and "off" for each operation. Thus for example, operator no. 8 who performs a grinding operation commenced at 1.32 and finished at 3.01. The time taken is calculated as 1 hr 29 mins. The rate of pay is £5·10, so the cost becomes £7·57. In this way the labour cost of the order 422 per drawing no. 90 is built up.

One practical difficulty of this method is that greasy hands tend to make the cost card rather messy to handle.

Making Up and Paying Out Wages

When a payroll is prepared department by department, as soon as the totals of the first have been cast and ruled off, it is possible to make up the pay packets for that section. Of course, this cannot be done unless the wages have already been drawn from the bank, and most of the larger firms have made an arrangement to do this on an imprest basis.

When the money is drawn from the bank, the bank cashier will want to know in what proportions of notes and coin he is to issue it, and this information is given to him on the basis of previous requirements. On return from the bank, the total amount drawn is immediately checked and arranged in convenient piles. After this the amount required for each department is obtained by analysis of the net pay column, and is counted out from the cashier's table.

The pay packets are then filled and, provided no discrepancy is found, they may be sealed. Some firms find that automatic coin-dispensing machines help in the task of filling the packets.

Each pay packet will contain the employee's pay slip, giving details of the gross pay, less deductions. When paying out it is a useful arrangement for it to be done in the departments, and in the presence of the departmental foreman, who knows the employees. The clock cards are also often handed out to the operatives in advance, so that they can check on the amount of their wages; the cards are then handed in, signed, in return for the pay packet.

Certain safeguards within the wages section are deemed advisable, and act as a form of internal check. For example, those who check the clock cards should not be concerned in the preparation of the payroll, and those who do that work should not be concerned in making up the pay or in paying out the wages. The duties should also be changed about at short notice.

Specimen Question

XYZ PLC estimate that their wages will amount to £2,000 per week as a maximum, and on April 1 transfer that sum from their main account at Midas Bank to a wages imprest account. On April 5 they draw the sum of £1,900 on account of wages, and subsequently find that the wages amount to £1,950·84 net. In the second week the wages cheque is drawn for £1,980, and actual net amount of wages payable amounts to £1,975·77. Write up the wages imprest account.

Answer

Wages Imprest Account

		£			£
Apr.	1 Transfer from		Apr.	5 Cheque	1,900·00
	No. 1 A/c	2,000·00		Balance c/d	100·00
Apr.	5 Balance b/d	100·00	Apr.	7 Cheque to	
	Transfer from			reimburse	
	No. 1 A/c	1,950·84		petty cash	50·84
				8 Balance c/d	2,000·00
Apr.	8 Balance b/d	2,000·00		12 Cheque	1,980·00
	14 Cash, wages			14 Balance c/d	24·23
	surplus	4·23			
Apr.	14 Balance b/d	24·23		15 Balance c/d	2,000·00
	Transfer from				
	No. 1 A/c	1,975·77			
	15 Balance b/d	2,000·00			

Examination Questions on Chapters 7 and 8 are given at the end of Chapter 8.

Chapter 8

Methods of Remuneration and the Effect on Costs

Problems of Remuneration of Labour

WHEN considering which method of remuneration should be adopted, a number of major questions have to be borne in mind. Low wages do not necessarily result in low costs of production, and innumerable instances may be given of manufacturers who pay high wages and whose costs are actually lower than those paying less wages to their employees. The reasons for this are not difficult to see, because apart from the fact that efficient workers earning good wages may produce better work and in greater volume, with less waste, there is the factor of the incidence of overhead expenses, and particularly of the fixed overhead. The saving in cost per unit due to the spreading of overhead over a greater number of units of production may, and often does, exceed the higher amount charged in the cost for well-paid labour.

Example

In factory A the wages paid are at the rate of £4·00 per hour. Hours worked are 40,000 per annum. The overhead, most of which is fixed, amounts to £100,000. Production amounts to 100,000 units per annum. It is estimated that if the rate of pay was increased to £5·00 per hour, greater productivity could be obtained, and the shop stewards have agreed to increase production to 125,000 units. Thus:

Case (1)

Wages	40,000 × £4·00	£160,000
Overhead		100,000
		£260,000

Cost per unit £260,000 ÷ 100,000 £2·60

73

Case (2)

Wages 40,000 × £5·00	£200,000	
Overhead	100,000	
	£300,000	

Cost per unit £300,000 ÷ 125,000 £2·40

Thus the total cost per unit would be reduced by £0·20.
The factors which have to be considered include the following.

(*a*) The need for having a satisfied staff of workers.

(*b*) The method which will produce the best work, from the point of view of (*i*) quality of work, (*ii*) quantity of output. In some cases quality and precision are comparatively more important than quantity, and vice versa.

(*c*) The cost of the method. Most wages systems are simple from the point of view of clerical work; others demand much detailed recording of times, quantities, etc., and correspondingly complex analysis and recording in the cost accounts.

(*d*) The flexibility of the scheme to permit of any necessary variations which may arise.

(*e*) The scheme must be readily understood by the employees. They understand straight time wages, piece-work rates, and simple bonus schemes, but not complex ones.

(*f*) The incidence of overhead, which can be linked with schemes involving consideration of output and time-saving in production.

(*g*) Loss arises when there are frequent changes in labour personnel. The expenses of finding new employees, attending to their engagement records, instructing recruits as to routine and detailed duties are often overlooked, yet these are losses inseparable from labour turnover. A satisfactory basis of payment to discourage labour changes is therefore advantageous.

Methods of Remunerating Labour

Methods of remuneration may be classified as follows.

(*a*) Time- or day-rate wages based on the time employed, including extra payment for overtime.

(*b*) Payment by results:

    (*i*)   piece-work;
    (*ii*) bonus schemes;
    (*iii*) profit-sharing schemes.

Payment by Flat Time-wages

Wages are paid at an agreed rate per hour, day, or week, without reference to the quantity of work done. Overtime is usually paid at higher rates, e.g. time and a quarter, time and a half, or double time.

There is no special inducement to attract more than average effort, except that the employee must work with sufficient diligence to ensure that his services will be retained.

The method is suitable in the following cases.

(a) Where supervision is close.

(b) For supervisors, inspectors, general labourers, and other classes of indirect labour.

(c) When measurement of work would not be simple, e.g. engine drivers, airline crew.

(d) For precision work, e.g. tool-makers and pattern-makers, where care is more important than speed and large output.

(e) Where high wages or rates are paid and standards of efficiency and output are set which the foremen must maintain.

Payment by Results

Piece-work

Individual piece-work. An incentive wage based on a fixed price per unit of work, regardless of the time taken. The unit may be an article, a batch of a stated quantity, or an operation.

The advantages are:

(a) a high speed is usually developed;

(b) a larger output generally results;

(c) constant repetition tends to uniformity of the product;

(d) the employer enjoys lower unit costs as output is increased, owing to the wider spread of the overheads over a larger number of units produced; the benefit is particularly important in regard to the fixed overheads, as in total they tend to remain the same, but the proportion falling to be borne by units produced becomes less as the output increases.

In the case of some workers careful work *may* be made a secondary consideration to quantity of output. Special inspection is thus required, which adds to the cost and thus reduces the savings otherwise obtained.

There are several piece-work schemes under which differential piece-rates are used, varying with the quantity produced, i.e. at stated increases in the number of units made the ordinary piece-work rate is increased. This serves as a special incentive for the worker to produce rapidly to earn the higher piece-rates offered. *Contract system.* A collective piece-work contract is made with a contracting workman, who engages the men and pays them their share. Again, when a group of, say, five workers feed and tend a machine, a price per 100 pieces (say) will be paid and is so fixed that the piece-rate provides wages which are equally divided among the workers, with, perhaps, the chargehand taking a double share.

Premium Bonus Scheme of Payment

Under piece-work systems the wages charge per unit in the costs remains constant, but labour's reward depends on the number of units produced, and output has a definite tendency to increase. The premium bonus schemes introduce a different principle, in that a bonus is given having regard to time saved over a pre-arranged time allowed per job.

Employees have an incentive to give their best efforts and save time on production orders, and the employer, knowing that he reduces his costs, seeks to maintain a sound organisation and efficient plant to ensure maximum production.

The various systems of premium bonus schemes differ chiefly in the method of computing the proportion of saving which is to be paid as bonus to the employees.

There is a reduced charge *per unit* for overhead, due to the spread of total shop expense over a greater number of units produced. The sum of the savings on all the units or jobs is the "fund" to be divided between the employer and his employees. There is thus a limit to the amount available for bonus. This limit is flexible, as it is determined by the extent to which production is in excess of normal production based on standard- or allowed-times for jobs.

The Halsey and the *Halsey–Weir premium bonus schemes.* These are similar, except that in the first the bonus paid is 50% of the time saved (valued at the employee's hourly rate of pay) over the time allowed for the job; and in the second the premium bonus is 30%. However, it is customary to assume that the bonus is 50%.

Example

An allowed time for a certain job of work is set at 3 hours, and employees Clark, Smith and Jones each do the job in 3, 2½ and 2 hours respectively, their ordinary wage rate being £4·00 per hour. The earnings under the Halsey scheme would be as below:

	Time allowed (hours)	Time taken (hours)	Basic pay at £4·00	Time saved (hours)	Bonus time (50%)	Bonus pay £	Total pay for job £
Clark	3	3	12·00	nil	nil	nil	12·00
Smith	3	2½	10·00	½	¼	1·00	11·00
Jones	3	2	8·00	1	½	2·00	10·00

At first sight it would appear that the slower workers are better paid, but although this is true for the individual job, it is not so for the amount earned per hour. Thus the amounts earned per hour are:

Clark £4·00
Smith £4·40
Jones £5·00

From this example it will be obvious that for a premium bonus scheme to work effectively there must be a sufficient number of jobs on hand to keep the workers continuously employed throughout the week.

The Rowan premium bonus scheme. Under this scheme the premium to be added to the pay-rate is the percentage that the time saved is of the time allowed.

It is often more convenient to calculate the wages at basic rates, and then add the percentage or proportion.

Thus, suppose the percentage to be added to the basic rate of £3·60 is 33⅓%. We may calculate:

(*a*) 8 hours at (£3·60 + £1·20) = 8 × £4·80 = £38·40
or (*b*) 8 hours at £3·60 = £28·80
Add 33⅓% = £9·60 = £38·40

To show the comparison between the Halsey and the Rowan systems, let us take the same example as before. Payments under the Rowan system will be:

	Time allowed (hours)	Time taken (hours)	Basic pay at £4·00	Time saved (hours)	Bonus time	Bonus pay £	Total pay £
Clark	3	3	12·00	nil	nil	nil	12·00
Smith	3	2½	10·00	½	⅙	1·67	11·67
Jones	3	2	8·00	1	⅓	2·67	10·67

The Rowan system is seen to be more favourable to the employees at first, for savings up to 50% of the time allowed. Thereafter the Halsey scheme becomes more favourable—at least in theory—but there are limitations to the speed a worker can sustain day in and day out.

Other Bonus Schemes

The fixed bonus system. A separate fixed bonus per hour or per unit is given in each department if output reaches or exceeds a stated quantity. This is, in effect, a bonus for collective time saved.

Cost premium method. A standard cost is set up, and if the actual cost proves to be less, a proportion of the saving is distributed to the employees on some agreed basis. This is a collective bonus scheme.

Production "points" system. A "point" is made to represent the amount of work an employee should do in one minute, giving a fair allowance for rest. The "point" is determined by a time study of each operation or even part of an operation.

Sixty points is thus the standard for one hour, or 480 for an 8-hour day.

An incentive rate is fixed "per point" and the employee is paid for his production measured in "points". In some cases only a proportion of his excess points over the daily standard—say 75%—is credited to him, the balance being allotted to a fund out of which the foremen and other indirect labour receive bonuses. This has not proved popular, and has largely been abandoned in favour of giving the operator his full earnings.

Example

A drilling operation is set up, the standard rate for which, in points, is 0·75 points per piece or 75 points per 100 pieces. The rate agreed is 8p per point. A guaranteed daily wage for an 8-hour day is in force, at the rate of £4·00. The standard is set at 480 points per day, i.e. 60 points × 8 hours, equivalent to 640 pieces.

One operator completes 800 pieces.

Another completes only 600 pieces.

The earnings will be

Operator 1   800 pieces × 0·75 = 600 points
600 points at 8p   £48·00

Operator 2 Below standard, therefore
guaranteed pay is due
     8 hours × £4·00   £32·00
He cannot claim to be paid £36·00 on the incentive points basis, which has been introduced
to encourage high production.
(600 × 0·75 = 450 at 8p)

Collective bonus schemes. These are intended to create collective effort. They are effective only in certain circumstances.

(a) Where the group is small, say 10 or 15 in number.

(b) When the group get on with each other and work as a team.

(c) When the group has some control over the replacement of members who leave.

(d) When the bonus is calculated and paid out without delay.

These schemes are based on such factors as production output measured in points (Priestman's production bonus), reduced labour costs (Towne gain sharing method), or reduced production costs, already referred to.

Profit-sharing Schemes

These schemes usually provide for a certain percentage to be paid to all employees, in agreed proportions, out of taxed profits remaining after the fixed dividends have been paid on preference shares, and an agreed percentage on the ordinary shares.

Example

Company A has an issued share capital, fully paid up, consisting of:

     10,000 9% preference shares of £1 each
     30,000 ordinary shares of £1 each.

It is agreed that 25% of the remaining taxed profits be paid to the employees after the payment of:

(a) the dividend due on the preference shares;

(b) a dividend of 15% on the ordinary shares.

The after-tax profits for the year are £20,000.
How much would be available for the profit-sharing scheme?
Dividends will absorb:

	£
Preference shares 9%	900
Ordinary shares 15%	4,500
	5,400

Deducting this figure from £20,000 leaves taxed profits
available for distribution of   £14,600
The profit-sharing scheme will absorb 25% of this   £3,650

In some cases an escalator clause is introduced into the scheme, so that, for example, the employees subsequently receive a further distribution if it is desired to authorise a higher dividend to the ordinary shareholders.

The payment of the share of profit cannot finally be made until the annual accounts have been audited and agreed, so that there is inevitably a considerable interval between the earning of the bonus and its receipt.

However, the advantage of receiving each year a lump sum bonus of substantial size, possibly coupled with an opportunity to acquire shares in the concern which rank for dividend, will be an attractive proposition to many employees, and profit-sharing schemes (and cooperatives) will tend to become more common.

Nowadays the annual reports of companies contain references to shares reserved for employees, substantial bonuses paid, etc. It is customary to take into account both earnings and length of service in fixing the scale of this additional remuneration.

From the employer's point of view such schemes powerfully help in increasing productivity and in keeping wages steady, since the amount of profit made, and consequently the amount to be shared out among the employees, will be governed largely by the efficiency of all departments. It is therefore in the interests of everybody to secure positive progress—both the maintenance and increase of sales and the reduction of total cost per unit produced.

Examination Questions
Also includes Questions on Chapter 7

1. Describe briefly the different types of machines which might usefully be employed in a large factory: (*a*) to record workers' times

within the factory, and (*b*) to assist in the cost and wages offices.
(*CAA*)

2. Detail the column headings of a pay-roll in a company which operates a premium bonus system and which organises many social and welfare activities. What checks would you install to test the accuracy of entries on such a pay-roll containing 2,500 names?
(*ICMA*)

3. Describe five methods of remunerating workmen. State the merits and demerits of each.   (*ICMA*)

4. Compare and contrast the Halsey–Weir and Rowan Premium system of payment bringing out differences in:

(*a*) formula;

(*b*) purpose and effects;

(*c*) advantages and disadvantages.

Illustrate with a calculation of earnings and cost per piece for each system.   (*ICMA*)

5. What is meant by a "collective bonus scheme"? In what circumstances is it effective?   (*CAA*)

6. Describe in detail a payroll procedure suitable for a manufacturing and assembly firm which employs:

(*a*) factory operatives paid at piece rates;

(*b*) site assembly workers on outside contracts;

(*c*) administrative and clerical staff paid at weekly rates.

(*IAADP*)

7. There is a growing opinion that piece-work or similar bonus systems of payment are failing to produce optimum efficiency. On the other hand, there is little evidence of departure from this method of payment. Give your opinions on this problem. (*SCCA*)

8. In what circumstances should overtime payments be charged to: (*a*) direct wages, or (*b*) overheads? Ilustrate your answer by general examples.   (*CAA*)

9. Outline the general principles which must be considered when a wage incentive scheme is being introduced.   (*LCCI*)

10. Your advice is asked as to the advantages and/or disadvantages of the following wages systems, which have been submitted to a manufacturer for the purpose of increasing the output and reducing the cost of production for the mutual benefit of employer and employee:

(*a*) Payment to the worker of a fixed premium of one-third of the saving for each hour saved in the standard time for the performance of a job.

(*b*) Payment to the worker of a premium bearing the same percentage to the wage-rate as the time saved bears to the standard time for the performance of a job.

Illustrate your answer by a suitable example.   (*CAA*)

11. What are the advantages and disadvantages of the piece-rate system of remunerating labour? Do you consider that workers remunerated by reference to this system should be required to maintain time records? (CAA)

12. As the recently appointed cost accountant to a small manufacturing company you are not satisfied that the existing method of remunerating workers on a time basis is economical.

Suggest two alternative methods of remuneration and the advantages which should accrue from their introduction. (CAA)

13. Submit a skeleton report (without figures) on Labour Turnover in any business with which you are familiar. (CAA)

14. What information would you provide to keep management fully informed on the following items:

(a) the number and grade of persons employed;
(b) the cost of labour;
(c) the efficiency and utilisation of labour? (ICMA)

15. A factory produces in large batches certain component parts, common to several of the company's finished products. Their progress through the shops may take several weeks. Job cards travel with the batch, each operative booking his time on such job cards.

How would you ensure that each operative's time is properly recorded for wage-payment purposes and wage-cost analysis purposes? (ICMA)

16. A company is considering the introduction of an incentive method of paying wages and asks your opinion of the following systems:

(a) The employee to receive a premium of one-half of the time saved against the standard time allowed, calculated at normal hourly rate.

(b) The employee to receive a premium on the hours worked at a rate which is in the same proportion to his normal rate as the time saved is to the time allowed.

Work out examples of each method and state which you recommend, giving reasons for your choice. (IAADP)

17. (a) What are the arguments for and against a collective bonus system for the payment of factory wages as compared with an individual bonus system?

(b) What are the objections to a profit sharing scheme from the employees' point of view? (IAADP)

18. Give an example of the calculation of wages under any premium bonus system of remuneration and add a short note indicating its advantages and disadvantages. (LCCI)

19. "The amount of wages paid on direct production should, for

efficient working, be as high a proportion as possible of the total wages paid."

Discuss this statement.   (*ICMA*)

20. The problem of avoiding payment of wages to "dummy" workers is an important feature in the organisation of a wages department. Describe:

(*a*) How you would expect the control by the wages department to obviate this danger.

(*b*) How you would expect the cost schedules to reveal the existence of such payments.   (*BIM*)

21. How do you account for the popularity, among employers and employees, of premium bonus wage schemes? Describe any two with which you are familiar.   (*BIM*)

22. Enumerate and discuss the factors to be borne in mind in the presentation of labour cost reports. Illustrate your answer by reference to a labour turnover report.   (*CAA*)

23. In a factory where workers under twenty years of age are paid weekly rates varying according to age, similar work is done by workers earning different rates. What methods of charging out wages costs can be used to ensure uniformity for different jobs?
                                                           (*CAA*)

24. How would you treat the increased labour cost consequent upon the introduction of overtime on the ascertainment of the costs of production of a manufacturing business? Distinguish between temporary overtime and permanent overtime.   (*CAA*)

25. Give an illustration of the working of a piece-work system of calculating wages with: (*a*) a guaranteed day-rate, and (*b*) a weekly guaranteed rate.   (*LCCI*)

26. Explain the working of a method of remunerating production labour where production can be measured and incentive to high productivity is necessary. Exclude straight piece-work method of pay.   (*SCCA*)

27. Do you consider overtime premium costs for direct and indirect labour should all be charged to oncost (or overheads), or should the costs be allocated to direct and indirect according to the type of labour involved? Give reasons.   (*SCCA*)

28. What is the object of a group bonus scheme? When is it a suitable plan and on what general rules is its application governed?
                                                           (*LCCI*)

29. Due to lack of popularity, night-shift work has become more costly in terms of labour cost. Give your opinions and reasons as to the circumstances under which night-shift work may still be justified.   (*SCCA*)

30. In most cases for the purposes of costing, as well as for other reasons, it is necessary to record the labour time spent on specific jobs, operations, or processes. Describe a system to take care of this. (SCCA)

31. (a) "The same cost may be classified in a variety of different ways for different purposes."

Identify three different ways of classifying the wages of an employee and give an example of the purpose of each method of classification.

(b) Discuss the possible effects, on a company's costs, of changing the method of remunerating its direct workers from a time-rate to a piece-rate based scheme. (ACA)

32. Payment by time is still the most prevalent method of remuneration in Great Britain. Give the advantages and defects of time rates and list the circumstances, and classes of work, in which remuneration on this basis is most favoured. (ICMA)

33. Describe a system of recording time spent against specific jobs, processes, or operations for the purpose of costing. (SCCA)

34. How would you deal in your cost accounts with wages paid for the following:

(a) the excavation of foundations for the installation of a large press, abandoned after several weeks' work, the site being discovered geologically unsuitable;

(b) transfer of direct labour from a slack department, the employees retaining their existing wage rates which exceed the rates normally paid in their new department;

(c) work on a project to manufacture an existing product more cheaply?

Give reasons. (LCCI)

35. What do you understand by "costs of idle time"? How would you present a statement showing time lost due to different occurrences? (LCCI)

36. A factory machine shop is divided into cost centres, each of which comprises a number of machines of similar type. Cost Centre D has four machines, each operated by a skilled worker. There is also one unskilled service man who conveys the work to and from the machines.

Basic hourly rates are: (Skilled) £3·00; (unskilled) £2·50.

The following conditions apply to the group incentive scheme in operation:

Skilled operators: One hour at basic rate is paid for every 12 units produced.

Unskilled service man: The bonus earned by the four operators is expressed as a percentage of their basic pay and the same percentage is applied to the service man's basic pay to determine his bonus.

In a certain week all five worked a full 40 hour week and 2,400 units were produced. Calculate the gross pay of the unskilled service man.   (*LCC*)

37. (*a*) The XYZ Company operates the Rowan premium bonus scheme for its production workers. During week ended November 8 employee A, whose basic hourly rate of pay is £4, was assigned the following jobs which he completed:

Job No.	Time allowed (hours)	Time taken (hours)
123	24	18
345	40	25

You are required to calculate:

(*i*) A's remuneration for the week in question; and

(*ii*) his effective hourly rate of pay for that week.

(*b*) What would A's remuneration for the week have been if the Halsey 50/50 premium bonus scheme had been in operation? *(ACA)*

38. (*a*) List the advantages to the *employee* of a premium bonus method of remuneration.

(*b*) An operator has a basic hourly rate of £3 and for every hour saved he is paid a bonus of 50% of the basic rate:

Calculate (1) the gross wage payable
                 (2) the bonus earned
if the time allowed for a job is 50 hours and the time taken is 40 hours.   *(LCCI)*

39. (*a*) Amongst the many schemes of incentive remuneration which have evolved over the last one hundred years, two of the better known are the Halsey or Halsey–Weir bonus scheme and the Rowan bonus scheme.

Briefly give your views on why you think each of these two schemes is not more widely used in industry.

(*b*) The details given below relate to an employee on job number 27. You are required to calculate his remuneration on this job based on:

(*i*) the Halsey 50% scheme;

(*ii*) the Rowan scheme.

Data:

Direct wage rate per hour	£4·00	
Time: allowed 40 hours		
taken 32 hours		*(ICMA)*

40. G Limited makes three products: H, J and K.

Data for the four weeks ended 2nd April relating to the three products and five employees, each paid on daywork at a rate of £2·20 per hour worked, are given below:

Employee	Actual hours worked	Production in units		
		Product H	Product J	Product K
Adam	170	97	80	—
Banks	146	38	12	120
Cann	162	—	54	156
Dell	164	188	10	—
Eve	183	2	134	44
Total	825	325	290	320

In an attempt to increase production G Limited is considering changing the basis on which employees are paid. The following suggestions are being considered:

1. piecework with rates as given below;
2. a rate of £2·00 per hour worked plus a bonus at a rate of £3·00 for each hour produced at standard time allowed in excess of actual hours worked.

Product	Piecework rate per unit	Standard hours allowed per unit
	£	
H	2·20	1
J	3·20	1½
K	1·50	¾

Using the information given you are required to calculate for each employee and total, the earnings on:
   (a) the present daywork system;
   (b) the proposed piecework system;
   (c) the proposed bonus system.   *(RSA)*

Chapter 9

Organisation for Overhead Control

A general idea of the nature of overhead has already been given in Chapter 2, and students are advised at this stage to turn back to p. 6 in order to refresh their memories.

Expense Headings

The main classification of overhead into:

(*a*) production overhead;
(*b*) administration overhead;
(*c*) selling overhead; and
(*d*) distribution overhead;

is straightforward enough, but in order to be informative, and to make control of expenditure easier, it is necessary to devise a suitable list of expense headings under each of these four main classifications. The particular headings will, of course, vary in some respects from one kind of business to another, but should be fairly uniform as between firms which are engaged in the same trade or industry. Two principles will act as a guide.

(*a*) There must be enough headings to cover every circumstance.
(*b*) None of them should be so narrow in scope as to allow some items of expense to fall into a somewhat similar heading.

Cost accountants often refer to the expense headings for production overhead as "standing order numbers", and to those under the other classifications as "cost account numbers". There is no magic in these names, and "expense numbers" or "nominal headings" would do equally as well.

For the sake of convenient reference the headings have to be coded. This may be done in any way desired, but there are two well-tried and acceptable methods.

87

The Mnemonic Method

This method uses as codes the letters of the alphabet in the form of memory aids. For example:

SA for sales;
MA for maintenance;
WA for wages;
AD for administration, and so on.

These letter combinations would then be used in conjunction with numbers.

The Decimal Method

This is a system of numerical codes somewhat similar to the Dewey method used in libraries.

Specimen Question

One of the service departments of H PLC is the boiler-house. The fuel used is coke. Devise a code of standing order numbers for the boiler-house.

Answer

```
09   SERVICE DEPARTMENTS
  09  01  Stores
      02  Tool-room
      03  Boiler-house, etc.
          _____

  09  03  BOILER-HOUSE
          01  Stokers' wages
          02  Stokers' overtime premium
          03  Employers' national insurance
          04  Coke
          05  Water
          06  Power for mechanical stoker
          07  Heating and lighting
          08  Depreciation
          09  Fire and explosion insurance
          10  Maintenance of boilers
          11  Maintenance of mechanical stokers
          12  Maintenance of boiler-house instruments
          13  Softening equipment supplies
          14  General expenses
```

Thus the invoice received for the insurance premium for the fire and explosion risk for the boilers would be coded 090309, and would be posted accordingly, either directly or via an overhead control account.

It will be seen from the above example that there can be as many divisions and subdivisions of the coding system as may be required. Obviously, it would be pointless to reproduce a whole coding manual in a book of this size, but it may be useful to the reader to have before him a short list of the kind of expense headings which could be expected under the four main classifications, and this has been given at the end of the chapter.

Fixed and Variable Overhead

At this stage the reader is asked to look more closely at the headings for the boiler-house given in the preceding illustration. Certain items of expenditure may be regarded as being fixed in amount, e.g. depreciation, while others are variable, e.g. coke. Even if the boilers are only lightly used during the summer months, the depreciation is still incurred; on the other hand, the use of coke would be greatly diminished. Other expenditures are partially fixed and partially variable.

The effect of these various qualities inherent in the nature of overhead is extremely important to all businesses, and the measurement of what the precise effect is in particular circumstances really constitutes the problem of overhead, which we will consider further in Chapter 10.

Depreciation

The reader will notice further from the boiler-house headings that almost all the expenditures are directly incurred. That is to say, there is a payment of cash involved. The one notable exception to this is depreciation. The reason for this is that plant and machinery, and other fixed assets, are bought and capitalised, and thereafter during the lifetime of the asset the cost is gradually written off to record the loss of value due to wear and tear.

In dealing with overhead, therefore, we must, among other matters, have a good system for recording particulars about our plant and other fixed assets; decide on a method of depreciation which we think is most suitable, schedule it, and transfer it by journal entry from the asset account to the appropriate expense heading. A ruling for a plant register is given in Fig. 24, and it will be seen that it combines a method for scheduling the annual depreciation.

The methods of depreciation most frequently encountered are enumerated below.

1. Straight-line Method

This simple and effective method is much used, and is to be preferred for costing purposes owing to the uniform charge. The life of the machine, or other asset, is estimated; also the residual value. The cost, less the residual value (plus the cost of fixing, in the case of a new machine), divided by the estimated years of life, determines the annual amount of depreciation to be charged. A separate calculation should be made for each machine.

PLANT REGISTER

Shop, or Department:.................   Machine Shop No.: 4
Sheet No.: 1.

Ref. No.	Description	Date of Purchase	Cost	Rate of Depre- ciation*	19....		19....		etc.
					Deprecia- tion £	Balance Value £	Deprecia- tion £	Balance Value £	
E1	Leader No. 2	3/1/19...	5,000	20%	1,000	4,000	1,000	3,000	
E2	10″ Centre Lathe	2/1/19...	2,500	10%	250	2,250	250	2,000	

FIG. 24.— *Plant register*

*Note—The examples provide depreciation by the straight-line method, which is usually more satisfactory. More complicated forms of plant register may show details of periodical major repairs and renewals, sales, and profits and losses on sales.

If, subsequently, capital additions and even abnormal expensive overhaul and repair are made to any asset the rate of depreciation will be adjusted by dividing the sum of the addition and the then value of the asset by the anticipated remainder of years of life.

Example

A machine costs £10,000, and it is estimated that its residual value at the end of ten years will be £500. At the end of five years the machine is completely overhauled at a cost of £3,000.

The depreciation for the first five years will be at the rate of £950 per annum, and the book value will have been written down to £5,250. The overhaul cost will be added to this, less the residual value, so that £7,750 must be written off over the next five years. The depreciation will therefore become £1,550 per annum.

2. Reducing Balance Method

A constant annual percentage rate of depreciation is determined, which is written off the reducing balance of the capital value, the rate being so fixed that at the end of the estimated life of the asset only the residual scrap value remains. In favour of this method it is argued that a heavier depreciation charge is borne in the earlier years, when repairs are lighter, and that the assumed increasing repair cost is counter-balanced, in later years, by the reduced annual charge of depreciation. The assumption is frequently incorrect.

Example

A machine costing £10,000 is to be depreciated by the reducing-balance method at the rate of 20% per annum.

£2,000 will be written off in year 1, leaving £8,000.
£1,600 will be written off in year 2, leaving £6,400 and so on.

3. Production Unit Method

When production can be estimated for the life span of a machine this method may be used to charge depreciation directly on to the products as a variable overhead.

Example

A soap company installs a toilet-soap tableting machine which produces 1 dozen tablets per operation. The cost of the machine is £60,000. It is estimated that production will be in the order of 12 million tablets before the machine has to be replaced.

The depreciation per dozen tablets will be:

$$\frac{£60,000}{12,000,000} \times 12 = £0 \cdot 06$$

4. Revaluation Method

This is the most convenient method to use for loose tools and patterns, because new items are often being made in the works and added to the stock, while others become worn out and are discarded. It would be too costly and time consuming to keep records about each tool, and a quick examination by an expert at the end of the year, with a clerk noting down his valuation, is a far easier task. The method of revaluation is also used by farmers in regard to their livestock, and by racing establishments in regard to their racehorses.

List of Typical Expenses Included under Main Classifications

1. Production Overhead

(*a*) Rent of buildings and land. When the manufacturer owns the property a charge equivalent to rent may be made.

(*b*) Rates imposed by local authorities.

(*c*) Insurance on:

(*i*) factory property;
(*ii*) machinery;
(*iii*) fixed annual charge (if any) for automatic fire alarms, sprinkler installation.

(*d*) Depreciation on:

(*i*) plant and machinery;
(*ii*) buildings.

(*e*) Salaries of managers and principal officials are often included.

(*f*) Interest on capital to the extent (if any) it is included as an item of cost.

(*g*) Maintenance and repairs (which includes materials and labour used by maintenance service departments plus the overhead apportioned to these departments) of buildings, plant, machinery, etc.

(*h*) Oiling and cleaning machinery, shafting, motors, etc.

(*i*) Miscellaneous operating supplies (consumable stores).

(*i*) Cotton waste, cloths for wiping.
(*ii*) Belt-dressing, fasteners, etc.
(*iii*) Brushes for sweeping, dusting, scrubbing.

(*iv*) Oil, benzine, emery and sand-paper, carborundum dust.

(*v*) Cleaning compounds.

(*j*) Perishable tools, small taps, dies, drills, files, emery wheels, polishing wheels, oil-stones, saw-blades, reamers, etc.

(*k*) Waiting time (= idle time), viz.:

(*i*) machinery breakdown;
(*ii*) power-supply failure;
(*iii*) waiting for work instructions;
(*iv*) accident to workers;
(*v*) waiting for material;
(*vi*) waiting for tools, etc.

(*l*) Holidays and sickness with pay.

(*m*) Stocktaking and stores physical check expenses.

(*n*) Inspection and testing.

(*o*) (*i*) Experimental and research work.

(*ii*) Designing for production.

(*iii*) Drawing-office expense.

(*p*) Timekeeping and gate control.

(*q*) Supervision: foremen, assistants, superintendents.

(*r*) Shop clerical work, labour and stationery.

(*s*) Shop labouring, general indirect; shop cleaning, etc.

(*t*) Stores expenses.

(*i*) Carriage inwards (unless added to the price of materials).

(*ii*) Storekeeper and assistants.

(*iii*) Other charges, e.g. branding, measuring and cutting off materials for issue, but not expenses particular to a specific order.

(*u*) Training and instructing new employees.

(*v*) Welfare; ambulance and first aid; canteens.

(*w*) Waste—spoilt and lost materials, stock discrepancies, faulty work, etc.

(*x*) Insurance.

(*i*) National.

(*ii*) Machinery breakdown, etc.

(*y*) Overtime expenses (except when a direct charge).

(*z*) Services.

(*i*) Power of all kinds.

(*ii*) Steam service.

(*iii*) Lighting.

(*iv*) Heating.

(*v*) Other services, e.g. fire protection, internal transport.

2. Administration Overhead

(a) Salaries of executives, managers, etc.
(b) Clerical expenses.
(c) Office expenses.

(i) Rent, rates, insurances (excluding the proportion applicable to the works).
(ii) Lighting, heating and cleaning.
(iii) Repairs and maintenance of buildings.
(iv) Repairs of equipment; machines.

(d) Stationery, postage, telephones.

3. Selling Overhead

(a) Sales office expenses.
(b) Travellers' salaries, commission, and expenses.
(c) Advertising; catalogues; price-lists; samples.
(d) Discounts allowed (sometimes excluded from costs).
(e) Estimating; preparing drawings and designs for tenders.

4. Distribution Overhead

(a) Warehousing of finished goods.
(b) Packing and warehouse trucking.
(c) Loading; loading conveyors, charges for cranes, hoists, etc.
(d) Delivery—upkeep and running of vehicles; outward freight and carriage.

Expenditure Excluded from Cost

Such items as income tax, cost of fixing new plant (except for a specific job), bonuses to employees voted at an annual meeting (being an apportionment of profit), dividends, cannot be included as items of cost. Various kinds of expense connected with financing, and exceptional losses such as abnormal waste and abnormal loss, are ordinarily also excluded. Some exclude cash discounts received and allowed; and, again, while bad debts are included in selling overhead by some accountants, others exclude them.

It is usual to exclude large abnormal losses such as, for example, obsolescence. Obsolescence is the process by which an asset loses its value by falling into disuse, other than by wear and tear. The term is generally used to indicate loss of value when, say, a machine or building is discarded before the expiration of its normal life, usually because of its inability to compete with one better adapted or of more modern type. There is a sudden, rather than gradual, diminution in value. If plant is scrapped before the original costs of plant and fixing have all been written off, the balance of the capital value is therefore transferred to obsolescence account, and from thence at the end of the year it is written off to profit and loss account.

Examination Questions on Chapters 9–11 are given at the end of Chapter 11.

Chapter 10

The Charging of Overhead to Departments

IN the previous chapter we dealt with the classification and coding of overhead, and we saw that this constituted the framework of organisation for overhead control. We now reach the stage in which we shall apportion the expenditure incurred for factory (or works) overhead to the various departments concerned, including production and service departments.

The advantage of collecting the overhead departmentally is twofold.

(a) The overhead expenditure of each department can be watched and the head of the department concerned is made aware of any overspending.

(b) The total departmental expenditure being known, there is a basis laid down for calculating a rate per unit or per hour which will recover the overhead as a charge against production.

Example

Suppose the total of the variable overhead of the marmalade boiling department of a factory amounts to £50,000. First, the detailed figures making up this amount may be compared with previous periods to check on undue growth. Secondly, the total of £50,000 may be taken as next year's estimate of expenditure and, if this figure is then divided by the estimated number of direct labour hours to be worked in the department, say, 10,000 hours per annum, a rate of £5·00 per direct labour hour is obtained. During the following year this rate will be used to absorb the overhead of the marmalade boiling department against production.

It will be realised, of course, that if in October in any year we wanted to fix in advance an overhead rate to be used in the following year we should have to estimate in advance both the total overhead expenditure and the total direct labour hours.

The Plan of Procedure

This may be set out as follows.

(*a*) All indirect expenses are collected under the selected separate headings of expense, as described in the preceding chapter.

(*b*) The totals so found are apportioned on suitable bases to each of the production departments and the service departments (if any), and, when appropriate, even to individual machines, in the manner described below.

(*c*) The total expenditure incurred in connection with each service department is apportioned fairly over the production departments in accordance with the services rendered.

(*d*) The total overhead for each production department is "recovered" by making a charge against every works order, contract, or other unit of production, which passes through or obtains the services of the departments, a separate charge being made in respect of each department or shop.

Observe that individual machines or groups of similar machines are regarded as "departments" for the purpose of expense analysis.

The Apportionment of Overhead to Departments

This must be made according to the way in which it occurs, and one or more of the following methods may be used.

(*a*) *A direct charge to a particular department* whenever an item of expense concerns that department only, e.g. power, when separate metering or measurement is available, jobbing repairs, expense overtime of men engaged solely in the department, foremen and general labour employed in the department.

Example

An invoice is received from L. Robinson for £45 in respect of repairs carried out to the calendering machine in a laundry. This would be allocated direct to the ironing department overhead.

(*b*) *An apportionment of production overhead proportionate to departmental wages paid.*

Example

The total production overhead of a company is £40,000 and the total direct wages £120,000. Department A direct wages are £30,000. The amount apportionable to Dept A would be

$$\frac{30,000}{120,000} \times 40,000, \text{ i.e. } £10,000$$

Although much used, this method is not satisfactory for general application, but only for such expenses as do in fact vary with the direct wages paid.

(c) *A percentage or proportion calculated on capital values of buildings and plant in each department.* Typical examples which may be dealt with in this way are depreciation of plant, machinery, and buildings, fire-insurance premiums relating to those assets, rates.

Example

The fire-insurance premiums paid by J. Smith & Co. amount to £950 and cover the following items:

	Insured values (£)	Apportion- ment of premiums (£)
3 capstan lathes	12,000	128
2 turret lathes	9,000	97
5 centre lathes	2,500	27
4 vertical millers	3,000	32
1 horizontal miller	4,000	43
Workshop building	25,000	268
Office building	30,000	322
Paint store	3,000	33
	£88,500	£950

The apportionment of premiums is done by simple proportion:

$$950 \times \frac{12,000}{88,500} = £128$$

(*d*) *Apportionment proportional to superficial floor area occupied* by each department. In some cases cubic capacity of departmental buildings is fairer.

Expenses such as lighting and heating (unless metered), night watchmen, rent, and fire-precaution expenses may be apportioned on this basis.

Example

The hot-water heating service supplied from the boiler-house via the calorifiers is estimated to cost £48,000 per annum. The following data are available.

Department	Dimensions	Area (sq. m)	Apportionment of cost (£)
General office	80 × 20	1,600	6,400
Sales office	40 × 10	400	1,600
Workshop	400 × 25	10,000	40,000
		12,000	£48,000

(*e*) *Apportionment proportional to departmental totals, of production hours of direct labour,* or, in some cases, of machines.

The amount charged on this direct-labour-hour basis, i.e. the proportion that the departmental hours bear to total factory direct hours, is usually a most equitable division, and whenever a more closely related basis cannot be found the method is a reliable one. It is suitable for most general expenses, such as works management, general overtime expense, timekeeping, inter-department transport, etc.

When both machine and bench work occur, separate division of totals as between machine and bench should be made, then the apportionment would be on the machine-hours and labour hours.

Example

The internal transport system of a furniture factory is estimated to cost £64,400 per annum. The following information is obtained.

Department	Direct labour (hours)	Apportionment of cost (£)
Saw bench	4,600	9,200
Planing shop	6,900	13,800
Mortise and tenon shop	9,200	18,400
Sanding shop	4,600	9,200
Assembly shop	6,900	13,800
	32,200	£64,400

(f) *Apportionment proportionate to the number of employees in each department.* This is a method which should be applied for those expenses which are dependent in magnitude on the *number* of employees, e.g. timekeeping expenses, canteen, rest room, central labour engagement office expenses, etc. Thus if there were 1,000 persons in the factory, and 100 of these were in department A, then one-tenth of the expenses named would be chargeable to department A.

Example

A factory making shoes has the following numbers of operatives in its departments, and the estimated deficit on running the canteen is £24,000 per annum.

Department	Numbers of operatives	Apportionment of canteen deficit (£)
Cutting	25	5,000
Bottoms	35	7,000
Uppers	30	6,000
Lasting	15	3,000
Heeling	5	1,000
Polishing	10	2,000
	120	£24,000

TABLE INDICATING HOW APPORTIONMENT TO DEPARTMENTS MAY BE
MADE FOR REPRESENTATIVE ITEMS

Expense item	Basis of apportionment	Workshops or departments			Administration	Selling
		A	B	C		
		£	£	£	£	£
Heating	Area or cubic capacity of each					
Rent	Ditto					
Depreciation	(a) Capital values, e.g. of machines and plant in each					
	(b) Floor area for depreciation of buildings					
Electricity:						
(a) Power	H.P.-hours in each shop					
(b) Light	Number of lights or watts; floor area or even number of workers					
Timekeeping and wages department	Number of workers in each shop					
(a) Buildings and plant	Capital values					
(b) National	Actual as shown in payroll of each department					
Sundry expenses	Direct labour-hours					
Stores expenses	Number of requisitions or values or weight, whichever most suitable					
Steam, hydraulic power, and compressed air	Consumption, either estimated or metered; or estimate based on potential demand					
Welfare, canteen, etc.	Number of workers or labour hours					
Overtime	Direct labour hours or direct from payroll					
Repairs	Direct					

Note. Additional columns should be added, in appropriate cases, for service department and distribution.

(g) *An approximate apportionment based on technical estimate, investigation or similar measurement.* Several specific methods fall under this heading.

(i) Charging electric light according to the number of lights or of watts in each department. This is, of course, alternative to the use of floor area.

(ii) Charging steam according to a consumption return or engineer's estimate of either actual usage or potential usage.

(iii) Estimation of certain items by the works engineer or chemist, sometimes in consultation with the cost accountant.

Example

The boiler-house cost of making live steam in a hospital is, say, £20,000. The total expenditure on this service department is then charged into power, lighting, and heating account, which is in turn apportioned to wards and departments according to the following technical estimate:

Department	Percentage use	Apportionment of power, lighting, and heating costs (including boiler-house costs) (£)
Wards	70	35,000
Out-patients	15	7,500
Catering	6	3,000
Radiotherapy	1	500
Diagnostic X-ray	3	1,500
Pathology	2	1,000
Physiotherapy	3	1,500
	100	£50,000

Inter-service Department Charges

In the above example it will be seen that one service department has been wholly charged to another, and that the costs of the second service department have been apportioned out to other departments. In this particular case the hospital evidently has no laundry of its own. If it had, we should have found a charge from power, lighting and heating account to the laundry, as well as to catering. Of course, the laundry would work for other departments, including service departments. Thus it would wash the linen from the wards, and nurses' and maids' homes, and also the boiler-house overalls, the white coats, the chefs' hats, the kitchen workers' protective clothing, from the catering department. Again the catering department provides meals not only for patients, doctors, nursing staff, ward orderlies and domestic staff but also for boiler men, laundry staff, engineers, painters, etc.

These cross charges between service departments are common in factory life as well, and the rule is to settle these charges first of all. Then when the totals of the overhead for the service departments are settled between themselves they may be further dealt with according to the nature of the undertaking. Thus:

(*a*) in a factory the finally agreed service department totals are apportioned to production departments according to the value of the services rendered to each;

(*b*) in a hospital, with some exceptions, such as power, lighting and heating service, no further apportionment has been thought to be either necessary or desirable.

Example

The departmental distribution summary has been prepared for Paulart PLC and is shown below.

Budget Period No. 1

		£
Production department	1	24,000
	2	18,000
	3	12,000
	4	6,000
Service department A		3,600
B		1,800
		£65,400

It has been estimated that the costs of running the service departments can be charged to the various departments according to the following percentages.

Details	*Production departments*				*Service departments*	
	1	*2*	*3*	*4*	*A*	*B*
	%	%	%	%	%	%
A	40	10	20	20	—	10
B	20	30	10	20	20	—

From this table it can be seen that department A services not only the four production departments, but also service department B. For example, department A could be a power station which provides power for the production departments and for the canteen. Similarly, department B services the production departments, and also department A, in this case the power station. Thus department B could be the canteen which provides meals for the employees of the factory, and also for those working in the power station.

This method of apportioning service department costs to production departments is called the repeated distribution method but there is a variety of methods which can be used. Interested readers are referred to *Wheldon's Cost Accounting.*[*]

Setting out the distribution statement, we arrive at the following result:

Details	Production departments				Service departments	
	1	2	3	4	A	B
	£	£	£	£	£	£
Budgeted						
cost	24,000	18,000	12,000	6,000	3,600	1,800
A	1,440	360	720	720	(3,600)	360
B	432	648	216	432	432	(2,160)
A	173	43	86	86	(432)	44
B	9	13	4	9	9	(44)
A	4	1	2	2	(9)	—
	£26,058	£19,065	£13,028	£7,249	—	—

From the above it can be seen that the total costs of £65,400 have been charged to the production departments, each of which has borne its share of the two service departments. Calculations are as follows.

Department A

Initial cost £3,600. This is shared between departments 1, 2, 3 and 4 and service department B according to the given percentages 40%, 10%, 20%, 20% and 10% respectively.

* *Wheldon's Cost Accounting,* L. W. J. Owler and J. L. Brown, Macdonald & Evans, 1984.

Department B

Initial cost £1,800 plus apportioned cost of £360. The total of £2,160 is shared according to the given percentages 20%, 30%, 10%, 20% and 20%.

Examination Questions on Chapters 9–11 are given at the end of Chapter 11.

Chapter 11

The Charging of Overhead to Production Units

In the previous chapter we noted that two important purposes were served by apportioning overhead to departments, namely:

(a) to facilitate comparison and control;
(b) to afford a means by which a rate could be calculated in order to charge an appropriate amount of overhead to each cost unit or works order.

Methods of Absorbing Overhead

We are now going to consider six methods by which overhead may be absorbed by the units of production. All are used in practice, but it should be observed that some of them are often not precise enough to be reliable. In some cases a particular method is selected because of its convenience, in others because of failure to realise that a better method exists.

One of the most important facts to be remembered is that the majority of expenses are incurred in time, and that the time spent by a worker or a machine on a job, and the time spent by the job in each department, have to be considered when deciding which method to use. Any method which does not either directly or indirectly provide for the time element can rarely result in correct cost accounting. For this reason the first two methods described below, although much used, are not sound from a cost accounting point of view.

1. Percentage on Cost of Direct Materials Method

The overhead for each department or shop is expressed as a percentage of the estimated total of direct material which it is considered will be treated in that department or shop for the period under review. The percentage rate so obtained is then applied to each works order in that department.

Example

If the total works overhead in respect of department A is £6,300 for 52 weeks and the amount of direct material which it is budgeted will be worked upon in that period is £18,900 the production overhead rate for department A would be

$$\frac{6,300}{18,900} = 33\tfrac{1}{3}\%$$

This means that for each and every order worked upon in department A there would be added to the prime cost an amount equal to 33⅓% of the value of direct material charged. In this way the total overhead of the department is absorbed. Similarly, as an order passes from department A to department B a further percentage addition will be made to absorb the overhead of that department, and so on.

Criticism of the method. This method is simple to apply and is much used, often with inaccurate results. The inaccuracy arises from the fact that there is no relation between production overhead and the cost of material. The overhead does not change because men and machines are working on brass instead of iron or white metal. But these metals are of very different values, so that by applying a fixed department percentage, different costs for expenses would result according to the metal worked upon, which is obviously incorrect.

Again the method takes no account of the length of time the job is in each department, so that two jobs having the same value for direct material would bear the same amount of overhead charge, even though one may occupy a bench or machine much longer than the other. The cost so found must be incorrect.

Again no difference in cost is shown, if this method is used, when one job requires the use of machines of different size and value, the running costs of which may show wide disparity.

To be accurate the value of material must be uniform, operating times must be strictly proportionate, and the equipment used must be of equal running cost and capital value.

2. Percentage on Cost of Direct Wages Method

A percentage of direct wages to be added to prime cost is calculated.

Example

Production overhead £160,000. Direct wages estimated for the same period £80,000.

Then the percentage will be $\dfrac{160,000}{80,000} \times 100 = 200\%$

In estimating the direct wages, allowance has to be made for any likely rise or fall in work in the department during the period under review.

Criticism of the method. In very many cases the method is inaccurate.

The time element may be reasonably well allowed for if workers are paid by uniform time rates, but when piece-work rates are used anomalous results arise.

Example

Consider two parallel jobs, disregarding materials:

(a) *Employee paid by the hour* (£5·00).

	£
The job takes 5 hours, hence the direct labour charge is	25·00
Overhead at 200%	50·00
Cost	£75·00

and if the job took 7½ hours the cost would be £112·50; the extra amount includes, as it should, a higher cost for overhead.

(b) *Employee paid piece-work rate.*

The job takes one employee 5 hours, piece-work pay, say, £20.

If the same job takes another man 7½ hours, the piece-work pay remains at £20·00 and in both cases the overhead addition would be 200%, and the cost £60·00, yet it is clear that the work by the second operator has cost more because space and equipment have been in use 2½ hours longer than for the first operator.

Other objections are:

(a) no difference in the overhead charges is made when different machines and bench work are employed;

(b) wages of employees on the same work may vary;

(c) allowance for the difference in time taken by slow and fast employees is not properly provided for, particularly when piece-rates are paid.

For the method to give precision in cost the units produced must be similar, employees must be paid by time wages of uniform rates, and the equipment used must not be very dissimilar in value.

3. Percentage on Prime Cost Method

In this method the percentage is arrived at as for the two previous methods, the divisor being the estimated value of prime cost of work for the period concerned, a separate calculation being made for each department.

The same criticisms apply as for the two methods already described.

Example

In respect of department X, the budgeted costs are as follows:

Direct materials	£60,000
Direct wages	£40,000
Production overhead	£300,000

The percentage will be:

$$\frac{300,000}{100,000} \times 100 = 300\%$$

Thus every job produced in department X will be charged 300% of its prime cost so as to absorb production overhead.

4. Rate Per Unit Produced Method

The rate to be used for recovering production overhead is determined by dividing the total production overhead for a period, say six or twelve months, by the number of units of production which it is expected will be produced in the period. This gives a rate per unit to be charged instead of a percentage addition.

In suitable circumstances the method gives equitable results, but it can be used only when the units produced are all uniform or can be made so by means of ratios. In some types of process and single output manufacturing this requirement is fulfilled. The method is simple and reliable in such cases.

Example

In respect of department Z, the budgeted production overheads amount to £400,000 and the budgeted output is 20,000 units. Each unit produced will be charged £20 so as to absorb production overheads.

5. Rate per Direct-labour-hour Method

The rate is obtained by dividing the total production overhead for the department by the total estimated direct labour hours for the same period. Careful estimating is necessary. This method gives very satisfactory results, and is probably the most suitable one to use in the majority of manufacturing concerns, excepting for shops where machinery is used, in which case the method next to be described is better. Where there is both bench work and machine work it is often better to divide the expenses of such a department as between the two classes of work and compute two separate rates for recovering overheads, as if the sections were separate departments.

It is usually desirable to calculate the direct-labour-hour rate over a period of twelve months, and by using such a period, the effect of seasonal fluctuations is eliminated.

Example

Departmental overhead for year:

Department A £45,000
Department B £33,750

Estimated number of direct labour hours in each department (assuming 45 effective hours per week and 50 effective weeks per year per employee):

Department A 10 men × 45 × 50 = 22,500
Department B   5 men × 45 × 50 = 11,250

The departmental rates will be:

A £45,000 ÷ 22,500 = £2·00
B £33,750 ÷ 11,250 = £3·00

These rates will be used thus:

Works Order No. 2913

		£
Materials		24·00
Labour		
Department A 4 hours at £4·00		16·00
Department B 5 hours at £4·80		24·00
	PRIME COST	64·00
Production overhead		
Department A 4 hours at £2·00		8·00
Department B 5 hours at £3·00		15·00
	PRODUCTION COST	£87·00

The method necessitates the recording and analysing of the time spent on each job by each worker, and although this involves additional clerical work, it ensures more precise costing, and affords better opportunities for control to be exercised.

It overcomes the objections mentioned in the methods previously described, as the allocation of overhead is not linked with the value of materials or with wages, whether time or piece-work.

6. The Machine-hour-rate Method

This method is similar to the preceding one, but instead of using labour hours as the divisor, the machine-hours are used. Again, the expenses are first apportioned by suitable analysis to each machine (or group of similar machines), and a separate rate is calculated for each machine.

When finding the cost of running a machine, it will be apparent that it falls into two divisions.

(a) The cost of the floor space occupied, including the proportion of general overhead expense commensurate with that floor space.

(b) The expense of operating the machine, depreciation, insurance, maintenance, repairs and power. (Some also include interest on the capital outlay on the machine.) The cost of operator's wages should not normally be included, this being, in most cases, charged as direct wages.

This machine-hour rate gives a fairly reliable basis for "recovering the expenses", i.e. for calculating the amount of overhead to be charged to a particular works order, whether that order represents a job, process or operation. Once the rate has been established, all that is necessary is to record the time spent by a job on each machine. This time valued at the machine-hour rate is the addition to be made to prime cost to cover overheads.

When machines are used intermittently it is advisable to estimate the total actual running hours for, say, a year, and to divide that total into the total expenses attributable to the machine for the same period. In this way proper allowance is made for the times when the machine is not employed. When there is much abnormal idle time it may be advisable to calculate the rate in three sections, viz. shop charges, machine expenses and power. The abnormal idle time expense can then be calculated, excluding the power charge.

Two examples of machine-hour-rate calculations are given below.

Example 1

A centre lathe was purchased on 1 January 19.., for £7,500. Its estimated life is 10 years, and no estimate of scrap value has been made. Depreciation is to be charged on a straight-line basis. The following additional information is available.

	Capital values (£)	Areas sq. m	H.P.	Machine-hours (estimated)
This lathe	7,500	100	1	1,800
Other machines	112,500	1,900		
	£120,000	2,000		

Insurance premium, £200.
Repairs and maintenance (based on past records), £800.
Rent apportioned to machine shop, £1,000.
Department expenses (estimated), £2,400.
Power, £0·05 per kilowatt hour (1 h.p. = 746 watts).

A machine-hour rate may be calculated as follows:

Machine shop A

Machine-hour rate for Machine No. A 21

Description: Centre lathe. *Maker's name:* Scamp & Scrimp. *No.:* 103489.
Date acquired: 1 January 19... *Power:* 1 h.p. *Cost* £7,500.
Depreciation: 10 years, straight line, i.e. £750 p.a.

	£
Depreciation	750·00
Insurance—on capital values—£7,500/£120,000 × £200	12·50
Repairs and maintenance	800·00
Rent—based on floor space—100/2,000 × £1,000	50·00
Department expenses (including supervision)—on floor space—100/2,000 × £2,400	120·00
Power—on units demanded, per estimate 746/1,000 × 1,800 hours × £0·05 per unit	67·50
	£1,800·00

Estimated running hours, 1,800.
Machine-hour rate £1,800 ÷ 1,800 = £1·00 per machine-hour.

Example 2

	Machine No. A 23 Shop E		2,000 hours
		Per annum	Per hour
		(£)	(£)
Department expenses			
Rent and rates		400	
Lighting		60	
Heating		280	
Supervision by foreman		740	
Miscellaneous		520	
		2,000	1·00
Machine expenses			
Depreciation		600	
Repairs and maintenance		500	
Sundries		400	
		1,500	0.75
Power			
10 units per hour at £0·05 per unit			0·50
TOTAL MACHINE-HOUR RATE			£2·25

Overhead Over- or Under-recovered

The difference between the actual expense incurred and that absorbed will be large or small according to the nearness of the various estimates which have to be made in arriving at the rates used, but there is always a balance under- or over-recovered.

The estimates which affect the position are:

(a) expense for each department—the fixed expenses are easily established, but not the variable expenses, which fluctuate in amount more or less with output;

(b) output of units of production;

(c) hours of labour (or machines).

The amounts under- and over-recovered are usually best treated by transfer from each department overhead account to an overhead expense adjustment account (sometimes called under- and over-recovered overhead account). The net difference on this account is then written off to production profit and loss account. It should not be carried forward and added to or deducted from the expenses for the following period, as this gives false results in that period and makes comparison between periods unfair.

The following example illustrates the principles enunciated, and shows the effects resulting from the use of a department rate based on budgeted figures which were subsequently found to be rather different from the expenditure actually incurred.

Example

It was estimated that the annual overhead in department M would be

Variable   £50,000
Fixed   £200,000

and that the direct labour hours would be 100,000. Rates for charging overhead to production orders passing through department M were therefore set up as follows:

Variable overhead £50,000 ÷ 100,000 = £0·50
Fixed overhead £200,000 ÷ 100,000 = £2·00

Department M actually worked 98,500 hours, and the overhead incurred was

Variable   £48,750
Fixed   £198,500

From this we have the following position:

	Actual expenses (£)	Overhead absorbed at predetermined rates (£)	Over-absorbed (£)	Under-absorbed (£)
Variable overhead	48,750	49,250	500	
Fixed overhead	198,500	197,000		1,500
	£247,250	£246,250	£500	£1,500

NOTE: 98,500 × £0·50 = £49,250
98,500 × £2·00 = £197,000

Administration, Selling and Distribution Overhead

It is not customary to charge these expenses to production units as part of the cost of production.

Administration overhead

This, as we have already seen (page 94), consists of executive salaries, office rent and rates, lighting, heating and cleaning the offices, and so on, and the usual method of dealing with them in the cost books is to regard them as periodic charges arising within the financial year. The amount applicable to the year on a time basis is then charged in total against the cost accounting profit for the year, as is done in all financial accounting.

Selling and distribution overhead

This is often considered collectively as one type of overhead, but a little thought shows that they are really quite different types of expense. Selling costs are incurred in order to obtain sales: distribution costs begin as soon as the finished goods are put into the warehouse, and continue until those goods are despatched or delivered to the customer.

Selling overhead is therefore often absorbed on the basis of sales values. By this means, those product lines which provide most profit take a larger proportion of overhead, and this seems reasonable. It could be, of course, that special sales effort has to be expended in connection with particular products, but unless details are kept which would enable an assessment to be made the method just explained should be adopted. The accounting entry will be:

      Cost of goods sold Dr
        To Selling overhead control account

Distribution overhead is more allied to production cost than to sales, and from one point of view could be regarded as an extra cost of production. However, it is usual to regard production cost as ending on the factory floor, and to deal with distribution overhead separately. It is generally absorbed as a percentage of production cost, but special circumstances, such as size and weight of products affecting the delivery charges, may cause a different basis of absorption to be used. The accounting entry will be:

      Cost of goods sold Dr
        To Distribution overhead control account

Examination Questions

Also includes Questions on Chapters 9 and 10

1. Into what categories is "Overhead" usually divided? Why is it so analysed? What item of expense would appear in each such sub-division? (*LCCI*)

2. (*a*) What do you understand by the term "cost centre" from the viewpoint of works overhead expenses?

(*b*) What is the significant distinction between a production department and a service department? (*CAA*)

3. How would you deal in the Cost Accounts with the following items:

(*a*) Experimental expenses.

(*b*) Packing materials.

(*c*) Holiday pay.

(*d*) Internal transport? (*CAA*)

4. List *five* documents that you would expect to find in connection with the collection, allocation, and apportionment of indirect expense, including labour and material. In respect of each document listed, mention briefly the function that it performs. (*ICMA*)

5. (*a*) What is meant by "indirect materials"? How do you consider they should be dealt with in the costing system?

(*b*) What principles determine whether expense is "direct" or "indirect"? (*IAADP*)

6. (*a*) Define the term "indirect labour" as an item of expense.

(*b*) Explain the various bases on which this expense may be apportioned to production cost in a factory engaged in mass production of a variety of small articles. (*BIM*)

7. Enumerate the various bases on which overheads may be apportioned to the cost of production and emphasise the dangers inherent in any of them. (*BIM*)

8. (*a*) Define depreciation.

(*b*) Annotate the various methods of computing depreciation.

(*c*) Would you consider that any one of these methods is adequate, under present conditions, in an old-established company? (*BIM*)

9. (*a*) Explain the nature and uses of the plant inventory.

(*b*) Prepare a draft form showing the relevant information in respect of a machine which was purchased in June. (*BIM*)

10. Prepare a departmental distribution summary, showing the expense usually obtaining in a factory. What purpose does such a summary serve? (*BIM*)

11. A firm has several departments, some entirely machine shops and others employing manual labour. On what basis would you charge overheads to the products? (*BIM*)

12. Tabulate the advantages and disadvantages of overhead absorption by: (*a*) direct labour hour rates, and (*b*) machine hour rates. (*CAA*)

13. Overhead has been defined as "the total of indirect materials, wages, and expense."

What do you understand by the word "indirect" in this context? Give examples of indirect items in your answer. (*LCCI*)

14. What items of expense would you expect to find under the heading "Selling Expenses"? Trace the relationship of each item to the sales of the firm's products, and state what arrangements you would make for the recovery of such expense. (*IAADP*)

15. Sales costs are divided into: (*a*) sales administration—concerned with sales policy; (*b*) sales promotion—dealing with the achievement of a budgeted programme of sales; (*c*) traveller effort—in obtaining orders; and (*d*) sales routine—dealing with the execution of orders and the keeping of sales ledger accounts. The whole cost is absorbed as a percentage of the sales value of each product.

How would you present a statement showing the items making up total sales costs and their apportionment to each of the four sections? (*LCCI*)

16. Defective work is inevitable in most factories, but must be kept under control in the interests of production efficiency. What records of scrap and waste would you keep, and to what uses would these records be put? (*CAA*)

17. In what form are records of plant and machinery usually kept? What costing information is obtained from them? (*LCCI*)

18. What do you understand by the alternative methods of costing depreciation by the "straight line" method and the "reducing balance" method? State your preference for costing purposes and give reasons. (*SCCA*)

19. Describe two methods of dealing with the apportionment of service department costs among service departments which, in addition to doing work for the production departments, also serve one another. (*CAA*)

20. (*a*) State four methods of calculating depreciation.

(*b*) Write a brief note describing the method of calculating any *one* of them and state any advantage or disadvantage it has.

(*ICMA*)

21. Describe the form in which records of plant and machinery

are usually kept and outline the costing information which can be obtained from them. (*LCCI*)

22. Define the term "overhead absorption." State the various methods which may be used for the absorption of overhead and for each method stated:

(*a*) show how it is calculated; and

(*b*) indicate the points that are in its favour and those which are against it. You may wish to associate the points you give with certain types of business. (*RSA*)

23. List the methods which could be used to absorb factory overheads and outline the circumstances in which each method might be used. (*LCCI*)

24. Cost centres may be divided into two main groups, those which refer to the main activities of the business, i.e. production, selling and distribution; and service cost centres. A number of costs which are not exclusive to one cost centre may have to be apportioned on some rational basis.

1. Define the term cost centre and comment on the possible size of a cost centre and how it could be named.

2. State what you understand by the term service cost centre.

3. Tabulate bases on which the undernoted items of budgeted overhead could be apportioned to cost centres, giving reasons for using the different bases:

Heating.
Electrical power.
Rates.
Medical and first aid.
Material storage.
Supervision. (*ICAS*)

25. (*a*) Define the term "overhead", state the two distinct objectives of overhead analysis and discuss the reasons for relating overhead to cost centres.

(*b*) List, with examples, the successive stages employed in overhead analysis to achieve the objectives referred to in (*a*) above.

(*c*) State why it is a common practice for a manufacturing business to budget or predetermine its overhead. Explain why this predetermined information is used. (*RSA*)

26. (*a*) Give two examples of production overhead which can be identified with and *allocated to* specific cost centres.

(*b*) State the basis of *apportionment* which should be adopted in the case of each of the following items of overhead:

(*i*) stores;

(*ii*) insurance (machinery);

(*iii*) works canteen;

(*iv*) rent and rates.

(c) State two commonly used bases for *absorbing* the overhead of a cost centre in the costs of products.   *(LCC)*

27. (a) Outline the procedures and information required in order to establish a set of predetermined production overhead absorption rates, for a company manufacturing a range of different products in a factory containing a number of production departments and several service departments.

(b) Critically examine the purpose of calculating overhead absorption rates.   *(ACA)*

28. You are appointed cost controller to a group of eight companies which make the same type of product but which deal with their cost items in varying ways.

(a) List five important aspects of overheads that you would need to examine to ensure that the product costs and the quarterly profit statements compiled by each company are comparable.

(b) Explain briefly why you would examine each aspect.   *(ICMA)*

29. Mr Allen purchased machinery in March 1983 and opened a small factory two months later. Preliminary accounts, made up to 31 May, showed a loss of £3,000. Mr Allen, discussing the situation with his accountant, expressed surprise and disappointment, pointing out that his firm had gradually increased its bank balance since commencing business. Mr Allen also complained that, had not £22,000 been charged for depreciation, a profit of £19,000 would have been shown.

Assume that you are Mr Allen's accountant and explain in concise terms:

(i) Why depreciation must be charged.

(ii) How provision for depreciation affects:

    (a) the reported profit;

    (b) the book value of assets;

    (c) the cash position.

(iii) The two most commonly used methods of calculating depreciation.   *(LCC)*

30. A company has four production cost centres, numbered 1 to 4, and three cost centres—stores, personnel and welfare, and factory heating.

(a) Draw up a suitable form of "overhead distribution sheet" *without* figures.

(b) State the basis on which each of the following items of expense would be apportioned over cost centres: insurance (plant and machinery), electrical power, rent and rates.

(c) State the basis on which the total of the expense of each of the service cost centres would be apportioned over the production cost centres.   *(SCCA)*

31. (a) Distinguish between overhead allocation and overhead apportionment.

(b) A factory is divided into three producing departments A, B and C, and one service department D. What would be the most equitable basis of apportioning the following expenses:

> Rent and Rates
> Canteen expenses
> Repairs to machinery
> Electric light
> Heating
> Insurance of buildings
> Supervision
> Directors' remuneration   (LCCI)

32. A multi-drilling machine has just been installed in an engineering factory and is designated plant register number 11/27. Details follow:

> Original cost including installation: £26,600
> Estimated life span: 10 years
> Estimated scrap value after 10 years: £600
> Floor space occupied: 250 square metres
> Number of operators: 2
> Estimated running hours: 1,800 hours per annum
> Estimated cost of maintenance: £480 per annum
> Estimated cost of power: £2,000 per annum

The following data relate to the department in which the machine is located:

> Floor area: 5,000 square metres
> Number of machine operators: 60
> Rent, rates, light and heat: £8,800 per annum
> Supervision: £7,200 per annum

Using the information given above, calculate a machine-hour absorption rate for machine 11/27.   (LCC)

33. The ABC Company Ltd. absorbs production by means of a predetermined rate per direct labour hour based upon the following budgets for the year:

> Production Overhead £32,000
> Direct Labour Hours 192,000

During the year, production overhead and direct labour hours worked are actually as follows:

	Production overhead incurred £	Direct labour hours
January	2,800	14,400
February	2,700	13,800
March	2,900	15,000
April	2,700	14,100
May	2,300	16,200
June	2,250	16,800
July	3,400	17,200
August	2,300	14,700
September	2,250	16,200
October	2,900	25,200
November	2,600	24,300
December	2,900	14,100

Prepare a table showing the overhead incurred, the overhead absorbed each month, and the cumulative under or over absorption at the end of each month. (*IAADP*)

34. The Grant Manufacturing Co. Ltd. estimated its factory overhead for the period at £45,000.

On an expected output of 30,000 units the production data is estimated at:

Materials	£90,000
Labour	£45,000
Number of labour hours	30,000
Number of machine hours	10,000

(*a*) Name three methods of overhead absorption and calculate the three rates using the data available.

(*b*) Calculate the total cost per unit under each of the methods.
(*LCCI*)

35. PQ Limited absorbs its production overhead by using predetermined rates—a percentage on direct labour cost for department P and a machine hour rate (calculated to three decimal places) for department Q.

The estimates made at the beginning of the financial year which ended on 31st October were as follows:

	Dept. P £	Dept. Q £
Direct labour cost	450,000	150,000
Production overhead	517,500	922,500

	Hours	Hours
Direct labour	172,500	40,000
Machines	20,000	180,000

For the month of October, the cost sheet for Job No. 186 shows the following information:

	Dept. P	Dept. Q
Materials used	£200	£800
Direct labour	£360	£190
Direct labour hours	120	47.5
Machine hours	20	260

Following the end of the financial year it was ascertained that actual production overhead incurred by department P was £555,000 and that incurred by department Q was £900,000.

You are required to:

(a) calculate the overhead absorption rates for each of the departments P and Q;

(b) determine the total production overhead cost to be charged to Job No. 186 for October;

(c) show the over/under absorbed overhead for each department and for the company as a whole for the year ended 31st October assuming that actual direct labour cost and machine hours worked were as originally estimated;

(d) comment on the choice of an overhead absorption rate based on direct labour cost for department P.   (ICMA)

36. E Limited makes one product, has two production departments, F and G and two service departments, H and J. The company's budget for the year commencing 1st July, contains the following information:

	Production department F £000	Production department G £000
Total direct wages	500	450
Total direct materials	1,000	750
Overhead incurred	380	240
	units	units
Production per direct labour hour	18	20

The direct wages rate in both departments is £2·50 per hour.

The costs of the service departments given below are apportioned to the production departments as follows:

	Service department H %	Service department J %
To production department: F	70	60
G	30	40

	Service department H	Service department J
	£000	£000
Overhead cost incurred	160	180

You are required to:

(a) calculate the budgeted overhead to be absorbed by each of the production departments F and G;

(b) calculate overhead absorption rates for each of the production departments F and G on the following bases:

(i) direct wages percentage rate;

(ii) direct labour hour rate;

(iii) direct materials percentage rate;

(iv) prime cost percentage rate;

(v) unit of production rate.

(c) state briefly why it may be preferable to absorb overhead into the product costs by direct labour hour rates rather than by direct wages percentage rates.   (RSA)

Chapter 12

Cost Control Accounts

IN most organisations, with the possible exception of very small firms, a cost department is operated in which detailed cost accounts, reports, etc., are produced. In cost accounting extensive use is made of control accounts which are based on the same principles as those used in financial accounting. For example, in the financial ledger the creditors' control account controls the individual creditors' accounts in the purchases ledger; in the cost ledger the stores control account controls the individual stores accounts in the stores ledger.

The cost department will operate ledgers on the double-entry system, but will differ from the financial accounts in that its work involves much more analysis. The cost accounts show not only the cost of a material or service utilised by the business but also how the cost affected a department or unit of production.

If the cost accounts are to inspire the confidence of management it is essential that they should be reconciled with the financial accounts. This reconciliation procedure is discussed in greater detail in the next chapter. However, many large firms have now adopted a system of integral accounts in which the accounting and costing departments operate together, using only one set of books; a full description of this system is outside the scope of this volume, and the reader is referred to *Wheldon's Cost Accounting.**

Ledgers Required

The cost department will probably operate a number of ledgers depending on the size of the business, type of industry, etc., but the following are in general use.

1. *Cost ledger*

This is the main ledger which controls all other ledgers in the cost department.

*Macdonald & Evans, 1984.

124

2. Stores ledger

All stores accounts are kept in this ledger, each account representing an item in store. This ledger was discussed in some detail in Chapter 5.

3. Work-in-progress ledger

In this ledger an account will be maintained for each job, process, department, or unit, in which will be recorded production during the period, the cost incurred in production, and stocks of work in progress.

4. Finished goods ledger

An account in this ledger will be opened for each type of finished product. In it will be recorded the completed production transferred from the work-in-progress ledger.

Control Accounts

In the cost ledger one control account should be operated for each subsidiary ledger, one representing the financial ledger and others as considered necessary, e.g. wages and materials.

1. Cost Ledger Control Account

This account is more correctly referred to as a general ledger adjustment account, but is widely used as such. In the cost ledger only impersonal accounts are recorded, because it is unnecessary to show personal accounts which are already shown in the financial books; thus, in effect, the cost ledger control account takes the place of the personal accounts. Into this account are posted those items of expenditure and income which are extracted from the financial accounts, the double entry being completed by posting to the appropriate cost accounts, e.g. wages, production overheads. In addition, any transfer from the cost books to the financial books, e.g. returns outwards or cost of capital work performed by the factory, will be entered into this account.

It is important to note that no entry should be made direct from the financial books to the cost books; entries must pass through the cost ledger control account. The balance on this account represents the total of all the balances of the impersonal accounts.

In the financial books a memorandum cost ledger control account is opened in which are recorded all the items of income and expenditure which affect the cost accounts (it will be shown on p. 148 that there are a few items which are regarded as purely financial items and are not shown in the cost accounts). The financial accountant will be requested to prepare the account, in addition to his usual accounts, so that the cost accountant can easily collect the transactions he needs for his control account.

Example

This procedure can be simply illustrated as follows:

During February materials valued at £5,000 are bought on credit.

In the financial books

	£	£
Dr Materials account	5,000	
Dr Cost ledger control account (memorandum)		
Cr Creditors		5,000

In the cost books

	£	£
Dr Stores ledger control account	5,000	
Cr Cost ledger control account		5,000

2. Stores Ledger Control Account

This account shows the total transactions of materials, e.g. total stocks of raw materials, total receipts and total issues. If all the accounts in the stores ledger are scheduled the figures should correspond with the figures shown in this control account. Sometimes a materials control account is also prepared which shows total purchases and transfers to stores. In this way, purchases and receipts of stores are reconciled before the stores ledger control account is posted.

3. Work-in-progress Ledger Control Account

This account represents the total work in progress at any time. In it is recorded expenditure on jobs and transfers to completed production. At the end of a period the total balances of the various job accounts should equal the balance shown on this account.

4. Finished Goods Ledger Control Account

The total value of finished goods in stock is represented in this account. In it are recorded receipts from production and transfers to distribution departments. The total balances of the various stock accounts should equal the balances on this account.

Specimen Book-keeping Entries

The main accounts used in the cost ledger are:

(a) cost ledger control account;
(b) stores ledger control account;
(c) wages account;
(d) production overhead account;
(e) administration overhead account;
(f) selling and distribution overhead account.

To these accounts is posted the expenditure appropriate to the account. To find the cost of production, charges are transferred to:

(g) work-in-progress ledger control account.

Completed jobs are then transferred to:

(h) finished goods ledger control account.

Finished goods which are sold are posted to:

(i) cost of sales account.

The cost of finished goods sold is transferred to:

(j) costing profit and loss account.

In this account the profit or loss is ascertained and transferred to cost ledger control account, thus completing the cycle.

Additional accounts may be opened as found necessary, such as, for example, accounts for capital work or special repairs.

Materials

(a) Materials purchased for store £5,000; for special jobs £1,000.

	£	£
Dr Stores ledger control account	5,000	
Work-in-progress ledger control account	1,000	
Cr Cost ledger control account		6,000

(b) Materials returned to suppliers £350.

	£	£
Dr Cost ledger control account	350	
Cr Stores ledger control account		350

(c) Direct and indirect materials amounting to £3,500 and £600 respectively are issued.

	£	£
Dr Work-in-progress ledger control account	3,500	
Production overhead account	600	
Cr Stores ledger control account		4,100

In the work-in-progress ledger individual job accounts will be debited; in the stores ledger individual stores accounts will be credited.

(d) Materials valued £100 were returned to stores from production.

	£	£
Dr Stores ledger control account	100	
Cr Work-in-progress ledger control account		100

In the stores ledger individual stores accounts will be debited; in the work-in-progress ledger individual job accounts will be credited.

(e) Materials valued at £50 were transferred from job no. 9 to job no. 10.

	£	£
Dr Job no. 10 account	50	
Cr Job no. 9 account		50

In the work-in-progress ledger only these two accounts are affected; no entry is required in the work-in-progress ledger control account.

Labour

(a) Wages earned amounted to £40,000.

	£	£
Dr Wages account	40,000	
Cr Cost ledger control account		40,000

(b) This figure was analysed as follows:

Direct labour	£32,000
Indirect labour: Production	£5,000
Administration	£1,000
Selling and distribution	£2,000

	£	£
Dr Work-in-progress ledger control account	32,000	
Production overhead account	5,000	
Administration overhead account	1,000	
Selling overhead account	2,000	
Cr Wages control account		40,000

In the work-in-progress ledger individual job accounts will be debited as per the analysis of job time records.

Overhead

(a) The cost of services supplied by creditors and by indirect labour amounted to £25,000, analysed as follows:

Production overhead	£15,000
Administration overhead	£6,000
Selling and distribution overhead	£4,000

	£	£
Dr Production overhead account	15,000	
Administration overhead account	6,000	
Selling overhead account	4,000	
Cr Cost ledger control account		25,000

(b) The actual cost of overhead has been ascertained and analysed; what is now required is the amount of overhead recovered. Recovery of overhead was discussed in Chapter 11. It is ascertained that production overhead, £16,000, has been absorbed by production.

	£	£
Dr Work-in-progress ledger control account	16,000	
Cr Production overhead account		16,000

In the work-in-progress ledger individual job accounts will be debited.

(c) Invariably there will be a difference between overhead incurred and overhead absorbed, due to increased or decreased production, etc. The balance of production overhead account is transferred to overhead adjustment account.

	£	£
Dr Production overhead account	1,000	
Cr Overhead adjustment account		1,000

(d) Administration overhead £6,500 has been absorbed by production of finished goods.

	£	£
Dr Finished goods ledger control account	6,500	
Cr Overhead adjustment account		6,500

Sometimes it may be preferable to transfer administration overhead direct to profit and loss account.

(e) The balance of administration overhead account is transferred:

	£	£
Dr Administration overhead account	500	
Cr Overhead adjustment account		500

(f) Selling and distribution overhead £3,400 has been recovered on goods sold.

	£	£
Dr Cost of sales account	3,400	
Cr Selling overhead account		3,400

It should be noted that selling and distribution costs do not form part of the cost of production, but part of the cost of goods sold.

(g) The balance of selling overhead account is transferred:

	£	£
Dr Overhead adjustment account	600	
Cr Selling overhead account		600

Specimen Question I

At the beginning of the year, the balances appearing in the books of the Paul Graeme Engineering PLC were as follows:

	£	£
Cost ledger control account		25,634
Stores ledger control account	16,236	
Work-in-progress ledger control account	3,478	
Finished goods ledger control account	5,920	
	£25,634	£25,634

Transactions for December were as follows:

	£	£
Purchases for stores		104,367
Purchases for special jobs		2,348
Returns to suppliers		684
Direct wages	46,269	
Indirect factory wages	12,327	
Production salaries	15,265	
Administration salaries	12,876	
Sales department salaries	6,142	
Distribution salaries	3,286	
		96,165

	£
Production expenses	11,187
Administration expenses	10,264
Selling expenses	5,418
Distribution expenses	6,524
Stores issued to production	95,816
Stores issued to maintenance	3,498
Production overhead absorbed by production	42,300
Administration overhead absorbed by finished goods	23,200
Selling overhead recovered on sales	21,300
Production finished during the year	186,015
Finished goods sold-at-cost	208,787
Sales	245,000

A physical inventory reveals the following balances at the end of the month:

Stores ledger	20,438
Work-in-progress ledger	4,196
Finished goods ledger	6,348

It is discovered that insured goods valued at £78 have been stolen; the balance in the stores ledger may be regarded as a normal loss.

Answer

Cost Ledger Control Account

		£			£
Dec. 31	Stores ledger control a/c	684	Dec. 1	Balance b/d	25,634
	Difference on stores a/c	78	Dec. 31	Stores ledger control a/c	104,367
	Cost accounting P & L			Work-in-progress	
	a/c—sales	245,000		control a/c	2,348
	Balance c/d	30,982		Wages a/c	96,165
				Production overhead	
				a/c	11,187
				Administration	
				overhead a/c	10,264
				Selling overhead a/c	5,418
				Selling overhead a/c	6,524
				Cost accounting P & L	
				a/c—profit	14,837
		£276,744			£276,744
			Jan. 1	Balance b/d	30,982

Stores Ledger Control Account

		£			£
Dec. 1	Balance b/d	16,236	Dec. 31	Cost ledger control a/c	684
Dec. 31	Cost ledger control a/c	104,367		Work-in-progress	
				control a/c	95,816
				Production overhead	
				a/c	3,498
				Difference in stores a/c	167
				Balance c/d	20,438
		£120,603			£120,603
Jan. 1	Balance b/d	20,438			

Wages Control Account

		£			£
Dec. 31	Cost ledger control a/c	96,165	Dec. 31	Work-in-progress	
				control a/c	46,269
				Production overhead	
				a/c	12,327
				Production overhead	
				a/c	15,265
				Administration	
				overhead a/c	12,876
				Selling overhead a/c	6,142
				Selling overhead a/c	3,286
		£96,165			£96,165

Production Overhead Account

		£			£
Dec. 31	Cost ledger control a/c	11,187	Dec. 31	Work-in-progress	
	Stores ledger control a/c	3,498		control a/c	42,300
	Wages a/c	12,327		Overhead adjustment	
	Wages a/c	15,265		a/c	66
	Difference on stores a/c	89			
		£42,366			£42,366

Administration Overhead Account

		£			£
Dec. 31	Cost ledger control a/c	10,264	Dec. 31	Finished goods control	
	Wages a/c	12,876		a/c	23,200
	Overhead adjustment				
	a/c	60			
		£23,200			£23,200

Selling and Distribution Overhead Account

		£			£
Dec. 31	Cost ledger control a/c	5,418	Dec. 31	Cost of sales a/c	21,300
	Cost ledger control a/c	6,524		Overhead adjustment	
	Wages a/c	6,142		a/c	70
	Wages a/c	3,286			
		£21,370			£21,370

Work-in-progress Ledger Control Account

		£			£
Dec. 1	Balance b/d	3,478	Dec. 31	Finished goods control	
	Cost ledger control a/c	2,348		a/c	186,015
	Stores ledger control a/c	95,816		Balance c/d	4,196
	Wages a/c	46,269			
	Production overhead				
	a/c	42,300			
		£190,211			£190,211
Jan. 1	Balance b/d	4,196			

Finished Goods Ledger Control Account

		£			£
Dec. 1	Balance b/d	5,920	Dec. 31	Cost of sales a/c	208,787
Dec. 31	Work-in-progress			Balance c/d	6,348
	control a/c	186,015			
	Administration				
	overhead a/c	23,200			
		£215,135			£215,135
Jan. 1	Balance b/d	6,348			

Cost of Sales Account

		£			£
Dec. 31	Finished goods control		Dec. 31	Cost accounting P & L	
	a/c	208,787		a/c	230,087
	Selling overhead a/c	21,300			
		£230,087			£230,087

Overhead Adjustment Account

		£			£
Dec. 31	Production overhead		Dec. 31	Administration	
	a/c	66		overhead a/c	60
	Selling overhead a/c	70		Cost accounting P & L	
				a/c	76
		£136			£136

Difference on Stores Account

	£			£
Dec. 31 Stores ledger control a/c	167	Dec. 31	Cost ledger control a/c—abnormal loss	78
			Production overhead a/c—normal loss	89
	£167			£167

Cost Accounting Profit and Loss Account for December

	£		£
Cost of sales a/c	230,087	Sales	245,000
Overhead adjustment a/c	76		
Cost ledger control a/c	14,837		
	£245,000		£245,000

Trial balance as at December 31

	Dr	Cr
	£	£
Cost ledger control a/c		30,982
Stores ledger control a/c	20,438	
Work-in-progress ledger control a/c	4,196	
Finished goods ledger control a/c	6,348	
	£30,982	£30,982

NOTES

1. Any difference in the stores account totals is transferred to a difference in stores account. Investigation will be made into discrepancies to find out the reasons, and if possible preventive action will be taken.

The loss by theft is considered abnormal, so is not included in cost of production, but is transferred out of the cost ledger via the cost ledger control account. There it is accounted for as an expense, e.g.:

	£	£
Dr Theft of materials account	78	
Cr Purchases account		78

When the insurance company agrees the claim, the amount will be transferred as follows:

	£	£
Dr Insurance co. account	78	
Cr Theft of materials account		78

If the materials had not been insured the theft would still be regarded as abnormal, so could not be absorbed as a production overhead. The accounting entry would be therefore:

	£	£
Dr Cost accounting profit and loss account	78	
Cr Difference on stores account		78

2. Under- or over-recovered overhead is transferred from the respective overhead accounts to overhead adjustment account, the balance of which is transferred to cost accounting profit and loss account. Sometimes the overhead adjustment account is not used, the balances of the overhead account being transferred direct to the cost accounting profit and loss account, but this is not to be encouraged.

3. The profit for the month, ascertained in the cost accounting profit and loss account, is transferred to the financial ledger, via the cost ledger control account. This figure should be reconciled with the profit for the month ascertained in the profit and loss account.

The problem of reconciling the cost and financial accounts is discussed in the next chapter.

Over- or Under-absorbed Overhead

In the above illustration over- or under-absorbed overhead was transferred to an overhead adjustment account, the balance of which was transferred to cost accounting profit and loss account. This was because many accountants consider that overhead incurred in a financial period should be absorbed during the same period. However, some accountants prefer to carry forward the balances on the various overhead accounts to the next period, which will necessitate the balances appearing in the trial balance; this results in a difference in profit shown in the cost accounting profit and loss account, compared with that in the financial profit and loss account. Thus in the reconciliation of the two accounts allowance must be made for such difference, if this second method is adopted. It is generally considered that this alternative method is not good cost accounting practice, because it passes the under- or over-absorption on to the next year's production.

Carriage Inwards

In theory it is desirable that the cost of carriage inwards be added to the purchase price of the materials. However, in practice it is very often impracticable to do this, because:

(a) transport charges may be ascertained long after the materials have been received in store;

(b) it may frequently be impossible to identify transport charges with specific materials;

(c) the transport cost per unit may be so small as to make the calculation meaningless and time consuming.

It is therefore usual to recover carriage inwards through production overhead, as a general charge against work in progress:

Dr Production overhead account
Cr Cost ledger control account

Capital Orders

Frequently employees are employed in the production of tools and equipment for a company's own use, or are engaged in improving plant, machinery, buildings, etc. Where this type of work is carried out it is absolutely essential that a record be kept of all expenditure incurred on these operations, so that charges are not included in the cost accounting profit and loss account. Such work, if successful, should be "capitalised", i.e. the expenditure transferred to an appropriate asset account.

A capital order would be opened for each item of capital work to be performed, and on this order would be recorded all expenditure incurred.

In the work-in-progress ledger all work performed, whether routine production, maintenance, or capital expenditure, will be recorded. Job accounts will be maintained for each job; possibly different colours will be used to distinguish the various types of jobs, e.g. red denoting capital, white denoting production, etc. When, for example, a capital order is completed the total material and labour cost can be transferred from the work-in-progress ledger to the capital order account in the cost ledger, which will thus reveal the cost of the project to be capitalised; e.g. in producing a machine for use in the factory it is ascertained that the cost of materials used was £2,500 and that the cost of labour was £1,200.

	£	£
Dr Capital order account	3,700	
Cr Work-in-progress ledger account		3,700

The asset when capitalised is transferred to the financial ledger by the following entry:

	£	£
Dr Cost ledger control account	3,700	
Cr Capital order account		3,700

It will be observed that no production overhead was charged to this capital order. Opinions differ on whether this ought to be done, but it is thought that provided such overhead is incurred in consequence of the capital order undertaken, it is legitimate to do so. It is obviously unsound practice, however, to load normal overhead on to capital projects to such an extent as to vitiate comparison of products manufactured.

Special Repair Orders

Special repair and maintenance work is recorded in a rather similar way to capital orders. A repair order is issued, and in the work-in-progress ledger a job account will be opened in which will be recorded all expenditure incurred on that job. On completion of the work, the repair order will be closed.

	£	£
Dr Special repair and maintenance order account	3,700	
Cr Work-in-progress ledger control account		3,700

The cost of the repair will then be charged to the department or departments for which the work was carried out, e.g. it is estimated that the cost of this special repair should be allocated as follows: production department £2,400; administration department £800; sales department £500.

	£	£
Dr Production overhead account	2,400	
Administration overhead account	800	
Selling overhead account	500	
Cr Special repair and maintenance account		3,700

Specimen Question II

On 1st December, the balances appearing in the books of the Jeremy Stuart Manufacturing PLC were as follows:

	£	£
Cost ledger control		344,823
Stores ledger control	185,624	
Work-in-progress ledger control	64,326	
Finished goods ledger control	94,873	
	£344,823	£344,823

Transactions during December were as follows:

	£	£
Purchases of materials		583,526
Return to suppliers		8,629
Issues of direct materials		559,906
Issues of indirect materials		42,617
Purchases for special jobs		10,342
Return to stores from production		3,427
Normal loss in stores		4,325
Abnormal loss in stores		2,468
Carriage inwards		36,489
Direct wages paid	248,372	
Direct wages accrued	5,688	
Indirect wages paid	49,362	
Indirect wages accrued	1,256	
Production salaries	58,763	
Administration salaries	99,634	
Sales department salaries	63,981	
Distribution department salaries	12,326	
Distribution department wages	34,976	
		574,358
Production expenses		156,328
Administration expenses		124,697
Sales expenses		63,425
Distribution expenses		24,973

Production overheads are absorbed by production at 150% of direct wages. Selling and distribution overheads are absorbed at 20% of the cost of sales. Administration overheads are not absorbed but are written off against profit. Capital orders completed at cost amounted to £54,000 and were "capitalised". Production completed £1,158,648. Finished goods sold at cost £1,166,730. Sales amounted to £2,000,000.

A physical inventory revealed the following balances at the end of the year:

Stores ledger control   £154,632
Work-in-progress ledger control   £53,649
Finished goods ledger control   £86,791

Answer

Cost Ledger Control Account

		£			£
Dec. 31	Stores ledger control	8,629	Dec. 1	Balance b/d	344,823
	Capital orders	54,000	Dec. 31	Stores ledger control	583,526
	Profit & loss (sales)	2,000,000		WIP ledger	10,342
	Balance c/d	295,072		Production overhead	36,489
				Wages control	574,358
				Production overhead	156,328
				Administration overhead	124,697
				S & D overhead	63,425
				S & D overhead	24,973
				Profit & loss	438,740
		£2,357,701			£2,357,701
			Jan. 1	Balance b/d	295,072

Stores Ledger Control Account

		£			£
Dec. 1	Balance b/d	185,624	Dec. 31	Cost ledger control	8,629
Dec. 31	Cost ledger control	583,526			
	WIP ledger	3,427		Abnormal loss	2,468
				Production overhead	4,325
				WIP ledger	559,906
				Production overhead	42,617
				Balance c/d	154,632
		£772,577			£772,577
Jan. 1	Balance b/d	154,632			

Wages Control Account

		£			£
Dec. 31	Cost ledger control	574,358	Dec. 31	Work in progress	248,372
				Work in progress	5,688
				Production overhead	49,362
				Production overhead	1,256
				Production overhead	58,763
				Administration overhead	99,634
				S & D overhead	63,981
				S & D overhead	12,326
				S & D overhead	34,976
		£574,358			£574,358

Production Overhead Account

		£			£
Dec. 31	Stores ledger control	42,617	Dec. 31	WIP ledger	381,090
	Stores ledger control	4,325			
	Cost ledger control	36,489			
	Wages control	49,362			
	Wages control	1,256			
	Wages control	58,763			
	Cost ledger control	156,328			
	Overhead adjustment	31,950			
		£381,090			£381,090

Administration Overhead Account

		£			£
Dec. 31	Wages control	99,634	Dec. 31	P & L account	224,331
	Cost ledger control	124,697			
		£224,331			£224,331

Selling and Distribution Overhead Account

		£			£
Dec. 31	Wages control	63,981	Dec. 31	Cost of sales	233,346
	Wages control	12,326			
	Wages control	34,976			
	Cost ledger control	63,425			
	Cost ledger control	24,973			
	Overhead adjustment	33,665			
		£233,346			£233,346

Work-in-progress Ledger Control Account

		£			£
Dec. 1	Balance b/d	64,326	Dec. 31	Stores ledger	3,427
Dec. 31	Cost ledger control	10,342		Capital orders	54,000
	Wages control	248,372		Finished goods	1,158,648
	Wages control	5,688		Balance c/d	53,649
	Stores ledger	559,906			
	Production overhead	381,090			
		£1,269,724			£1,269,724
Jan. 1	Balance b/d	53,649			

Finished Goods Ledger Control Account

		£			£
Dec. 1	Balance b/d	94,873	Dec. 31	Cost of sales	1,166,730
Dec. 31	WIP ledger	1,158,648		Balance c/d	86,791
		£1,253,521			£1,253,521
Jan. 1	Balance b/d	86,791			

Cost of Sales Account

	£		£
Dec. 31 Finished goods	1,166,730	Dec. 31 Profit and loss	1,400,076
S & D overhead	233,346		
	£1,400,076		£1,400,076

Overhead Adjustment Account

	£		£
Dec. 31 Profit and loss	65,615	Dec. 31 Production overhead	31,950
		S & D overhead	33,665
	£65,615		£65,615

Abnormal Loss in Stores Account

	£		£
Dec. 31 Stores ledger	£2,468	Dec. 31 Profit and loss	£2,468

Capital Orders Account

	£		£
Dec. 31 WIP ledger	£54,000	Dec. 31 Cost ledger control	£54,000

Cost Accounting Profit and Loss Account for month ended 31st Dec.

	£		£
Cost of sales	1,400,076	Sales	2,000,000
Administration overhead	224,331	Overhead adjustment	65,615
Abnormal loss in stores	2,468		
Net profit	438,740		
	£2,065,615		£2,065,615

NOTES

1. Normal loss in stores is transferred to production overhead account so that the cost can be absorbed in the cost of production.

2. Abnormal loss is transferred to abnormal loss in stores account, which is eventually shown as a specific item in the profit and loss account; this "highlights" the loss.

3. Production overhead is absorbed in work in progress at 150% of cost of direct wages. Direct wages amount to £254,060 (paid £248,372 + accrued £5,688), so the amount recovered is 150% of £254,060.

4. Selling and distribution overhead is absorbed at 20% of cost of sales. Thus 20% of £1,166,730 is £233,346.

5. Administration overhead has not been recovered so has been written off directly to profit and loss account.

6. Work on capital projects completed has been "capitalised", so capital orders have been transferred to cost ledger control account.

Examination Questions

1. Outline a system of control accounts for costing ledgers and summarise the results achieved thereby.   (*CAA*)

2. Describe briefly the control accounts you would set up when you are introducing a costing system where none formerly existed, and state the sources of debit and credit to these accounts.   (*RSA*)

3. Explain the working of stores control accounts. If at the time of stocktaking the quantity of counted stock should be found to differ considerably from the total shown in the control account, what conclusions would you draw, and why?   (*LCCI*)

4. Describe briefly a work-in-progress account and illustrate its relation to the financial accounts.   (*RSA*)

5. You wish to institute control accounts in respect of materials purchased and used in your factory. What purposes do control accounts serve? What accounts would you institute, and from what sources would the entries be derived?   (*ICMA*)

6. J Limited keeps cost accounts separate from its financial accounts. The debit balances on the cost ledger at 1st January were as follows:

	£000
Stocks: Raw material	190
Work-in-progress	200
Finished goods	260

The following is a summary of the transactions for the three months ended 31st March:

	£000
Purchases:	
Raw materials	350
Indirect supplies, production	28
Issues: direct material to production	320
Wages and salaries incurred and paid	
Production: direct	232
indirect	114
Selling and distribution	52

	£000
Expenses:	
Production, indirect	88
Selling and distribution	24
Depreciation provision for three months:	
Production, plant and machinery	50
Selling and distribution, vehicles	20
Sales	1,200

Production overhead is absorbed into work-in-progress at a pre-determined rate of 125% on direct wages.

At 31st March, the stock of:

work-in-progress was   £178,000, and of
finished goods   £220,000

You are required for the three months ended 31st March to:

(*a*) open the accounts in the cost ledger of J Limited and post into them the transactions given for:

(*i*) stocks of raw materials, work-in-progress and finished goods;

(*ii*) production overhead and selling and distribution overhead;

(*b*) prepare a profit and loss account   (*RSA*)

7. The balances in the cost ledger of a manufacturing company on January 1 were as follows:

	£
Stores ledger control	7,560
Work in progress (at factory cost)	12,600
Finished stock (at factory cost)	2,250
Cost ledger control	22,410

You are given the following information for the year:

	£
Purchases of materials	43,200
Direct factory wages	61,200
Manufacturing expenses	36,216
Materials issued to production	42,480
Selling expenses	5,760
Manufacturing expenses recovered	35,700
Selling expenses recovered	5,610
Sales	148,800
Stock of finished goods, December 31, at factory cost	3,390
Work in progress, December 31, at factory cost	16,920

144   12. COST CONTROL ACCOUNTS

There was no loss or wastage of materials or of finished or partly finished goods.

You are required to show the accounts in the cost ledger for the year, to prepare the costing profit and loss account for the year, and to extract a trial balance as at December 31.   (*ICSA*)

8. The manufacturing and trading accounts of B Limited for the year are as follows:

Manufacturing account:

	£	£	£		£
Raw material:				Trading account:	
Opening stock		15,634		Cost of goods	
Purchases	98,746			manufactured	265,796
Returns	6,324				
		92,422			
		108,056			
Closing stock		14,831			
			93,225		
Direct wages			84,723		
Overhead			87,531		
			172,254		
Work in progress:					
Opening stock		8,375			
Closing stock		8,058			
			317		
			£265,796		£265,796

Trading account:

	£	£	£
Finished goods:			Sales	417,548
Opening stock	24,326		
Cost of goods			
manufactured	265,796		
	290,122		
Closing stock	24,941		
		265,181	
Gross profit		152,367	
		£417,548	£417,548

The statement prepared to reconcile the gross profits in the financial and the cost accounts at the end of the year is as follows:

	£	£	£
Gross profit in financial accounts			152,367
Difference in stock valuations:			
Add: Raw material, closing stock		176	
Work in progress, opening stock		265	
Finished goods, opening stock		321	
		762	
Less: Raw material, opening stock		198	
Work in progress, closing stock		243	
Finished goods, closing stock		365	
		806	
			44
Gross profit in cost accounts before			
adjustment of overheads			£152,323

The cost accounts revealed that overheads had been under-absorbed by £2,808.

Show the following control accounts in the cost ledger:

(*a*) Raw material.

(*b*) Work in progress.

(*c*) Finished goods. (*ICMA*)

9. From the information given below relating to P Manufacturing Company Limited you are required to:

(*a*) write up the accounts in the cost ledger for the month of April;

(*b*) extract from the accounts prepared in answer to (*a*) above a trial balance as at 30th April.

The trial balance of the cost ledger as at 31st March, was as follows:

	£	£	£
Stores control		45,200	
Work-in-progress control, process 1:			
direct materials	4,100		
direct wages	3,200		
production overhead	11,200		
		18,500	
Work-in-progress control, process 2:			
direct materials	15,600		
direct wages	4,400		
production overhead	11,000		
		31,000	

Work-in-progress control, process 3: £   £   £
  direct materials   28,800
  direct wages   6,400
  production overhead   9,600
                                                44,800
Finished goods control   44,500
Production overhead, under/over
  absorbed   2,400
Sales   340,000
Cost of sales   264,600
General ledger control   110,700
Abnormal loss   4,500

                                              £453,100 £453,100

During the month of April, the following transactions took place:

                                                          £
Materials returned to supplier   780
Actual cost of materials purchased on credit   21,250
Materials issued to process: 1   10,600
                            2   5,200
                            3   3,400
Materials issued to production maintenance department   640
Direct wages incurred in process: 1   8,400
                                 2   10,800
                                 3   12,200
Production salaries incurred   24,100
Production indirect expenses incurred   56,000
Sales   210,000
Production reports included the following:

	Direct materials £	Direct wages £
Abnormal loss in process: 1	240	200
2	700	140
3	1,450	220
Transfer from process: 1	12,300	9,800
2	55,000	10,260
3	84,260	12,780

The value of finished goods in stock at 30th April, was £49,100.

Overhead is absorbed by means of direct wages percentage rates. Production is transferred from one process to the next and in the accounts of the receiving process is treated as an item of materials cost.   (*ICMA*)

Chapter 13

Reconciliation of Cost and Financial Accounts

IN many large businesses a system of integral accounting has been adopted, whereby only one set of accounts is operated.* This system has been used to replace a separate financial accounting and cost accounting system. Where integral accounting is in operation there will obviously be no need for any reconciliation between the cost and financial accounts. However, where separate cost accounting and financial accounting departments are maintained it is essential that the accounts produced by these departments are reconciled, otherwise management would have no faith in the system. For this purpose, a memorandum reconciliation account is prepared, which will be illustrated in this chapter.

In Chapter 12 the procedure adopted by the cost accountant for ascertaining the cost accounting profit was outlined. It may be recalled that the profit was transferred from the cost accounting profit and loss account to the cost ledger control account. At this stage it may be expedient to consider again this account.

Cost Ledger Control Account

		£			£
Dec. 31	Stores ledger control a/c	684	Dec. 1	Balance b/d	25,634
	Difference on stores a/c	78	Dec. 31	Stores ledger control a/c	104,367
	Cost accounting P & L			Work-in-progress control	
	a/c—sales	245,000		a/c	2,348
	Balance c/d	30,982		Wages control a/c	96,165
				Production overhead a/c	11,187
				Administration overhead	
				a/c	10,264
				Selling overhead a/c	5,418
				Selling overhead a/c	6,524
				Cost accounting P & L	
				a/c—profit	14,837
		£276,744			£276,744
			Jan. 1	Balance b/d	30,982

*Reference may be made to *Wheldon's Cost Accounting*, L. W. J. Owler and J. L. Brown, Macdonald & Evans, 1984, and *Managerial Accounting and Finance*, J. L. Brown and L. R. Howard, Macdonald & Evans, 1982.

It will be observed that the profit for the year as ascertained by the cost accountant is £14,837. The financial accountant will also have computed the profit for the year, which will no doubt be quite different, so it will be necessary to effect a reconciliation.

In the above account most of the items shown will be identical with those shown in the financial accounts, the exceptions being:

(*a*) opening and closing balances, which represent stocks of raw materials, work in progress, and finished goods;
(*b*) cost accounting profit.

Thus, when preparing a memorandum reconciliation account these items must be considered. In addition, consideration must be given to items which are peculiar to one set of accounts only.

Items shown only in the Financial Accounts

There will invariably be certain items which appear in the financial accounts and not in the cost accounts. The main items are as follows.

1. *Purely financial charges*

(*a*) Losses of capital assets, arising from sale, exchange, or insured destruction. Fees of assessors and advisors on such destruction losses (fire, etc.) come under this heading, being unrelated to operating cost.
(*b*) Stamp duty and expenses on issues and transfers of capital stock, shares and bonds, etc.
(*c*) Losses on investments.
(*d*) Discounts on bonds, debentures, etc.
(*e*) Fines and penalties.
(*f*) Interest on bank loans, mortgages, etc.

2. *Purely financial income*

(*a*) Rent receivable; if, however, the rent is received from sub-letting part of the business premises, the allowance will probably have been made in the cost accounts.
(*b*) Profit arising from sale of fixed assets, if not capitalised.
(*c*) Fees received on issues and transfers of shares, etc.
(*d*) Interest received on bank deposits, loans, etc.
(*e*) Dividends received.

3. *Appropriations of profits*

(*a*) Donations to charities.
(*b*) Items which appear in the profit and loss appropriation account.

Items shown only in the Cost Accounts

There are very few items which appear in the cost accounts only. All expenditure incurred, whether for cash or credit, passes through the financial accounting system, so the type of entry which can appear in the cost accounts only is a notional charge.

1. *Interest on capital*

Sometimes management policy is to charge interest on capital employed in production so as to show the notional cost of employing the capital rather than investing it outside the business.

2. *Charge in lieu of rent*

Again it is sometimes policy to charge a notional amount for rent of premises owned, so as to be able to compare the cost of production in a factory owned by a company with similar costs in a leasehold or rented factory.

However, these two items will not affect the agreement with the financial profit and loss account, because they are merely a transfer in the cost accounts:

Dr Production overhead account
Cr Interest on capital/notional rent account
Dr Work-in-progress account
Cr Production overhead account
Dr Interest on capital/notional rent account
Cr Cost accounting profit and loss account

The reader should appreciate the significance of these entries. The first journal entry creates the notional charge and inflates the production overhead. Production overhead will be absorbed into production in the normal manner, e.g. as a machine hour rate or as a percentage of direct wages. Eventually, this charge to work in progress will be transferred to finished goods, cost of sales, and then to cost accounting profit and loss account. The final journal entry shown above closes off the notional account by transferring it to cost accounting profit and loss account. The notional charge has served its purpose of inflating production costs, without appearing in the financial accounts. The financial accounts are, of course, not affected, because the transaction is an internal arrangement in the cost accounting books, no cash or credit being involved.

Memorandum Reconciliation Account

It will now be apparent to the student that the cost accounts and financial accounts will not agree automatically. The two main differences may be summarised:

(a) items peculiar to one set of accounts only;
(b) stocks may be valued in one set of accounts on a different basis from that used in another.

Examples of a memorandum reconciliation account illustrating the particular points mentioned above are now given.

1. *Items peculiar to one set of accounts only*

Specimen Question

The financial accountant of Susaeme Products PLC has prepared the following profit and loss account:

Profit and Loss Account for the Month Ending December 31

	£		£
Office salaries	7,241	Gross profit b/d	38,462
Office expenses	5,346	Dividend received	325
Salesmen's salaries	4,365	Profit on sale of	
Sales expenses	7,489	machinery	240
Distribution salaries	2,436	Bank interest	50
Distribution expenses	5,648		
Fines	150		
Interest on mortgage	200		
Net profit c/d	6,202		
	£39,077		£39,077

	£		£
Corporation tax	2,000	Balance b/d	3,000
Dividends	2,500	Net profit b/d	6,202
Reserve	1,500		
Balance c/d	3,202		
	£9,202		£9,202

The cost accountant has prepared a cost accounting profit and loss account for the same period, which revealed a profit of £5,937. Notional rent charged for the period was £500, and interest on capital charged was £2,000. Reconcile the two sets of amounts.

Answer

Memorandum Reconciliation Statement

	£	£		£	£
Items not debited in cost accounts:			Profit as per cost accounts		5,937
Fines	150		Items not credited in cost accounts:		
Interest on mortgage	200		Dividends received	325	
		350	Profit on sale of		
Profit as per financial accounts		6,202	machine	240	
			Bank interest	50	
					615
		£6,552			£6,552

It should be noted that notional rent and interest on capital do not appear in the memorandum reconciliation account. As explained previously, if the accounting entries illustrated above have been carried out, the cost accounting profit and loss account will have been directly credited and indirectly debited with the amount of the notional charges, so that the entries have been eliminated from profit. There is therefore no necessity to reconcile these transactions.

2. Different bases of stock valuation

It frequently happens that stocks of raw materials are valued in the financial accounts at a figure quite different from those in the cost accounts. In the financial accounts stock is invariably based on the principle of the lower of cost or replacement price as a matter of financial prudence. On the other hand, in the cost accounts stock will be valued according to the system adopted in the stores accounts, e.g. FIFO or LIFO.

Stocks of work in progress may be valued differently in the financial accounts from those appearing in the cost accounts. Valuation of work in progress often proves to be very difficult, due to the different stages in production which each unit may have reached. If one excludes marginal costing, where overheads are not absorbed by production, there are three main bases of valuation:

    (a) Prime cost;
    (b) Prime cost + Production overhead;
    (c) Prime cost + Production overhead + Administration overhead.

Policy of the firm will dictate which method is considered most suitable, taking account of the circumstances peculiar to the industry.

Stocks of finished goods would normally be valued in the cost accounts at cost price (adopting one of the above methods), while in the financial accounts stocks would be recorded at cost or replacement price, whichever is the lower.

As will be appreciated, differences in stock valuations will affect the profits or losses shown by the two sets of accounts.

Specimen Question

The abbreviated final accounts of Graesan Manufacturing PLC are as follows:

Manufacturing Account for the Month Ended December 31

	£	£		£
Raw materials:			Trading account:	
Opening stock	34,268		Cost of goods manufactured	381,652
Purchases	186,456			
	220,724			
Less Closing stock	37,189			
Raw materials				
consumed		183,535		
Wages—direct		106,385		
Prime cost		289,920		
Factory overhead		94,316		
Gross production cost		384,236		

	£	£		£
Deduct Work in progress:				
Closing stock	21,326			
Less Opening stock	18,742			
		2,584		
		£381,652		£381,652

Trading Account for the Month Ended December 31

	£	£		£
Finished goods:			Sales	450,000
Opening stock	15,246			
Goods manufactured	381,652			
	396,898			
Less Closing stock	17,485			
		379,413		
Gross profit c/d		70,587		
		£450,000		£450,000

Profit and Loss Account for the Month Ended December 31

	£		£
Expenses	49,246	Gross profit	70,587
Net profit	21,341		
	£70,587		£70,587

The cost accounts revealed the following information:

	Raw materials	Work in progress	Finished goods
	£	£	£
Opening stock	34,142	18,875	15,246
Closing stock	37,356	21,467	17,485

Profit for the period was £21,642.
Reconcile the two sets of accounts.

Answer

Memorandum Reconciliation Account

	£	£		£
Differences in stock:			Profit as per cost accounts	21,642
Raw materials—			Differences in stocks:	
Opening stock	126		Work in progress—opening	
Closing stock	167		stock	133
Work in progress—				
Closing stock	141			
		434		
Profit as per financial				
accounts		21,341		
		£21,775		£21,775

NOTES

Raw material—opening stock

Cost accounts, £34,142; financial accounts, £34,268.

Thus £126 more was charged in the financial accounts, so cost profit must be reduced or financial profit increased (as far as memorandum reconciliation account is concerned).

Raw material—closing stock

Cost accounts, £37,356; financial accounts, £37,189.

Thus £167 more was credited in the cost accounts, so cost profit must be reduced or financial profit increased.

Work in progress—opening stock

Cost accounts, £18,875; financial accounts, £18,742.

Thus £133 more was charged in the cost accounts, so cost profit must be increased or financial profit reduced.

Work in progress—closing stock

Cost accounts, £21,467; financial accounts, £21,326.

Thus £141 more was credited in the cost accounts, so cost profit must be reduced or financial profit increased.

Finished goods—opening stock

Cost accounts, £15,246; financial accounts, £15,246.
No reconciliation required.

Finished goods—closing stock

Cost accounts, £17,485; financial accounts, £17,485.
No reconciliation required.

Overhead

Indirect expenses are recorded in the financial accounts at actual cost; in the cost accounts they are recovered as overhead based on estimated expenditure aligned with estimated production: thus if either expenditure or production is different from that estimated, as is very likely to happen, overhead recovered would be either more or less than actual cost. Such differences should be written off to an overhead adjustment account, as was shown in Chapter 11. The result of this adjustment is that the actual amounts in the financial accounts will now agree with those in the cost accounts.

However, in some systems over- or under-recovered overhead is not written off to an adjustment account, but is carried forward as a balance in the overhead accounts. This results in the amount recovered in the cost accounts being different from the actual amount in the financial accounts. This procedure is regarded by many as bad accounting practice, but when adopted it is then necessary to allow for the difference in the memorandum reconciliation account.

Again, in some systems the recovery of selling and distribution overhead is ignored. Where this occurs, it is obvious that the financial accounts, which record actual expenditure, could not agree with the cost accounts, which record recovered expenditure, so it is necessary to account for this in a reconciliation.

Specimen Question

The manufacturing, trading and profit and loss accounts of J. D. PLC for the month ending December 31 are as follows:

	£	£		£
Raw materials:			Trading account:	
Opening stock	15,628		Cost of goods manufactured	227,135
Purchases	97,432			
	113,060			
Less Closing stock	17,465			
Raw materials consumed		95,595		
Wages—direct		78,463		
Prime cost		174,058		

	£	£		£
Production overhead:				
Wages—indirect	24,213			
Power	15,326			
Rent and rates	6,328			
Heat and light	2,145			
Depreciation	5,300			
Expenses	876			
		54,188		
Gross production cost		228,246		
Deduct Work in progress:				
Closing stock	17,432			
Less Opening stock	16,321			
		1,111		
		£227,135		£227,135

	£	£		£
Finished goods:			Sales	400,000
Opening stock	15,346			
Goods manufactured	227,135			
	242,481			
Less Closing stock	17,243			
		225,238		
Gross profit c/d		174,762		
		£400,000		£400,000

	£		£
Office salaries	28,346	Gross profit b/d	174,762
Office expenses	15,245	Dividend received	225
Salesmen's salaries	12,348	Bank interest	100
Sales expenses	17,432		
Distribution salaries	3,468		
Distribution expenses	9,523		
Discount on debentures	500		
Fines	100		
Loss on sale of machinery	650		
Net profit c/d	87,475		
	£175,087		£175,087

	£		£
Corporation tax	20,000	Balance b/d	24,320
Goodwill written off	1,000	Net profit b/d	87,475
General reserve	25,000		
Ordinary share dividend	15,000		
Preference share			
dividend	10,000		
Balance c/d	40,795		
	£111,795		£111,795

The cost accounts revealed the following information:

	Raw materials	Work in progress	Finished goods
	£	£	£
Opening stock	15,786	16,196	15,346
Closing stock	17,297	17,549	17,243

Selling and distribution expenses had been ignored.
Profit for the month was £131,087.
Notional rent for the period was £2,000 and interest on capital was £5,000. Reconcile the two sets of accounts.

Answer

Memorandum Reconciliation Account

	£	£		£	£
Items not debited in cost accounts:			Profits as per cost accounts		131,087
Discount on debentures	500		Items not credited in cost accounts:		
Fines	100		Dividends received	225	
Loss on sale of machinery	650		Bank interest	100	
		1,250			325
Overheads not recovered in cost accounts:			Differences in stocks: Raw materials— opening	158	
Salesmen's salaries	12,348		Raw materials— closing	168	
Sales expenses	17,432				326
Distribution salaries	3,468				
Distribution expenses	9,523				
		42,771			
Differences in stocks:					
Work in progress— opening	125				
Work in progress— closing	117				
		242			
Profit as per financial accounts		87,475			
		£131,738			£131,738

It should be noted that, for reasons explained earlier in this chapter, no entries are recorded for the notional charges shown in the cost accounts.

Examination Questions

1. State shortly the means by which you would reconcile the cost accounts with the financial books of the business. (*IA*)

2. Explain the methods to be adopted in order to prove that the cost records are in agreement with the financial books. (*LCCI*)

3. "It is fundamental that there should be complete integration between the cost and financial records in a manufacturing business." Comment on this statement. (*AIA*)

4. At the end of its accounting period the net profit shown in a company's cost accounts is considerably in excess of that disclosed in the audited financial accounts.

(*a*) From what sources is this difference likely to have arisen?

(*b*) What recommendations would you make in order to avoid similar differences in the future? (*IAADP*)

5. Indicate the reasons why it is usually necessary for the cost and financial records of a factory to be reconciled and explain the main sources of difference which might enter into such a reconciliation.

(*CAA*)

6. (*a*) Why is it important that cost and financial accounts should be capable of reconciliation one with the other?

(*b*) Give three examples of items which would not normally appear in the cost accounts though they would quite properly be taken into account in the financial revenue accounts. (*ICAEW*)

7. Outline a system of cost accounts with which you are familiar and indicate the manner in which the cost accounts should be co-ordinated with the financial accounts. (*CAA*)

8. In cases where there is a discrepancy between results disclosed by financial and cost accounts the latter sometimes gives the more favourable result. How would you account for this and what would you advise to ensure closer correspondence between the two sets of accounts? (*CAA*)

9. Discuss the relative merits of the following methods of valuing stock and work in progress:

(*a*) labour and materials (prime cost);

(*b*) prime cost plus factory overheads (factory cost);

(*c*) factory cost plus administration overheads;

(*d*) selling price less net profit. (*IAADP*)

10. During the year a company's profits have been estimated from the costing system to be £23,063 whereas the final accounts prepared by the auditors disclose a profit of £16,624. Given the following information you are required to prepare a reconciliation statement showing clearly the reasons for the difference.

The costing records show:

(a) A stock ledger closing balance of £78,197.

(b) A direct wages absorption account with a closing credit balance of £24,867.

(c) A factory overheads absorption account with a closing credit balance of £19,714.

(d) Administration expenses calculated at 3% of the selling price.

(e) Selling prices including 5% for selling expenses.

(f) No mention of sundry income.

Profit and Loss Account for Year Ended September 30

	£	£		£
Opening stocks	247,179		Sales	346,500
Purchases	82,154			
	329,333			
Closing stocks	75,121			
		254,212		
Direct wages		23,133		
Factory overheads		20,826		
Gross profit c/d		48,329		
		£346,500		£346,500

	£		£
Administration expenses	9,845	Gross profit b/d	48,329
Selling expenses	22,176	Sundry income	316
Net profit	16,624		
	£48,645		£48,645

(CAA)

11. The L Manufacturing Co. Ltd. maintains separate cost and financial accounts. In the cost ledger for the six months ended June 30, the stock control accounts were as follows:

Stores Ledger

	£		£
Balance b/d	44,800	Returns	9,000
Purchases	216,900	Work in progress	205,600
		Balance c/d	47,100
	£261,700		£261,700
Balance b/d	47,100		

Work-in-Progress Ledger

	£		£
Balance b/d	10,200	Finished goods	430,800
Stores	205,600	Balance c/d	10,600
Wages	71,400		
Production overhead	154,200		
	£441,400		£441,400
Balance b/d	10,600		

Finished Goods Ledger

	£		£
Balance b/d	22,100	Cost of sales	430,900
Work in progress	430,800	Balance c/d	22,000
	£452,900		£452,900
Balance b/d	22,000		

Production overhead has been absorbed in the above work-in-progress control account on the basis of 75% of direct material costs. A charge of £5,000 for the six months ended June 30 in respect of capital invested in stocks has been added in the cost ledger to the actual production overhead incurred.

A simplified revenue account prepared from the financial accounts for the six months ended June 30 was:

	£	£		£
Direct materials:			Production cost carried down	427,800
Opening stock		43,600		
Purchases	216,900			
Less Returns	9,000			
		207,900		
		251,500		
Less Closing stock		46,200		
		205,300		
Direct wages		71,400		
Production overhead		151,400		
Gross production cost		428,100		

	£	£			£
Work in progress:					
Closing	11,300				
Opening	11,000				
		300			
Net production cost		£427,800			£427,800
Finished goods:			Sales		747,800
Opening stock		22,400			
Production cost					
brought down		427,800			
		450,200			
Less Closing stock		21,900			
		428,300			
Gross profit		319,500			
		£747,800			£747,800

You are required to:

(a) state the accounting treatment of interest on capital invested in stocks used in the cost ledger and discuss results arising from its inclusion;

(b) enumerate briefly the possible reasons for, and the recognised methods of dealing with, the under-absorption of production overhead in the cost accounts;

(c) calculate the profit shown in the cost accounts and prepare a statement to reconcile the profits shown in the financial accounts and the cost accounts   (ICMA)

12. J Limited maintains its accounts on a non-integrated basis. Both the financial accountant and the cost accountant have completed their accounts for the year ended 30th November, and a memorandum account reconciling the two profit figures has been prepared.

During the year production overhead has been absorbed into the costs as a percentage of direct wages at a rate of 250%.

You are required to show:

(a) the following control accounts as they would appear in the cost ledger:

(i) raw material stores;

(ii) work-in-progress;

(iii) finished goods;

(b) the over- or under-absorption of production overhead.

The financial accountant has prepared the following account:

Manufacturing, Trading and Profit and Loss Account
Year ended, 30th November

	£	£	£		£
Raw materials:				Trading account:	
Opening stock		25,648		cost of goods	
Purchases	102,346			manufactured	
less Returns	2,679			c/d	237,386
		99,667			
		125,315			
less Closing stock		23,691			
			101,624		
Direct wages		38,794			
add Accrued		1,242			
			40,036		
Prime cost			141,660		
Production overhead					
Indirect wages		12,645			
Power		21,278			
Supervision		16,349			
Depreciation		24,251			
Heat and light		14,326			
Sundry expenses		6,491			
			95,340		
			237,000		
Work-in-progress:					
Opening stock		12,248			
less Closing stock		11,862			
			386		
			£237,386		£237,386

	£	£			£
Finished goods:			Sales		316,262
Opening stock	31,945		*less* Returns		3,462
Goods manufac-					
tured b/d	237,386				312,800
	269,331				
less Closing stock	32,851				
		236,480			
Gross profit c/d		76,320			
		£312,800			£312,800

	£		£
Administration expenses	26,529	Gross profit b/d	76,320
Sales expenses	15,281	Discount received	895
Distribution expenses	8,463		
Debenture interest	1,000		
Discount allowed	1,482		
Net profit c/d	24,460		
	£77,215		£77,215

The memorandum account reconciling the profits shown in the financial and cost accounts for the year ended 30th November, is as follows:

	£			£
Profit as shown in the		Profit as shown in		
financial accounts	24,460	the cost accounts		50,150
Differences in stock		Differences in stock		
valuation:		valuation:		
opening stock: £		opening stock: £		
work-in-progress 175		raw materials 160		
finished goods 326		closing stock:		
closing stock:		finished goods 341		
raw materials 211				501
work-in-progress 148		Discount received		895
	860			
Debenture interest	1,000			
Discount allowed	1,482			
Sales expenses	15,281			
Distribution expenses	8,463			
	£51,546			£51,546

(*ICMA*)

13. (*a*) The cost accountant and the financial accountant of C Limited have each completed their final accounts for the year. Shown overleaf are the manufacturing, trading and profit and loss accounts, together with a statement reconciling the cost and financial profits. You are required to show the following accounts in the cost ledger:

(*a*) raw materials;
(*b*) work-in-progress;
(*c*) finished goods;
(*d*) profit and loss.

Manufacturing, Trading and Profit and Loss Account
for the year ended 31st December

	£000	£000		£000	£000
Raw material:			Trading account,		
Opening stock	110		cost of goods		
Purchases	640		manufactured		1,000
	750				
less: Returns	20				
	730				
Closing stock	130				
		600			
Direct wages					
Paid	220				
Accrued	20				
		240			
Prime cost		840			
Production expenses		162			
Work-in-progress:					
Opening stock	25				
Closing stock	27				
		(2)			
		1,000			1,000

	£000	£000		£000	£000
Finished goods:			Sales	1,530	
Opening stock	82		*less:* Returns	30	
Manufactured	1,000				1,500
	1,082				
Closing stock	72				
		1,010			
Gross profit		490			
		1,500			1,500
Administration expenses		200	Gross profit		490
Sales expenses		70	Discount received		10
Discount allowed		20			
Debenture interest		10			
Net profit		200			
		500			500

Reconciliation Statement

	£000	£000	£000
Profit shown in the financial accounts			200
Items not shown in the cost accounts:			
Discount allowed		20	
Debenture interest		10	
Sales expenses		70	
Discount received		(10)	
			90
			290
Difference in stock valuation:			
Opening stock, raw materials	7		
Opening stock, finished goods	9		
Closing stock, raw materials	15		
		31	
Closing stock, work-in-progress	(5)		
Opening stock, work-in-progress	(3)		
Closing stock, finished goods	(4)		
		(12)	
			19
Profit shown in the cost accounts			309

NOTES:

Production overhead is absorbed at a rate of 66⅔% of wages.

Administration overhead is written off in the period in which incurred.

(b) Discuss briefly the reasons for including in a cost accounting system notional interest on capital locked up in stock and its treatment in preparing a reconciliation of cost and financial profits.

(ICMA)

Chapter 14

Job Costing

Introduction

JOB costing is the method used for two types of work:

(a) contracts such as are undertaken by builders, civil engineering contractors, shipbuilders, etc.;

(b) job orders undertaken in factories and workshops.

The principle is the same in both cases, but there are a few points of difference in procedure, owing to the different nature of the work involved. In the one case there are a few large contracts, whereas in the other there are likely to be numerous smaller jobs.

Job Numbers

A distinguishing number is given to each order received. This is essential in order to identify the cost account to which the items of expenditure have to be charged; it also facilitates reference for posting purposes in the ledger, and is conveniently short for use on various forms.

Contract Costs

As questions on contract costs frequently appear in examinations, it is thought desirable to give the following examples.

Example 1

Paulart Construction PLC began work on December 1 upon a contract for sewerage for the East Fincham District Council, amounting to £70,000. The retention is 10%. At December 15 the certificates of work done (gross) amounted to £32,000. The following information regarding the contract is available:

166

	£
Materials delivered direct to contract	8,000
Materials issued from stores	1,200
Wages	15,000
Apportionment of overhead to December 31	2,500
Plant sent to contract, at valuation	135,000
Plant returned from contract on November 30, at valuation	89,000
Plant remaining on contract at December 31, at valuation	43,000
Accrued wages to December 31	650
Work done not yet certified, at December 31, at cost	2,400
Materials on site at December 31	1,750

You are required to complete the contract accounts and to show the amount of profit which might be taken into the annual accounts to December 31.

Before completing the formal answer, the question mentions several matters which require to be understood clearly.

(a) *Plant sent to contract.* Contractors sometimes adopt the practice, which is not thought to be a very good one, of charging the contract account with the value of the plant sent to the contract, and later on, when it is sent off the contract, a reduced valuation is credited to the contract account, thus leaving a net charge for depreciation. A better method is to charge for the hire and use of the plant by means of monthly internal debit notes, but examiners seem to expect the other method, overlooking the practical difficulties which are involved when contract statements are to be prepared at regular intervals.

(b) *Accrued wages.* Often wages are paid up to a week in arrear, in order to give the staff time to prepare the payroll, and to make up the wage packets. This is called "lying time". At the end of a given period it is therefore necessary to accrue for the wages due but not yet paid.

(c) *Work done not yet certified.* The measurement of the work done under the contract is carried out to suit the mutual convenience of the engineer and surveyor appointed by the contractees and the contractor. It does not necessarily coincide with the end of a financial period, but the work continues from day to day, and so an adjustment has to be made for the cost incurred during the interval from the date of the last certificate to that of the end of the financial period. This adjustment is usually done on the certificates account, so that the cost of the work in progress is shown at that date, and the certificates are increased by an amount which brings them to the same date.

(*d*) *Materials on site.* This is the valuation placed on materials delivered to the site, but which have not yet been made use of in the constructional work. The cost is therefore carried forward to the next period. In a very few cases the contractor is allowed to add the value of the materials on site to the amount due to him on certificates each month, and, subject to deduction of the amount included the previous month, is paid for them as the contract proceeds.

(*e*) *Retention.* Large engineering contracts are carried out at some risk to the contractees, for there is the chance that the contractor may have made an error in his tender price, or may come up against unusual difficulties, and be unable to complete the work. Even if the contractor completes the work, defects may show themselves in what he has done, and will have to be rectified at his own expense. If he lacks resources the cost would have to be borne by the contractees. To safeguard themselves against risks of loss, it is usual for a percentage of the certificates to be withheld until a year or more after the official completion date has been agreed. The engineer for the contractee then meets the contractor on the site, and they agree on the amount of additional work necessary to rectify any faulty work. This is done to the satisfaction of the contractees, and the release of the retention money is then authorised. In the meantime the retention money must on no account be treated as a debtor in the balance sheet, because the amount is not immediately due.

(*f*) *Profit on uncompleted contracts.* On small jobs no profit is brought into account until the job has been satisfactorily completed and paid for. The case has to be somewhat different in the case of large contracts, but the contractor has to be careful not to take in too much as profit at the end of his financial year, especially if there is the possibility of future loss on the contract through the discovery of hazards still unknown. There is no set method which can be quoted as being "correct" in all circumstances, but there are two well-known ones which may be used in safety:

(*i*) Notional profit $\times$ $\frac{2}{3}$ $\times$ Cash received/Work certified;
(*ii*) Work certified/Contract price.

With these preliminary explanations, the following accounts can be prepared.

Method 1

Contract no. 37 account—sewerage works for East Fincham District Council—contract price £70,000—retention 10%—official date of commencement December 1. Completion due by January 31.

Contract Account

	£		£
Materials direct	8,000	Plant returned	89,000
Materials ex stores	1,200	Plant on site c/d	43,000
Wages	15,000	Materials on site c/d	1,750
Overhead	2,500	Work in progress at	
Plant	135,000	December 31 at cost	
Accrued wages c/d	650	c/d	28,600
	£162,350		£162,350
Balances b/d		Balance b/d	
Work in progress	28,600	Accrued wages	650
Plant on site	43,000		
Materials on site	1,750		

Contract No. 37—Certificates Account

	£		£
Balance c/d	34,400	Certificates 1–6	32,000
		Work done not yet	
		certified at cost c/d	2,400
	£34,400		£34,400
Balance b/d	2,400	Balance b/d	34,400

Contract No. 37—Retentions Account

	£		
Certificates 1–6	3,200		

Contract No. 37—East Fincham District Council Account

	£		£
Certificates 1–6	28,800	Cleared by cheques	
		received	28,800

Contract No. 37—Profit Provision Account

	£		£	£
Transfer to contracts profit and		Notional profit at		
loss a/c	3,480	December 31:		
		Certificates	34,400	
		Work in progress	28,600	
				5,800
		£5,800 × ⅔ × 90% c/d		3,480
	£3,480			£3,480
Balance b/d	£3,480			

The outstanding balances would be grouped in the following manner for balance sheet purposes, but the student should note that the details given in parentheses would not be shown:

	£	£
Plant on contract		43,000
Work in progress at December 31, including profit		
to date (£28,600 + £3,480)	32,080	
Less Cash received on account		
(£34,400 − £2,400 − £3,200)	28,800	
		3,280
Materials on site		1,750
and, among the current liabilities		
Accrued wages		650

Method 2

In view of the fact that examiners seem to expect to see a particular form of layout, it is considered advisable to illustrate it here.

Contract No. 37 Account

	£	£		£
Materials direct		8,000	Plant returned	89,000
Materials ex stores		1,200	Plant on site c/d	43,000
Wages	15,000		Materials on site c/d	1,750
Add Accrued c/d	650	15,650	Cost c/d	28,600
Overhead		2,500		
Plant to contract		135,000		
		£162,350		£162,350
Cost b/d		28,600	Value of work certified	32,000
Profit:			Cost of work not yet certified c/d	2,400
Profit and loss a/c	3,480			
Balance c/d	2,320	5,800		
		£34,400		£34,400

Balance b/d:	£	Balance b/d:	£
Plant on site	43,000	Wages	650
Materials on site	1,750	Profit	2,320
Work not yet certified	2,400		

East Fincham District Council

	£		£
Certificates 1–6	32,000	Cash on account	28,800
		Balance c/d	3,200
	£32,000		£32,000
Balance b/d	3,200		

Apart from the impracticable method of dealing with plant which is common to both methods, the specific objections to method 2 are as follows.

(*a*) It tries to do in one Contract Account what would be more clearly seen in separate accounts. It is the auditor's quick answer to incomplete records.

(*b*) It brings into account as a provision the balance of notional profit, when it would be better not to do so. This balance is not merely deferred: there is considerable doubt if it has been made.

(*c*) It leaves the retention as a balance on the Personal Account of the contractee, as though it were due from him, whereas under the conditions of contract it is clearly not yet due.

Example 2

A further example is given which is based on a typical examination question. For illustration purposes, method 2 which was shown above, is used; the interested reader may care to answer the question using method 1, which was also discussed above.

Jeraul Construction PLC began work on July 1 on a contract for the building of an extension to a college for the Kingsham District Council amounting to £600,000. The retention money is agreed at 10%. On November 20 the certificates of work approved amounted to £400,000. The following information is available:

	£
Materials sent to site	150,000
Labour engaged on site	120,000
Plant installed at cost	60,000
Direct expenditure	24,000
Establishment charges	50,000

	£
Materials returned to store	5,000
Cost of work not yet certified	30,000
Materials on site at December 31	15,000
Wages accrued at December 31	5,000
Direct expenses accrued at December 31	1,000
Value of plant at December 31	40,000

You are required to complete the contract account, to show the amount of profit which may be taken into the annual accounts to December 31 and to calculate the value of the work in progress.

Method 1

Contract Account

	£	£		£
Direct materials		150,000	Materials returned to store	5,000
Direct wages	120,000		Stock c/d	15,000
Accrued c/d	5,000		Plant c/d	40,000
		125,000	Cost to date c/d	350,000
Plant		60,000		
Direct expenses	24,000			
Accrued c/d	1,000			
		25,000		
Establishment charges		50,000		
		£410,000		£410,000
Cost b/d		350,000	Contractee—work certified	400,000
Notional profit c/d		80,000	Cost of work not yet certified c/d	30,000
		£430,000		£430,000
Profit and loss		48,000	Notional profit b/d	80,000
Profit provision c/d		32,000		
		£80,000		£80,000
Stock b/d		15,000	Direct wages accrued b/d	5,000
Plant b/d		40,000	Direct expenses accrued b/d	1,000
Cost of work not yet			Profit provision b/d	32,000
certified b/d		30,000		

Contractee—Kingsham District Council

	£		£
Work certified	400,000	Cash	360,000
		Balance c/d	40,000
	£400,000		£400,000
Balance b/d	40,000		

Included in the balance sheet of Jeraul Construction PLC would be the following:

	£	£
Plant on contract		40,000
Work in progress:		
Cost	350,000	
Profit	48,000	
	398,000	
Cash	360,000	38,000
Stock on site		15,000
And among the liabilities		
would be:		
Accrued wages	5,000	
Accrued expenses	1,000	6,000

The amount shown for work in progress (£38,000), can be shown in an alternative way as follows:

	£
Contractee	40,000
Cost of work not yet	
certified	30,000
	70,000
Profit provision	32,000
	£38,000

NOTE

The establishment charges shown in the contract account refer to the charges made by the head office of a contractor. Where a contracting company has a number of contracts in operation, the cost of running the head office is absorbed by the contracts.

Factory Job Costing Procedure

Instead of opening a few contract accounts in the main books of account, it is usual in factory work to open a work-in-progress ledger control account in the main books, and keep the details in job cost ledger accounts in a subsidiary ledger. The work-in-progress ledger control account gives, *in totals only*, the elements of cost incurred on all the jobs done in the works. The procedure is as follows.

1. Charging Materials

(*a*) *Stores material.* The materials issue notes show the quantities of material of various kinds which have been issued from stores. When copies of these documents reach the cost office they are priced and entered in the stores ledger accounts, in the "out" column, a new balance then being struck on each account affected.

The total value of these stores issues is obtained, either by means of an adding machine or by entry into a stores materials abstract (Fig. 25) and this total will be posted:

Dr   Work-in-progress ledger control a/c
      Production overhead control a/c
Cr   Stores ledger control a/c

The allocations to the various jobs as given in the stores materials abstract are also totalled, and will be posted to the various job cost ledger accounts. Indirect materials will be posted to the standing order numbers for production overhead.

If control accounts are understood, it will be readily gathered that the totals posted to work-in-progress ledger control account and production overhead control account are reflected in the details found in the subsidiary accounts.

Example

Stores valued at £2,000 are allocated from stores requisitions as follows:

Job no. 312	£500
Job no. 313	£400
Job no. 314	£800
Production overhead code no. 02569	£300

Entries required:

Main books

Dr   Work-in-progress ledger control   £1,700
      Production overhead control a/c   £300
Cr   Stores ledger control a/c   £2,000

No. 12

Week ending: February 7, 19...

Job No. 90		Job No. 91		Job No. 98		Job No. 100		R.13		N.31		Summary		Cost Ledger folio
I.R. No.	£	I.R. No.	£	I.R. No.	£	I.R. No.	£	I.R. No.	£	I.R. No.	£	Job No.	£	
91	4·45	93	1·10	92	7·75	94	2·05	96	8·30	88	6·15	90	7·45	
95	3·00	97	3·35			98	0·75	99	3·10	89	5·95	91	4·45	
								90	1·27			98	7·75	
												100	2·80	
												R.13	12·67	
												N.31	12·10	
	7·45		4·45		7·75		2·80		12·67		12·10		47·22	

FIG. 25.—*Material issue analysis sheet*

A form such as this is admirable for summarising stores requisitions when the office has no equipment to provide machine-added summaries.

Subsidiary books

Job cost ledger accounts
Standing order number 02569
Debit from foot of columns concerned after summarising in the
stores materials abstract
Stores ledger accounts
Credit accounts affected, for outgoing stores. Exercise care in
doing this kind of posting, as mistakes are not easily found, and may
cause serious situations, such as running out of vital raw materials.
The total of your entries would in this case amount to £2,000.

If students do not understand these control account entries they
are recommended to come back to this again after Chapter 12 has
been revised.

(*b*) *Special materials.* In the case of contracts for public works, as
we have seen, materials are usually delivered direct to the site by the
suppliers. In factory work, too, components are bought ready-made
and are sent, on receipt, straight to the department in which they are
to be used. In neither case is the stores affected, and it is usual to
debit, as a direct charge, work-in-progress ledger control account
and also the cost account for the particular job, crediting creditors.

2. Charging Wages

As explained in Chapter 7 (to which reference should be made),
the gross and net wages to be paid to the workers will usually be
calculated upon clock cards or other gate time records, piece-work
tickets, or time sheets, according to the arrangements in force.

An analysis and summary of job tickets, illustrations of which
were given in Figs. 22 and 23, is made for the direct labour, and an
analysis of the payroll entries for the indirect labour. This is carried
out in a wages abstract, so that the number and hours chargeable to
each contract, job, or expense account in respect of each worker
employed are obtained. The reasons for recording hours as well as
wages is that it is necessary to obtain the total direct labour hours for
each job in a shop so that the correct amount of shop overhead may
be charged. A portion of a wages abstract is shown in Fig. 26. The
abstract is usually arranged in sections, following the sections of the
payroll, so that in a factory there will be:

(*a*) the cost centres showing wages chargeable to jobs done;
(*b*) types of indirect labour showing wages chargeable to expense
headings.

No. 32

Week ending: February 7 19...

Job No. 90			Job No. 91			Job No. 98			Job No. 100			R.13			N.31			Summary			Cost Ledger folio
Clock No.	Hr	£	Clock No.	Hr	£	Clock No.	Hr	£	Clock No.	Hr	£	Clock No.	Hr	£	Clock No.	Hr	£	Job No.	Hr	£	
12	4	12·80	22	5	16·00	23	4	12·80	12	4	12·80	22	3	9·60	14	8	25·60	90	15	48·00	
13	8	25·60	23	4	12·80	17	40	128·00	18	2	6·40	18	14	44·80	17	8	25·60	91	9	28·80	
18	2	6·40							21	2	6·40	21	2	6·40	21	3	9·60	98	44	140·80	
21	1	3·20										12	20	64·00	22	40	128·00	100	8	25·60	
												19	6	19·20				R. 13	45	144·00	
																		N. 31	59	188·80	
	15	48·00		9	28·80		44	140·80		8	25·60		45	144·00		59	188·80		180	576·00	

FIG. 26.—*Wages analysis sheet*

This is useful for the analysis of job tickets and idle-time cards of workers whose wages are charged as direct labour. The total will be posted partly to work-in-progress ledger control account and partly to production overhead control account, probably via the wages analysis book.

When the payroll has been completely analysed as to gross wages, bonus payments, overtime premium, employers' national insurance, etc., the columns of the wages abstract will be totalled and cross-cast, and agreed with the payroll. The entries required in the main books will be:

> Dr   Work-in-progress ledger control a/c
>   Production overhead control a/c
>   Administration overhead control a/c
>   Selling and distribution overhead control a/c
> Cr   Wages control a/c

In the subsidiary books the entries required are:

> Job cost ledger accounts
> Standing order numbers
> Cost account numbers
>   Debit from foot of columns concerned in the wages abstract.

Suitable and commonly used rulings for job cost ledger accounts are shown in Figs. 27 and 28.

3. Charging Overhead

It has been explained in Chapters 9 and 10 how shop overhead expenses are apportioned over the respective shops and machines, and how, from the totals so arrived at, a separate shop rate in the form of a direct labour hour rate or a machine-hour rate is calculated. The time taken by a job to pass through a cost centre is shown in the job cost ledger account (*see* Fig. 27), and thus it is simple to debit the appropriate amounts of works overhead in the column provided. Other overhead, e.g. administration, selling and distribution is also often added to production cost. The basis used to absorb administration overhead is usually a percentage on production cost; that to absorb selling overhead may be a percentage on the cost of production—that is—on production cost plus administration overhead; while distribution overhead, being directly incurred in respect of sales made, may be absorbed as a percentage of sales values. The modern tendency, however, seems to favour the idea that administration, selling and distribution overhead should not be added to product cost, but, as in ordinary financial accounting, treated as a charge against gross trading profit.

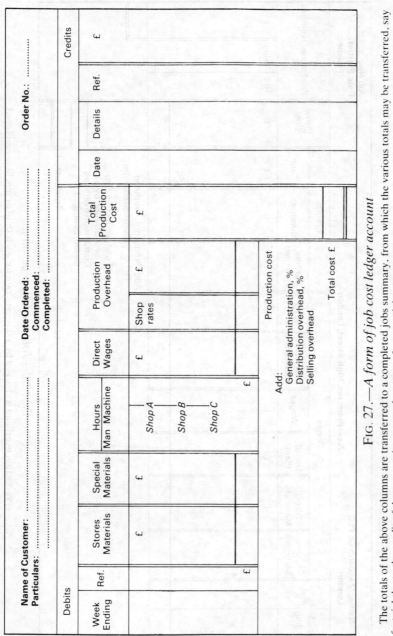

FIG. 27.—*A form of job cost ledger account*

The totals of the above columns are transferred to a completed jobs summary, from which the various totals may be transferred, say fortnightly, to the credit of the appropriate control accounts for materials, wages, etc.

Name: Mandarin Co PLC   **New Premises, High Street, London**
London

Job No.: ....
Date Started: ...
Finished:

Week Ending	Ref.	Debits						Credits			Prime Cost	Production Overhead		
		Stores Materials	Direct Materials	Use of Plant	Wages	Direct Expenses	Total	Stores Returned	Sundries	Total		Hrs	Rates	
		£	£	£	£	£	£	£	£	£	£		£	£

Add: Production overhead
(from last column)

Total production cost
Add: Administration overhead
Distribution overhead
Selling overhead

Total cost £

FIG. 28.—*Job cost ledger account*

Note—Production overhead is charged by a separate rate for each shop or machine employed.

4. Completed Jobs

As each job or production order is completed the various columns are totalled, and transferred to a jobs summary account, ruled on the same lines as the job cost ledger accounts. The value of this jobs summary account is that it provides a total of each class of expenditure for each accounting period, and acts as the basis of a journal entry:

> Dr Finished work a/c
> Cr Work-in-progress a/c

A suggested ruling for the jobs summary account is given in Fig. 29. As completed jobs are taken out of work in progress, the balance remaining on that account represents the cost of the work now being done in the factory.

Example

A typical examination question in job costing is shown now. It should be noted that in this type of question one is usually given the prime cost details of the job, but one is required to estimate the additional costs. This involves working from the general to the specific; in other words, one is using data which relate to the company in general and applying them to a specific job being performed by the company.

J. Paul PLC has been asked by S. David PLC to quote a price for manufacturing job no. 6. The cost estimator of J. Paul PLC has produced the following data:

> Direct materials: 16 units at £10 per unit
> Direct wages: Dept X 12 hours at £4·00 per hour
>   Dept Y 20 hours at £3·60 per hour

Information extracted from the company's budget for the year is as follows:

> Dept X variable overhead £9,000. Hours to be worked 18,000
> Dept Y variable overhead £18,000. Hours to be worked 20,000
> Fixed overhead for the company £180,000
> Total hours to be worked 60,000
> Profit is taken at 20% of the selling price.

Date	Job No.	Stores Material	Direct Material	Direct Wages	Production Overhead			Total
					Department 1	Department 2	Department 3	
		£	£	£	£	£	£	£
Totals		£	£	£	£	£	£	£
Control Account Ref.								

Fortnight Ending:..............

FIG. 29.—*Completed Jobs Summary Account*

J. Paul PLC
Estimated selling price of Job No. 6 for S. David PLC

		£	£
Direct materials:	16 units at £10 per unit		160
Direct wages:	Dept. X 12 hours at £4·00	48	
	Dept. Y 20 hours at £3·60	72	
			120
Prime cost			280
Variable overhead:	Dept. X 12 hours at £0·50	6	
	Dept. Y 20 hours at £0·90	18	
			24
Variable cost			304
Fixed overhead:	32 hours at £3·00		96
Total cost			400
Profit			100
Selling price			£500

NOTES

1. Variable overhead is calculated for each department through which the job is processed. For example:

$$\text{Dept. X} \quad \frac{\text{Variable overhead}}{\text{Hours worked}} \quad \frac{£9,000}{18,000}$$

2. Fixed overhead is absorbed as an hourly rate by each job produced in the company:

$$\frac{\text{Fixed overhead}}{\text{Hours worked}} \quad \frac{£180,000}{60,000}$$

3. Profit is one-fifth of selling price, which is equal to one-quarter of cost price:

One-quarter of cost price £400 = £100
One-fifth of selling price £500 = £100

Examination Questions

1. PQR Limited make shop counters, display stands, shelving units, etc., to customers' special requirements. It follows, therefore, that a system of job costing is operated.

Draw a suitable form of *job card* and insert imaginary cost figures.
(LCCI)

2. Examine the different concepts which may be applied to the valuation of work in progress and their influence on reported results. What particular problems are associated with the valuation of work in progress of long-term contracts? *(ICSA)*

3. (*a*) You are required to state briefly the general manufacturing features you would expect to find where the following systems would be appropriate:

(*i*) a job costing system;

(*ii*) a process costing system.

(*b*) Most local authorities in the United Kingdom have a direct labour organisation (D.L.O.), sometimes called direct works department. This department employs craftsmen who carry out improvements and extensions together with maintenance both of a planned and of a day-to-day nature on properties owned by the authority such as housing, schools, offices, libraries and art galleries. In recent years legislation has been introduced to make the direct labour organisations become profit orientated, that is, a return of 5% is expected to be earned on the assets employed by D.L.O.s. Now they have to tender, in competition with private firms, for all local authority maintenance contracts having a value of over £10,000.

You are required to write a report, addressed to the Director of the D.L.O. of a local authority, listing the principal control aspects relating to the ascertainment of cost appropriate to each maintenance contract over £10,000 which is undertaken, and stating the documents or vouchers which would be used. *(ICMA)*

4. Equipment is manufactured to customers' special requirements by DEF Limited. Job No. 171 was in progress on 31 March when accumulated costs were materials £900, wages £288 and overhead £258.

The following costs were charged to jobs in April:

Job No.	171	172	173
	£	£	£
Materials	216	864	1,242
Wages	720	1,080	630

Overhead expenditure in April amounted to £2,250 but jobs were charged at the predetermined rate of 90% of direct wages. The following two jobs were completed in April:

Job No.	Contract price
171	£3,550
172	£3,475

(a) Ascertain the cost of each job to 30 April.

(b) Ascertain the profit earned in April, taking under-absorbed overhead into account. (LCCI)

5. F Limited is under contract to build a new factory for LP Limited. The contract price has been agreed and work on the new site commenced on January 1. Data relating to this contract is shown below, from which you are required to value the work in progress as necessary for balance sheet purposes as at December 31.

	£000s
Cash received from contractee	720
Direct materials:	
Issued to contract	340
Returned to central store	8
Returned to supplier	7
Transferred to other contracts	15
On site at December 31	20
Direct wages:	
Paid on site	220
Accrued on site at December 31	10
Direct expenses:	
Paid	25
Accrued at December 31	5
Cost of work not yet certified at December 31	60
Value of work certified at November 30	800
Plant: installed, at cost	100
on site, valued at December 31	75
Overhead incurred on contract	85
Establishment charges	60

(ICMA)

6. EFG (Contractors) Ltd. are building an office block for Riverdale Development Ltd. at a price of £110,000. The contract (No. 320) was only partially completed at the end of the contractors' financial year and the following items then appeared in the books:

£

Materials purchased and delivered to site 38,000
Materials issued from store   4,000
Materials returned to store   600
Site wages   15,000
Site expenses   2,000
Plant sent to site   5,000
Plant returned from site   600
Architects' fees   2,000
Sub-contract work   7,000
Head office overhead absorbed   4,000

Year end valuations were:

Materials on site   1,300
Plant on site   3,000
Work-in-progress not yet certified   4,000

The sections of the work which were completed during the year and passed by the architects were assessed as representing 75 per cent of the whole contract price. The contractee made progress payments to this extent, less 10 per cent retention moneys. For the purpose of the annual accounts of EFG (Contractors) Ltd. the management decided to make a provision of one-third of the apparent profit to date against the possibility of defects and other contingencies arising later in respect of the work already passed for payment.

You are required:

(a) to calculate the amount to be transferred to the main profit and loss account of EFG (Contractors) Ltd. for the year, and

(b) to detail all items related to contract No. 320 which would be included in the balance sheet.   (SCA)

7. X Ltd. manufactures a number of products, including product D, which is sold under contract to J Ltd. Using information given below:

(a) calculate the selling price of 100 units of D;

(b) evaluate 1,000 units of D held in stock by X Ltd.

This valuation is for inclusion in the Balance Sheet. Give brief reasons in support of the method you recommend.

Standard production data for 100 units:

£

Direct materials   200 kg of material Z at 0·5 per kg
Direct wages   10 hours at   4·00 per hour
Variable production overhead   20·00
Machine hours   30

Budgeted data for year:

	£000s
Production variable cost	1,000
Overhead: Fixed production	400
Administration	350
Selling and distribution	700
Profit 25% of selling price	
Machine hours 100,000	

(*ICMA*)

8. The data given below refers to contract M101 for the construction of a section of a motorway.

The contract was commenced on 1st April at an agreed price of £20,000,000. The contract was expected to take four years to complete. Retention money was agreed at 10% of work certified.

Details of the contract during the first year are as follows:

		£000s
Direct materials:	received on site	2,560
	returned from site	25
	lost from site, but insured	30
	on site at 31st March	355
Direct wages:	paid	1,320
	accrued at 31st March	30
Direct expenses:	paid	240
	accrued at 31st March	10
Plant:	in use on site at cost	2,000
	valuation at 31st March	1,500
Site overhead		370
Allocated head office charges		180
Cash received in respect of work certified		4,500
Cost of work completed but not yet certified		700

You are required to:
   (*a*) prepare the account of the contract; and
   (*b*) evaluate the work-in-progress as at 31st March

(*ICMA*)

Chapter 15

Unit Costing

SINGLE, output, or unit costing is a simple method of process costing per unit of production, where manufacture is continuous and the units are identical, or can be made so by means of ratios. It may be applied to particular processes in conjunction with process accounts, or to operation and batch costing, and is used in undertakings where there is a uniform product of which there is a natural unit of cost.

The accounts are designed to show:

(a) the total cost and the cost per unit of the output for any required period;

(b) the unit cost in respect of each heading of expense entering into the cost.

Examples of industries in which the method may be used are

Industry	Unit of cost
Steel works	Tonne of steel
Quarries	Tonne of stone or sand
Collieries	Tonne of coal raised
Breweries	Barrel of beer
Textile factory	Metre of material
Brick making	Thousand bricks

Procedure

A manufacturing account in the form of a cost statement is prepared at short regular intervals, e.g.:

(a) at the completion of production of a particular volume of work—at the end of each "brew" in a brewery, after the completion of a particular production order, such as for 10 kilograms of azure notepaper;

(b) weekly, fortnightly or monthly when there is continuous production, such as in a brickworks or a coal-mine.

The account is charged with all materials issued, wages paid, and overhead apportioned to the period under consideration, and the total cost thus ascertained. The unit cost is obtained by dividing the total units produced into the total cost, and for further information

	Week ending			
Production this Week: ....tonnes	**Last week:** ..... tonnes			
	This week		Last week	
	Totals £	Cost per Tonne £	Totals £	Cost per Tonne £
Materials used: 1.......... 2.......... 3..........				
Total materials	£	£	£	£
Wages Direct expenses				
Prime cost				
Production overhead *Fixed:* Rent Depreciation Insurance Other *Variable:* Indirect Wages Power Light Heat Sundries				
Production cost	£	£	£	£
Administration overhead: Salaries Office rent Office expenses, etc.				
Production and Administration Cost	£	£	£	£
Selling and distribution overhead: Sales office Advertising, etc.				
Total Cost				

FIG. 30.—*Cost sheet*

the total of units produced is also often divided into the individual items of expense.

These features of this type of costing will be more readily understood by references to the *pro forma* cost sheet shown in Fig. 30, and to the examples shown in Figs. 31 and 32, which relate to the working of a foundry, and to a manufacturing chemist, respectively.

In the *pro-forma* example (Fig. 30) the addition of administration

Labour & Overhead	Time or Piece Price	Bonus %	Labour £	%	Overhead £
Moulding (Piece)	£3·00	115	6·45	130	8·38
Moulding (Day)					
Dressing (Floor)	£0·50	85	0·93	181	1.68
Passing (Floor)				7	0.80
Coremaking	£0·30	50	0·45	125	0·56
Pattern Maintenance				18	2·00
Shot Blasting	120 kg	22 kg	1·10	500	5·50
Machining	22 mins		0·90	115	1·04
Sheet iron	£1·00	130	2·30	85	1·96
Smiths	5 mins		0·20	70	0·14
Engineers	10 mins		0·40	130	0·52
Grinding					
Surface grinding					
Welding	7 mins		0·30	70	0·21
Polishing	£0·20	119	0·44	95	0·42
Painting	£0·30	130	0·69	94	0·65
Stove enamelling					
Fettling					
Enamelling	120 kg	2·5 kg	8·00	515	41.20
Fitting	£4·00	125	9·00	75	6·75
Packing	£0·60	35	0·81	125	1·01
TOTALS			31·97		72·82
Total labour and overhead					104·79
Direct material					103·80
Enamel material					8·00
Production Cost					216·59
Loading and Despatch					8·02
Establishment charge					50·25
Total cost					274·86

FIG. 31.—*Foundry cost sheet*

COST SHEET

Cost Period: No. 4

Production Order No.: 3972
Sod. Co. Tablets, in bottles of 100
Corked, waxed and capped

Production: 100,000 tablets

		Total	Per 100
	£	£	£
1. PROCESS COSTS			
Ingredients			
Chemical A, as materials abstracts			
Chemical B, as materials abstracts			
Chemical C, as materials abstracts			
Chemical D, as materials abstracts			
Starch, as materials abstracts			
Flavouring, as materials abstracts			
Colouring, as materials abstracts			
Total ingredients cost (process loss...% included)		1,450·500	1·45
Labour			
Mixing, etc.	425·500		
Drying	5·875		
Tableting	167·250		
Total direct labour cost		598·625	0·60
Production Overhead Expenses (Processes)			
Mixing	2·108		
Drying	24·900		
Milling	2·458		
Tableting	64·258		
General	45·625		
Total process overheads		139·349	0·14
Total production cost of tablets		2,188·474	2·19
2. PACKING COSTS			
Materials, as materials abstracts			
Bottles, including 0·6% wastage	6,502·134		
Corks including 0·52% wastage	405·216		
Labels	12·300		
Wool	73·400		
Wax	16·950		
Screw caps	830·000		
Total packing materials		7,840·000	7·84
Labour, as per labour abstract			
Labelling	342·000		
Filling	988·525		
Corking	330·075		
Wax dipping	295·025		
Capping	215·450		
		2,171·075	2·17
Overheads, 20% on direct labour		434·200	0·43
Total cost of tablets bottled		12,633·749	12·63
3. DESPATCH (cartons, cases, banding, stencilling, and handling)		996·800	1·00
4. ADMINISTRATIVE OVERHEAD EXPENSES, 10% on cost of filled tablets		1,263·367	1·26
Total cost		14,893·916	14·89

FIG. 32—*Cost sheet for medicinal tablet manufacture*

overhead, and selling and distribution overhead as part of the product cost is open to some criticism, and modern practice seems to be moving away from this method.

Figure 31 perhaps requires a little explanation. The various operations to be carried out are shown in the left-hand column. Moulding is carried out by piece-work, and so nothing is recorded for day work.

The piece work price is shown as	£3·00
Add Bonus at 115%	3·45
Total labour cost	£6·45

Overhead at 130% of labour cost, i.e. 130% of £6·45

£8·38

Figure 32 is another example of a cost sheet, in this case one used by a drug company making medicinal tablets. The details of the cost of ingredients have not been shown, presumably because it is not company policy to allow all employees using the cost sheet to have information in this rather sensitive area.

Unit operation costing is particularly useful when a factory is operating on mass-production lines, where production is of a continuous nature. An example of this would be a mass-production furniture factory, in which parts for tables, sideboards, etc., are being made and later assembled to fulfil orders received. Scrap and waste will be involved at various stages, but the continuous nature of the work would make it difficult to separate this scrap as arising from different batches. All operations are in process simultaneously, and the quantities passing through each operation, at any one time, are in no direct relation to one another.

Example

A firm is making components in three operations, and as operation 1 is completed, the work passes into a stores for partly processed components, from whence the accumulated stock is drawn upon at irregular intervals for the completion of operation 2. Similarly, the work then passes again into the stores, and the stock is drawn upon for operation 3 to be completed.

On the basis of past records it is estimated that:

(*a*) of every 100 units put into process at operation 1 there will be 10% rejects on inspection at the end of the operation, leaving 90 to pass into stores available for re-issue;

(*b*) of every 100 units put into process at operation 2 there will be 3% rejects, leaving 97 to pass into stores for re-issue to operation 3;

(*c*) of every 100 units put into process in operation 3 there will be 5% rejects, leaving 95 to be transferred to Finished Stock.

This information may be rearranged as follows:

Operation	Put into process	Rejects	Percentage rejects to gross quantity	Percentage rejects to net quantity
1	100	10	10	11·111
2	100	3	3	3·092
3	100	5	5	5·263

The necessity of obtaining the percentage of rejects to the net quantity is that it enables us to work out the scale of manufacture at each operation.

Thus, working backwards from operation 3.

(*a*) If 1,000 good products pass into finished stock after operation 3 there would be the following rejects:

$$1,000 \times 5·263\% = 53$$

so that 1,053 would have to be processed to produce 1,000.

(*b*) If 1,053 units have to be available for operation 3 we must provide for the following rejects at the end of operation 2:

$$1,053 \times 3·092\% = 33$$

so that 1,086 would have to be put into process.

(*c*) Finally, if 1,086 units have to be available for operation 2 we must provide for the following rejects at the end of operation 1:

$$1,086 \times 11·111\% = 120$$

so that 1,206 units would have to be put into process.

Continuing our illustration, let us suppose that the following information in regard to labour costs is available for the month of March.

Operation	Units put into process	Rejects	Net units passing inspection	Labour cost (£)
1	120,000	12,000	108,000	1,200
2	112,500	3,375	109,125	950
3	105,000	5,250	99,750	1,120

We are now in a position to build up our unit operation costs, for labour only, as follows:

Opera-tion	Gross units	Rejects	Net units	Per-centage rejects to net	Ratio figure per 1,000 for cost of final net	Value (£)	Labour costs per 1,000		
							On gross	On net	On final net
(1)	(2)	(3)	(4)	(5)	(6)	(7)	(8)	(9)	(10)
						£	£	£	£
1	120,000	12,000	108,000	11·111%	1,206	1,200	10	11·11	12·06
2	112,500	3,375	109,125	3·092%	1,086	950	8·44	8·71	9·17
3	105,000	5,250	99,750	5·263%	1,053	1,120	10·67	11·23	11·24
					1,000	£3,270	£29·11	£31·05	£32·47

NOTES

1. The figures in column (8) are obtained by dividing the wages in column (7) by the gross numbers in column (2) and multiplying by 1,000. This gives the labour cost per operation per 1,000 gross.

2. The figures in column (9) are found by dividing the wages in column (7) by the net good output at each operation as shown in column (4) and multiplying by 1,000. This gives the labour cost for each operation per 1,000 net.

3. The figures in column (10) showing the labour cost per 1,000 on the quantities finally passed as good are obtained by multiplying the gross cost per column (8) by the ratio in column (6), e.g. 1,206/1,000. Thus we obtain the actual rate of cost allowing for rejects.

INTERPRETATION OF COST SHEET

1. The final direct labour cost of 1,000 finished components is £32·47.

2. Column (6) shows the number of units to be put in hand at each operation to secure 1,000 units properly finished.

3. The total loss sustained through rejections is £3·36, i.e. column (10) less column (8).

4. The effect of having losses at each operation which are cumulative is £1·42, i.e. column (10) less column (9).

Examination Questions

1. Draw up a cost estimate sheet for a simple product, making provision for the comparison of actual costs at a later date. (*LCCI*)

2. Draft a monthly cost statement for a small works producing one product only (figures are not required). State briefly the source of each type of information shown. (*ICMA*)

3. A cycle manufacturer receives, from an outside supplier, a quotation for cycle frames at a price considerably lower than the cost shown by his own costing records for making frames of the same design and quality.

You have been asked to investigate and report on the advisability of the manufacturer obtaining his future requirements of cycle frames from the outside supplier.

You are required to state:

(*a*) what investigations you would make to satisfy yourself whether or not the purchase of cycle frames from the outside supplier would in fact result in a saving of expense to the manufacturer; and

(*b*) the points you would bring to the attention of the manufacturer when making your report. (*CAA*)

4. By what method would you cost an article, the manufacture of which went on uninterruptedly, and where wastage occurred at various stages of manufacture and assembly? (*RSA*)

5. A number of articles varying in size and style can only be completed after an interval between each process. The articles may be batched for certain processes, but the time involved varies for each article, and in some cases is of short duration. How would you ascertain the cost of each article when complete? (*ICMA*)

6. The following are the recorded costs of the same machine operation during six months.

	Number of operations	Wages cost	Machine overheads	Other overheads	Total
		£	£	£	£
January	1,250	624	938	94	1,656
February	636	356	478	52	886

	Number of operations	Wages cost £	Machine overheads £	Other overheads £	Total £
March	1,584	936	1,188	140	2,264
April	858	484	644	72	1,200
May	1,026	606	770	90	1,466
June	1,384	600	1,038	90	1,728
	6,738	£3,606	£5,056	£538	£9,200

Calculate the monthly cost per operation of two or three months in which the figures appear to be most significant; compare these with the average unit cost over the whole period, and state very briefly what may be the causes of such wide fluctuations. *(CAA)*

7. Housesales Ltd. manufactured and sold 2,250 domestic refrigerators during the year ended September 30, 19–1. The summarised Trading and Profit and Loss Accounts set out below relate entirely to the manufacture and sales of these domestic refrigerators during the year ended September 30, 19–1, when the whole output of finished appliances was sold; opening and closing work-in-progress has been ignored:

	£		£
Materials consumed	18,000	Sales	90,000
Direct wages	27,000		
Manufacturing overheads	11,250		
Gross profit c/d	33,750		
	£90,000		£90,000
Management and staff salaries	13,500	Gross profit b/d	33,750
Rent, rates and insurance	2,250		
Selling expenses	6,750		
General expenses	4,500		
Net profit	6,750		
	£33,750		£33,750

For the year ended September 30, 19–2 it is estimated that:

(a) Output and sales will be 2,700 domestic refrigerators.

(b) Prices of materials will rise by 20% over the previous year's level.

(c) Wages rates will rise by 5%.

(d) Manufacturing overheads will rise in proportion to the combined cost of materials and wages.

(e) Selling expenses will remain unchanged.

(f) Other expenses will remain unaffected by the rise in output.

You are required to submit a statement to the Directors showing the price at which the domestic refrigerators should be marketed so as to show a profit of 20% on the selling price. (SCCA)

Chapter 16

Operating Costing

OPERATING costing is applied to the cost of operating services such as are provided by:

(a) hospitals;
(b) railways;
(c) airlines;
(d) buses;
(e) goods haulage;
(f) local authorities;
(g) steam service;
(h) canteens;
(i) personnel department of a factory.

The precise headings of the accounts used to record the expenditure will vary with the kind of undertaking, but the methods of accounting used will be similar to unit costing. The chief difference is, in fact, that here we are costing the operation of a service, whereas before we were finding the cost of manufactured articles. The units to use when goods are being manufactured are simple enough, but the units of measurement to use to express the cost of a service are somewhat more difficult, and open to various decisions.

Nature of Expenditure

In an undertaking operating a service, the expenditure will fall under the following headings.

1. *Capital expenditure*

This includes the buildings, plant, vehicles, and equipment from the use of which the service is provided. Other revenue expenditure will arise following the expenditure on capital assets, by way of depreciation, insurance, etc.

2. *Direct expenses*

Among such expenses may be:
medical and nursing salaries (hospitals);
drivers' and guards' wages (railways);
pilots' and navigation officers' salaries (airlines);
fuel oil (buses);
petrol (cars and vans);
provisions (canteens).

3. *Fixed overhead*

This heading will contain:
depreciation;
rent and rates;
insurance;
road fund licences, etc.

To explain more clearly the way in which operating costing is made use of in practice, we may take the example of motor transport.

The accounts are usually designed to show the cost of operating each vehicle or groups of similar vehicles of the same age, from which total the desired unit costs may be derived. The costs serve the following purposes.

(*a*) To afford comparison between the cost of using motor vehicles owned and that of using other types of transport, either owned or hired.

(*b*) To determine what should be charged against departments, or others, using the service.

(*c*) To assist in deciding at what price the use of a vehicle can be charged, profitably, to anyone hiring a vehicle.

(*d*) To promote efficiency by comparing the cost of maintaining and running one vehicle with that of another of the same type and capacity.

Collection of Information

When a fleet of vehicles is maintained, daily report or log sheets should be obtained for each vehicle. These may be completed by the drivers, or in suitable cases by a foreman or checking clerk at the depot, and state in the space provided at the top of the card (*see* Fig. 33) the vehicle number, driver's name, date, route, and time of departure and return after each trip.

DAILY REPORT SHEET

Vehicle No.: ....   No. of Sheet: ....
Route (or District): ....   Date: ....
Driver: ....   Time, Start: ....
                                                                                    Finish: ....

TRIP RECORD

Trip No.	From	To	Tonnes Packages or Passengers		Kilo-metres	Time	
			Out	En Route		Out	In
1							
2							
3							
4							
etc.							

Employee's Time	Delays	Supplies and Services	Office References
Driver:	Loading:	Petrol:	
Assistant:	Traffic:	Oil:	
Cleaners:	Accidents:	Grease:	
Mechanics:	Breakdown:	Tyres:	
		Repairs:	

FIG. 33.—*Report sheet*

At the foot are recorded details of:

(*a*) petrol, oil, and other supplies provided by the garage;

(*b*) time spent on the vehicle for washing, cleaning, and attending to minor adjustments by the mechanics;

(*c*) the length of time on duty of the driver and his assistant; also of time spent on the vehicle by cleaners, mechanics, etc., at the depot;

(*d*) time lost through exceptional delays.

Times and speedometer readings may be made by the driver for each trip, or by the checking clerk.

Details of repairs may be noted on the back of the sheet, or a reference made to the mechanics' repair job tickets, from which the office completes the cost.

These daily reports are summarised on to analysis sheets, upon which statistics and costs are collected for transfer to a monthly cost summary.

Some costs involved in transport costing are of a semi-variable nature; in other words, part of the cost is fixed, while part is variable per kilometre or per hour. For example, the maintenance cost of operating a fleet of vehicles will be determined in part by the fixed costs of operating the maintenance department, and in part by the distance recorded for the transport vehicles. This behaviour of costs is illustrated on page 242.

The Monthly Cost Summary

This is compiled for each vehicle from the analysis sheets entered up from the daily records, providing the information shown in Fig. 34.

Units of Cost in Transport Costing

A number of units of cost have been used to measure the efficiency of running vehicles, and among the most frequent are:

1. THE TONNE-KILOMETRE

There are two varieties of this unit:

(a) *The absolute tonne-kilometre.* This is the unit of cost of carrying 1 tonne over a distance of 1 kilometre. Thus

$$2 \text{ tonnes} \times 6 \text{ kilometres} = 12 \text{ tonne-kilometres (absolute)}$$

Again

A lorry carries 4 tonnes: it unloads 1 tonne after 7 km, and the balance after a further 5 km, then returning empty.

$$(1 \text{ t} \times 7) + (3 \text{ t} \times 12) + (0 \text{ t} \times 12) = 43$$

That is, 43 absolute tonne-kilometres, the "weight carried × kilometres run" for each section of the trip.

(b) *The commercial tonne-kilometre.* The difficulties in computing the absolute tonne-kilometre for trips broken frequently for unloading led to the search for a simpler method. This was found

COST SUMMARY AND PERFORMANCE STATEMENT

No. of Car: 19   **Month ended** April 19....
Chassis No.: 14966A   **Capacity in lbs.........**

MONTHLY CHARGES

A. Operating Charges		B. Maintenance Charges	
	£		£
Petrol		Tyres	
Oil		Repairs	
Grease etc.		Overhaul	
Driver		Spare Car	
Assistant		Garage Charge etc.	
Mechanics			
Total	£502·622	Total	£526·762

C. Fixed Charges	Proportion for Month
	£
Insurance at £...... per year	
Interest at ...... % per year	
Depreciation at ...... % per year	
Tax, licence at £...... per year	
Other items at £...... per year	
Total	£568·616

MONTHLY COST SHEET

1. Total Capital cost, complete	£5,300

Performance Record	
2. Days operated	26
3. Days idle	4
4. Days maintained (Item 2 + Item 3)	30
5. Total hours operated	232
6. Total kilometres covered	803
7. Total trips made	28

Performance Averages	
8. Average kilometres per day maintained (Item 6 ÷ Item 4)	26·76
9. Average kilometres per day operated (Item 6 ÷ Item 2)	30·88
10. Average kilometres per trip (Item 6 ÷ Item 7)	28·67

Costs for the Month	
11. Total expenses for month (sum of Items A, B, and C above)	£1,598·00
12. Cost per day operated (Item 11 ÷ Item 2)	£61·46
13. Cost per day maintained (Item 11 ÷ Item 4)	£53·27
14. Cost per kilometre operated (Item 11 ÷ Item 6)	£1·99
15. Cost per hour (Item 11 ÷ Item 5)	£6·89

FIG. 34.—*Cost summary and performance statement*

This provides summarised details in regard to the running of each vehicle or group of similar vehicles. Comparison of period with period and of one vehicle with another should yield useful information for control purposes.

in the idea of the commercial tonne-kilometre, which in its simplest form is

$$\frac{\text{Tonnage loaded on lorry} \times \text{Distance travelled}}{2}$$

This is a compromise, but it is sufficiently accurate if it is adapted to the circumstances of each carrier. It is based on the theoretical assumption that the vehicle is working, on an average, half loaded.

Specimen Question

A vehicle sets off with 6 tonnes on a round trip, and delivers as follows: 2 tonnes after 10 km; 1 tonne after a further 8 km; 1 tonne after a further 4 km; and the remaining 2 tonnes after a further 5 km. It then returns empty, covering a distance of 13 km. Calculate: (*a*) the absolute tonne-km; (*b*) the commercial tonne-km.

Answer

(*a*) The absolute tonne-km are:

$$(6 \times 10) + (4 \times 8) + (3 \times 4) + (2 \times 5) + (0 \times 13)$$
$$= 60 + 32 + 12 + 10 + 0$$
$$= 114$$

(*b*) The commercial tonne-km are:

$$\frac{6 \times 40}{2} = \underline{120}$$

2. THE KILOMETRE RUN

This is the unit most frequently used for costing vehicles' performance when the carrying of goods is not involved. The expenditure on running staff cars might therefore be related to this unit of cost.

3. COST PER HOUR

When vehicles are hired out to customers at so much an hour it is convenient to know the costs per hour, so that adequate charges may be made to cover all the cost plus profit. The "hour" is in this case the "hired-out hour".

Examination Questions

1. A company owns a fleet of vans, and the directors wish to examine the costs of (a) each van; (b) the fleet as a whole.

Prepare a report on the accounting arrangements that are needed and draft specimens of the forms that you recommend for presentation to the directors.

Show separate rates for fixed and variable expenditure and state how these should be used. (*IAADP*)

2. State the advantages and disadvantages of using the following units for comparing the operating costs of road transport: (a) per tonne; (b) per kilometre; (c) per absolute tonne-kilometre; (d) per commercial tonne-kilometre. (*SCCA*)

3. Assuming the steam heating for a whole factory is generated at a central boiler-house, what basis would you use for allocating the heating costs to the various departments? (*SCCA*)

4. A company has a large boiler-house with a number of water-tube boilers and supplies steam to several departments for use in manufacturing operations. The boiler-house has its own Cost Centre Account.

What form would this account take and what units of cost be established? What means could be used to apportion the total cost over the various main locations? (*LCCI*)

5. A factory operates a fleet of 5-tonne, 3-tonne and 1½-tonne vehicles for delivery of its own goods.

You are required to draft a monthly cost and statistical statement for the assistance of the management. (Figures are not required.) (*ICMA*)

6. On what basis would you prepare the costs of a road-transport business using different types of vehicles, carrying different kinds of loads to a variety of destinations, sometimes returning empty and sometimes bringing back return loads; assuming the management must be furnished with means of comparing the relative cost and efficiency of the different types of vehicle? (*ICMA*)

7. A bus service operates on five separate routes in and around a small country town.

The following particulars apply:

Fares are fixed on the basis of £0·05 per *passenger-mile*.

Running costs average £0·30 per *mile*.

Annual vehicle costs (licences, depreciation, maintenance, etc.) average £6,000 per vehicle.

General Administration costs amount to £74,000 per annum.

	Routes			
	1	2	3	4
Number of vehicles used	3	4	2	2
Total annual mileage (thousands)	150	160	60	70
Average number of passengers carried	14	15	8	12

(a) Present a columnar statement showing, for each route and in total, the *contribution* towards the general administration cost and profit.

(b) Calculate a revised contribution for Route 3 if fares on that route are reduced by 25% to meet competition from a rail service, with a consequent doubling of the number of passengers carried.

(*LCCI*)

8. The transport department of the Norwest Council operates a large fleet of assorted vehicles. These vehicles are used as the need arises by the various departments of the Council. Each month a statement is prepared for the transport department comparing actual results with budget.

One of the items in the transport department's monthly statement is the cost of vehicle maintenance. This maintenance is carried out by the employees of the department.

To facilitate his control the transport manager has asked that future statements should show vehicle maintenance costs analysed into fixed and variable costs.

Data for the six months from January to June inclusive are given below:

	Vehicle maintenance cost £	Vehicle running hours
January	13,600	2,100
February	15,800	2,800
March	14,500	2,200
April	16,200	3,000
May	14,900	2,600
June	15,000	2,500

You are required to:

(a) analyse the vehicle maintenance costs into fixed and variable costs, by means of a graph, based on the data given;

(b) discuss briefly how you would propose to calculate rates for charging out the total costs incurred to the user departments.

(*ICMA*)

9. Data:

	£
Cost of motor car	5,500
Trade-in price after 2 years or 60,000 miles is expected to be	1,500

£

Maintenance—6-monthly service
   costing   60
Spares/replacement parts, per
   1,000 miles   20
Vehicle licence, per annum   80
Insurance, per annum   150
Tyre replacements after 25,000 miles,
   four at   37·50 each
Petrol, per gallon   1·90
Average mileage from one gallon is 25 miles.

(*a*) From the above data you are required:

(*i*) to prepare a schedule to be presented to management showing for the mileages of 5,000, 10,000, 15,000 and 30,000 miles per annum:

1. total variable cost
2. total fixed cost
3. total cost
4. variable cost per mile (in pence to nearest penny)
5. fixed cost per mile (in pence to nearest penny)
6. total cost per mile (in pence to nearest penny)

If, in classifying the costs, you consider that some can be treated as either variable or fixed, state the assumption(s) on which your answer is based together with brief supporting reason(s).

(*ii*) on the graph paper provided, to plot the information given in your answer to (*i*) above for the costs listed against *1, 2, 3* and *6*.

(*iii*) to read off from your graph(s) in (*ii*) and state the approximate total costs applicable to 18,000 miles and 25,000 miles and the total cost per mile (in pence) at these two mileages.

(*b*) "the more miles you travel, the cheaper it becomes." Comment briefly on this statement.   (*ICMA*)

Chapter 17

Process Costing

Introduction

THIS method of costing is completely different from those systems described in the preceding chapters. Mention has already been made of the fact that basically there are two types of cost accounting systems (*see* Chapter 3):

(a) job cost; and
(b) process cost.

In the job costing system each job is complete within itself, in other words, prime cost and overheads are calculated for a specific order; the identity of any order is maintained throughout the production cycle. The result may be that the cost of one completed job may be different from that of another completed job of the same type.

However, in a process costing system the type of production is such that a continuous flow of output of identical products results; there is no unit with an individual identity, because each unit is part of a process. Because, in a process system, products are manufactured in a continuous process the name "continuous" costing was introduced. The result of this system is that costing an individual unit is impossible; it is therefore necessary to adopt a period of time as the basis for determining the average cost per unit of production, e.g.:

Production during August was 100,000 units
Direct materials consumed amounted to £25,000
Direct labour costs were £10,000
Production overhead incurred was £15,000
The average cost per unit is determined by dividing the total cost by the total number of units produced:

$$\frac{£50,000}{100,000} = £0.50 \text{ per unit}$$

The average cost of £0·50 per unit will be applied to each of the 100,000 units produced during the period, irrespective of the fact that on one day materials consumed may have been more expensive than those on another day. It it because of this averaging of costs during a period that the name "average" costing originated.

Application of the Method

Process costing is used to ascertain the cost of a product at each process, operation, or stage of manufacture, where processes are carried on having one or more of the following features.

(*a*) Where the product of one process becomes the material of another process or operation.

(*b*) Where there is simultaneous production, at one or more processes, of different products, with or without by-products.

(*c*) Where, during one or more processes or operations of a series, the products, or materials, are not distinguishable from one another, as, for instance, when finished products differ finally only in shape or form.

The industries in which process costing may be used are many; in fact, except where job or operating costing is necessary, a process costing system can usually be devised. In practice, process costing is used in such industries as chemical, soap-making, food products, and distillation plants.

In most cases process costing requires fewer forms and less details than are needed for job costs, but a closer analysis of operations is needed. For example, there is not the need for the allocation of labour to so many order numbers, and material is issued in bulk to departments, rather than to many specific jobs. In continuous processes employees are engaged continuously on each process, so it is relatively easy to allocate wages.

General Features

The factory is divided into departments or processes, which are limited to a certain operation, e.g. in an oil refinery one department will separate the crude oil by distillation into a number of primary products, another department will convert low-quality oils into high-quality oils by the application of heat and catalysts, etc. The process may consist of a certain operation or operations, each of which completes a special stage in the production cycle. Each process is usually the responsibility of one person, who may be a foreman or a supervisor.

An account is kept for each process or operation. Materials, labour, and production overheads are debited, and by-products and scrap are credited, while the material as modified at the operation concerned is passed on to the next process. The "finished" product of the first process becomes the "raw material" of the next one, and so on, until the final products are completed. Each process cost account, in fact, represents a subdivision of a manufacturing account, so that the production cost of each process is separately ascertained, and from this the unit cost of each operation may be calculated.

Any normal loss suffered in a process is borne by the good production, thus increasing the average cost per unit, e.g. if 100 units are produced at a cost of £45 the cost per unit would be £0·45; however, if there is a normal loss of 10% of production the cost per unit would be £0·50. Any abnormal loss is valued at the ordinary rate and the amount transferred to an abnormal loss account, which reveals to management the cost of losses due to inefficiency, accidents, etc.

Standard Costs in Process Costing

In industries where process costing is suitable standard costs may be used with great advantage. Standard costs provide a measure against which actual costs may be compared. Standard costing in connection with process costing gives management an excellent measure of the efficiency of production, and it may be mentioned that cost accounting systems on these lines are being more widely used every year. Standard costing is discussed more fully in Chapter 21.

The Elements of Production Cost

Direct Materials

Broadly speaking, there are two types of production cycle in process costing.

(a) Material is introduced in process 1, is processed, then passed to process 2, where further processing takes place; then it is transferred to the next process; and so on.

(b) A routine similar to the above, except that, in addition, direct materials are added to the original material at each stage.

The production control department must ensure that adequate supplies of direct materials are available, when and where required; the procedure for requisitioning materials was discussed in Chapter

5, and this routine should be followed, unless bulk requisitioning is used, in which case the stores issues materials in bulk to the process department, where the materials are held in store until required.

Direct Labour

This element of cost is usually the smallest item in process costing. Most of the industries which operate this production cycle have adopted, and are adopting more and more, the automatic plant or equipment which is invaluable where mass-production techniques are used. The result is that direct labour cost per unit becomes smaller, while the overhead cost per unit increases.

In comparison with job costing, the recording and allocation of time spent on production is relatively easy. Usually employees are continuously engaged on one process, and labour costs are analysed and posted to the debit of the appropriate process account. Where employees are engaged on more than one process it will be necessary to record or estimate the time spent on each process, then allocate the cost to each process concerned.

Direct Expenses

This type of expenditure is not frequently experienced, but if any expenditure is directly attributable to a product it should be debited to the relative process account. An example of such expenditure is the hire of a bean-sorting machine in a department processing beans in a food factory.

Production Overhead

It was mentioned above that most industries in which process costing is operated are able to introduce mechanised production lines to a considerable extent. This results normally in high production overhead costs. In many cases the cost of using certain equipment will be allocated directly to the department concerned, but in other cases careful apportionment of overheads to departments affected will be necessary.

An example of process costing now follows, to illustrate the elements of cost previously discussed and transfer of "finished product" of one department to "raw material" in the next process, until completion of production.

Example

The manufacture of product Peejay requires three distinct processes, numbered 1–3. On completion, the product is passed from process 3 to finished stock. During May the following information was obtained in respect of the product:

Element of cost	Total	Process		
		1	2	3
	£	£	£	£
Direct material	7,600	5,600	1,250	750
Direct labour	3,360	620	860	1,880
Direct expense	1,000	800	200	—
Production overhead	5,040			

There was no stock of raw material or work in progress, either at the beginning or end of the period.

Production overhead is absorbed by processes on the basis of 150% of direct wages.

Production during the period was 100 units.

Process 1

Description: Period: May
                                                                            Output: 100 units

	Amount	Cost per unit		Amount	Cost per unit
	£	£		£	£
Direct material	5,600	56·00	Output transferred to		
Direct labour	620	6·20	process 2	7,950	79·50
Direct expense	800	8·00			
Production overhead	930	9·30			
	£7,950	£79·50		£7,950	£79·50

Process 2

Description: Period: May
                                                                            Output: 100 units

	Amount	Cost per unit		Amount	Cost per unit
	£	£		£	£
Output transferred from			Output transferred to		
process 1	7,950	79·50	process 3	11,550	115·50
Direct material	1,250	12·50			
Direct labour	860	8·60			
Direct expense	200	2·00			
Production overhead	1,290	12·90			
	£11,550	£115·50		£11,550	£115·50

Process 3

Description: Period: May
                                                               Output: 100 units

	Amount	Cost per unit		Amount	Cost per unit
	£	£		£	£
Output transferred from			Output transferred to		
process 2	11,550	115·50	finished stock	17,000	170·00
Direct material	750	7·50			
Direct labour	1,880	18·80			
Production overhead	2,820	28·20			
	£17,000	£170·00		£17,000	£170·00

Finished Stock

	Amount	Cost per unit		Amount	Cost per unit
	£	£		£	£
Output transferred from					
process 3—100 tons	£17,000	£170·00			

Process Loss

In many processes a loss of weight arises in the course of manufacture, and this is particularly the case where distillation or disintegration by heat or chemical action is involved. In many cases such loss is inherent and inevitable. However, even though loss is inevitable, it is still essential that accurate records are maintained to enable management to minimise the loss incurred. It should be pointed out to foremen and supervisors that scrap, etc., should be measured and recorded, otherwise production costs will be adversely affected.

Materials which have been processed and are then found to be defective and scrapped have incurred their share of labour and variable overhead up to the point of rejection, so obviously the financial loss to the firm increases with each stage of production reached. Keen inspection at each stage should help to reduce losses, because sub-standard units will not be further processed.

Normal Process Loss

In most process industries the loss of material which is inherent in the processing operation can be worked out in advance; usually this is calculated by formula or by past experience. Process loss is often caused by such factors as evaporation and that loss inherent in large-scale production, but may often include scrap and waste.

Scrap refers to products or materials which are found to be not up to standard and may be used in other departments of the firm, or sold at a much lower price than the cost.

Waste refers to anything which has no value.

Thus normal process loss represents the loss which would be expected under normal conditions.

Abnormal Process Loss

In many process industries loss of material may be experienced due to unexpected conditions, e.g. supply of sub-standard raw materials, carelessness, and accidents. All losses under this category must be recorded and thoroughly investigated, and where possible, steps taken to prevent any recurrence.

This abnormal process loss represents the loss which occurs under abnormal conditions.

Accounting for Process Loss

Accounting procedure for normal and abnormal loss differs. When normal loss occurs the cost is absorbed in the cost of production of good products, so no account for normal loss is required. However, in the event of abnormal loss a separate account must be opened, to which is debited the cost of material, labour, and appropriate overhead incurred up to the point of rejection. Abnormal losses should be written off to the cost accounting profit and loss account.

The accounting procedure can now be illustrated.

Example

In the manufacture of product Jaydee 500 kg of raw material at £1·00 per kg were supplied to process 1. In this process labour costs amounted to £75, and production overheads of £100 were incurred. The normal process loss due to waste has been estimated at 10%. Actual production for the third period was 440 kg.

It will be observed that the full cost of production is charged to abnormal loss, while the cost of normal loss is absorbed by finished output. It has been assumed that the rejection occurred at the finished stage of this process; if it had occurred earlier the abnormal loss would have been charged only the expenditure incurred up to that point.

Process 1

Description: Period: No. 3
                                                                             Output: 460 kg

	kg	Cost per kg	Amount		kg	Cost per kg	Amount
		£	£			£	£
Direct material	500	1	500	Normal loss	50	—	—
Direct labour	—	—	75	Abnormal loss	10	1·5	15
Production overhead	—	—	100	Process 2—output	440	1·5	660
	500		£675		500		£675

Abnormal Loss

		£			£
Process 1		£15	Profit and Loss a/c		£15

If the loss in the above illustration had been saleable as scrap at £0·90 per kg the position would be as follows:

Process 1

Description: Period: No. 3
                                                                             Output: 360 kg

	kg	Cost per kg	Amount		kg	Cost per kg	Amount
		£	£			£	£
Direct material	500	1	500	Normal loss	50	0·90	45
Direct labour			75	Abnormal loss	10	1·40	14
Production overhead			100	Process 2—output	440	1·40	616
	500		£675		500		£675

Abnormal Loss

		£			£
Process 1	10	14	Debtors	10 0·90	9
			Profit and loss a/c		5
		£14			£14

NOTES

1. Normal loss is calculated as follows:

Estimated loss of 10% of production (500 kg) = 50 kg
Scrap value of 50 kg at £0·90 per kg = £45

2. Abnormal loss is calculated:

Estimated production	450 kg
Actual production	440 kg
Abnormal loss	10 kg

Cost of normal production =
$$\text{Total cost} - \text{Scrap value of normal loss}$$
$$= £675 - £45$$
$$= £630$$

$$\text{Cost of normal production per kg} = \frac{£630}{450 \text{ kg}} £1 \cdot 40$$

Cost of abnormal loss: 10 kg at £1·40 per kg = £14.

3. Abnormal loss account is debited with the cost of abnormal loss. Assuming the scrap can be sold at £0·90 per kg, there will be a credit to the account for 10 kg at £0·90 per kg = £9, which amount will be recovered from debtors. The balance of the account is then written off to cost accounting profit and loss account.

4. Debtors account in the financial accounts will be debited with £54 for sale of scrap; this figure is made up of £45 normal loss and £9 abnormal loss.

Abnormal Gain

It was mentioned earlier that normal process loss represents the loss which would be expected under normal conditions. Frequently the loss is greater than expected, in which case an abnormal loss occurs. Sometimes, however, the loss is not as much as was expected, the result of which is that, in effect, a gain is obtained. This abnormal gain will be calculated in a similar manner to an abnormal loss, then posted to an abnormal gain account.

Example

In the manufacture of product Jaydee, during period 4, 400 kg of raw material at £1 per kg were supplied to process 1. Labour costs amounted to £60 and production overheads of £80 were incurred. The normal process loss is 10% which can be sold as scrap at £0·90 per kg. The actual production during the period was 365 kg.

Process 1

Description: Period: No.4
                                                               Output: 385 kg

	kg	Cost per kg	Amount		kg	Cost per kg	Amount
		£	£			£	£
Direct material	400	1·00	400	Normal loss	40	0·90	36
Direct labour			60	Process 2—output	365	1·40	511
Production overhead			80				
Abnormal gain	5	1·40	7				
	405		£547		405		£547

Abnormal Gain

	£		£
Process 1	4·50	Process 1	7·00
Profit and loss a/c	2·50		
	£7·00		£7·00

NOTES

1. Normal loss has been calculated as follows:

Estimated loss of 10% of production (400 kg) = 40 kg
Scrap value of 40 kg at £0·90 per kg = £36

2. Abnormal gain is calculated:

Estimated production	360 kg
Actual production	365 kg
Abnormal gain	5 kg

Cost of normal production = Total cost − Scrap value of normal
                    Total cost − Scrap value of normal
                            = £540 − £36
                            = £504

Value of normal production per kg = $\dfrac{£504}{360 \text{ kg}}$ = £1·40

Cost of abnormal gain = 5 kg at £1·40 per kg = £7.

3. Abnormal Gain Account is credited with the value of abnormal gain. However, this gain is partly offset by the loss in scrap realised; it was expected that scrap would be 40 kg at £0·90 per

kg, but in fact only 35 kg at £0·90 per kg materialised. This difference of 5 kg at £0·90 per kg = £4·50 represents loss in scrap value, so is debited to Abnormal Gain Account to reduce the gain transferred to Profit and Loss Account at the end of the period.

4. Debtors Account in the Financial Accounts will be debited with £29·50 for sale of scrap; this figure is made up of £34 normal loss, minus £4·50 abnormal gain.

It should be observed that in the last two illustrations the cost per kg of output transferred to process 2 has not changed: £1·40 per kg in each case. The introduction of abnormal loss and abnormal gain accounts should ensure that minor variations in production do not cause the cost of production to fluctuate. In addition, the attention of management is drawn to these accounts, which may reveal efficiencies or inefficiencies, or possible need for revision of allowances.

A comprehensive illustration of process costing, involving topics discussed in this chapter, is now given.

Example

Product Emmess passes through three processes to completion. In period 6 the cost of production was as follows:

Element of cost	Total	Process		
		1	2	3
	£	£	£	£
Direct material	4,166	1,256	2,124	786
Direct labour	2,204	505	742	957
Direct expense	234	234	—	—
Production overhead	2,204			

500 units at £6 per unit were issued to process 1.

Normal loss of units per process was estimated at

Process 1	10%
Process 2	10%
Process 3	5%

The loss in each process represented scrap which could be sold to a merchant at a value as follows:

Process 1	£2 per unit
Process 2	£4 per unit
Process 3	£5 per unit

Actual output of each process was:

Process 1	440 units
Process 2	400 units
Process 3	382 units

There was no stock of materials or work in progress in any process, either at the beginning or the end of the period. The output of each process passes direct to the next process and finally to finished stock. Production overhead is allocated to each process on a basis of 100% of the cost of direct labour.

Process 1

Description:

Period: No. 6
Output: 440 units

	Units	Cost per unit	Amount		Units	Cost per unit	Amount
		£	£			£	£
Units introduced	500	6	3,000	Normal loss	50	2	100
Direct material			1,256	Abnormal loss	10	12	120
Direct labour			505	Process 2—output			
Direct expense			234	transferred	440	12	5,280
Production overhead			505				
	500		£5,500		500		£5,500

Process 2

Description:

Period: No.6
Output: 400 units

	Units	Cost per unit	Amount		Units	Cost per unit	Amount
		£	£			£	£
Process 1—output	440	12	5,280	Normal loss	44	4	176
Direct material			2,124	Process 3—output			
Direct labour			742	transferred	400	22	8,800
Production overhead			742				
Abnormal gain	4	22	88				
	444		£8,976		444		£8,976

Process 3

Description:

	Units	Cost per unit	Amount		Units	Cost per unit	Amount
		£	£			£	£
Process 2—output	400	22	8,800	Normal loss	20	5	100
Direct materials			786	Finished stock—			
Direct labour			957	output transferred	382	30	11,460
Production overhead			957				
Abnormal gain	2	30	60				
	402		£11,560		402		£11,560

Finished Stock

	Units	Cost per unit	Amount		Units	Cost per unit	Amount
		£	£			£	£
Process 3—output	382	30	£11,460				

Abnormal Loss

	Units	Cost per unit	Amount		Units	Cost per unit	Amount
		£	£			£	£
Process 1			120	Debtors			20
				Profit and loss a/c			100
			£120				£120

Abnormal Gain

	Units	Cost per unit	Amount		Units	Cost per unit	Amount
		£	£			£	£
Process 2			16	Process 2			88
Process 3			10	Process 3			60
Profit and loss a/c			122				
			£148				£148

NOTES
Process 1

Normal loss $500 \times \dfrac{10}{100} = 50$ units

Scrap value 50 units at £2 per unit = £100
Abnormal loss:
Normal cost £5,500 − £100 = £5,400.
Normal production 500 units − 50 units = 450 units

$$\dfrac{£5,400}{450} \times 10 = £120$$

Process 2

Normal loss $440 \times \dfrac{10}{100} = 44$ units

Scrap value 44 units at £4 per unit = £176
Abnormal gain:
Normal cost £8,888 − £176 = £8,712
Normal production 440 − 44 = 396 units

$$\dfrac{£8,712}{396} \times 4 = £88$$

Process 3

Normal loss $400 \times \dfrac{5}{100} = 20$ units

Scrap value 20 units at £5 per unit = £100
Abnormal gain:
Normal cost £11,500 − £100 = £11,400
Normal production 400 − 20 = 380 units

$$\dfrac{£11,400}{380} \times 2 = £60$$

Abnormal gain account

In respect of process 2, abnormal gain account is debited with £16. This represents the loss in scrap value as a result of scrap being less than expected. It was estimated that 44 units would be scrapped, but in fact only 40 units were scrapped, so 4 units scrap value is not realised from the scrap merchant, i.e. 4 units at £4 per unit = £16. Consequently, £16 will reduce the gain of increased production of 4 units, which represents a value of 4 units at £22 per unit = £88. Therefore the net gain transferred to profit and loss account is £72.

A similar calculation would be made in respect of process 3. In the financial accounts the debtors account would show, in respect of scrap sales:

Debtors

	£		£
Process 1	120	Cash	370
Process 2	160		
Process 3	90		
	£370		£370

This figure of £370 is represented in the cost accounts as follows:

	£	
Process 1 Normal loss	100	
Process 2 Normal loss	176	
Process 3 Normal loss	100	
Process 1 Abnormal loss	20	
		396
Process 2 Abnormal gain	16	
Process 3 Abnormal gain	10	
		26
		£370

Work in Progress

In the examples shown in this chapter the problem of work in progress has been ignored until now. The problem is a difficult one, but should be discussed in a study of process costing. It is not proposed, in this text, to go deeply into this topic; anyone who wishes to do so is referred to *Wheldon's Cost Accounting.**
However, the basic concepts will be discussed and some simple illustrations given.

* Macdonald & Evans Ltd, 1984.

In process costing one is dealing mainly with a flow-line type of production, e.g an oil refinery, brewery, or dairy, where there is a more or less continuous flow of production. If at the end of an accounting period it is necessary to calculate the value of the product in the pipeline this creates quite a problem. Different products may have reached varying stages of completion, so that it is necessary to evaluate each element of cost at the varying stages of output. A technique which has been developed to facilitate this operation is one known as equivalent units, or effective units of production.

Equivalent Units

The amount of work in progress is estimated by an expert, such as a production controller, in terms of units in the pipeline and the degree of completion reached. For example, it may be estimated that 600 units of product Emmess have reached a stage of completion analysed as to: direct materials 100%, direct labour 50%, production overhead 25%. These 600 units of work in progress would be regarded as being the equivalent of finished units as follows: direct materials 600 units, direct wages 300 units, and production overheads 150 units. In this simple case it can be observed that, by expressing these unfinished units in terms of equivalent units of finished product, it is then possible to evaluate these units quite easily. The standard or normal cost should be ascertained from the cost records, and then, by multiplying the equivalent units by the cost of each element of cost, the work in progress can be evaluated.

Example 1

During July 5,000 units were introduced to process 1.

Normal loss in process was estimated at 10%.
Cost of direct materials introduced was £0·92 per unit.
Cost of direct wages was £1,075.
Cost of production overhead was £2,100.
Units scrapped realised £0·20 per unit.

Inspection takes place at the end of the process, so any units which are scrapped have been through the entire process.

At the end of July it was estimated that output was as follows:

Work in progress	400 units
Scrap	600 units
Finished output	4,000 units

It was also estimated that work in progress had reached the following stage:

Direct materials	100%
Direct wages	50%
Production overhead	25%

Evaluate the output.

Statement of Production

Process 1   *July*

Input		Output		Element of Cost					
				Direct materials		Direct labour		Production overhead	
Details	Units	Details	Units	Units	%	Units	%	Units	%
Materials	5,000	Normal loss	500	—	—	—	—	—	—
		Abnormal loss	100	100	100	100	100	100	100
		Finished goods	4,000	4,000	100	4,000	100	4,000	100
		Work in progress	400	400	100	200	50	100	25
	5,000		5,000						
		Equivalent units		4,500		4,300		4,200	

Statement of Cost

Element of Cost	Cost	Equivalent Production	Cost per unit
	£	Units	£
Direct materials	4,600		
Less Scrap	100		
	4,500	4,500	1·00
Direct wages	1,075	4,300	0·25
Production overheads	2,100	4,200	0·50
Total cost	£7,675		£1·75

Statement of Evaluation

Production	Element of Cost	Equivalent Production	Cost per unit	Total cost	
		Units	£	£	£
Normal loss	Direct materials	—	1·00	—	
	Direct wages	—	0·25	—	
	Production overheads	—	0·50	—	
Abnormal loss	Direct materials	100	1·00	100	
	Direct wages	100	0·25	25	
	Production overheads	100	0·50	50	
				—	175
Finished goods	Direct materials	4,000	1·00	4,000	
	Direct wages	4,000	0·25	1,000	
	Production overheads	4,000	0·50	2,000	
				—	7,000
Work in progress	Direct materials	400	1·00	400	
	Direct wages	200	0·25	50	
	Production overheads	100	0·50	50	
				—	500
					£7,675

NOTES

1. The cost of normal loss is absorbed by the good production. It will be recalled that earlier in this chapter this point was explained in some detail.

2. The abnormal loss is evaluated at the full cost, so that management are aware of what this cost is for the period. Presumably an explanation for this inefficiency would be required.

In this simple illustration inspection took place at the end of the process, so that these units had received 100% of the cost of production. It will not always follow that inspection will occur at the end of the process, and so, depending on the stage reached, the abnormal loss will be charged accordingly.

3. Scrap. The value of scrap received from normal loss units was subtracted from the cost of the direct materials input, to obtain the net cost of direct materials. Earlier in this chapter it was explained that the cost of normal loss, and the value of scrap received therefrom, is absorbed by the good output. The sales value of scrap received from the abnormal loss units must not be credited to the process; it must be credited to the abnormal loss account so as to reduce the loss on units which were scrapped unexpectedly.

The accounts in respect of the process would appear as under:

Process 1

	Units	£		Units	£
Direct materials	5,000	4,600	Normal loss	500	100
Direct wages		1,075	Abnormal loss	100	175
Production overheads		2,100	Process 2	4,000	7,000
			Work in progress	400	500
	5,000	£7,775		5,000	£7,775
Bal. b/d	400	500			

Process 2

	Units	£			
Process 1	4,000	7,000			

Abnormal Loss

	Units	£		Units	£
Process 1	100	175	Debtors	100	20
			Profit and loss		155
	100	£175		100	£175

Debtors account would include an amount in respect of scrap for process 1. Taking process 1 in isolation, debtors account would appear as follows:

Debtors

	Units	£		Units	£
Process 1	500	100	Cash	600	120
Abnormal loss	100	20			
	600	£120		600	£120

The next example is based on an examination question set by an accountancy body, and is intended to illustrate the introductory type of question which may appear involving this technique of equivalent units. The opportunity is taken also to introduce a new layout of the statements required, which it is hoped will facilitate the presentation of information. A simple introduction to the problem of evaluating the opening stock in a process is given also.

Example 2

For the month of August, the following particulars are submitted in respect of process 1:

> Opening stock: 800 units valued at £600
> Direct materials £2,450
> Direct wages £980
> Production overhead £1,470

During the month 5,200 units were begun, and 4,600 units were passed to process 2. Certain losses were incurred in process, but are not to be regarded as part of the cost of production of the finished units. The inspection department discovered the faulty units when the units were 75% completed. Opening and closing work in progress were as follows:

> Opening stock　75%
> Closing stock　60%

It can be assumed that each element of cost accrues evenly over time, so that if a unit is half completed it can be assumed to have absorbed half its elements of cost. Draft the process account.

Statements of Production, Cost, and Evaluation
Process 1　　　　　　　　　　　　　　　　　　　　　　　　　August

| Input | | Output | | Element of Cost | | | | | | Total £ |
Details	Units	Details	Units	Direct materials Units	%	Direct labour Units	%	Production overhead Units	%	
Opening stock	800	Opening stock	800	200	25	200	25	200	25	
Input	5,200	CPDP*	3,800	3,800	100	3,800	100	3,800	100	
		Abnormal loss	400	300	75	300	75	300	75	
		Closing stock	1,000	600	60	600	60	600	60	
	6,000		6,000							
		Equivalent units		4,900		4,900		4,900		
				£		£		£		
		Cost		2,450		980		1,470		4,900
		per unit		0·5		0·2		0·3		1·0
		Evaluation								
		Opening stock		100		40		60		200
		CPDP		1,900		760		1,140		3,800
		Abnormal loss		150		60		90		300
		Closing stock		300		120		180		600
				£2,450		£980		£1,470		£4,900

Process 1 Account

	Units	£		Units	£
Balance b/d	800	600	Process 2	4,600	4,600
Direct materials	5,200	2,450	Abnormal loss	400	300
Direct wages		980	Balance c/d	1,000	600
Production overhead		1,470			
	6,000	£5,500		6,000	£5,500
Balance b/d	1,000	600			

NOTES

1. Opening stock. The opening stock of work in progress was 75% complete, so during August only 25% of the elements of cost are required to complete this stock.

2. Abnormal loss. In this question there are no normal loss units, so that the entire loss of units is to be treated as abnormal loss. This loss must bear its full share of the cost up to the inspection and rejection point.

3. *CPDP. The term "completely processed during period" has been introduced to distinguish those units which came into the process and were passed out of the process during the accounting period, as distinct from those such as opening stock units which came into the process last month and were completed this month. Obviously this distinction is important for apportioning the costs for each accounting period.

4. Process 2 transfer is made up of the units of opening stock and those which were completely processed during the month. (Cost £600 + £200 + £3,800.)

5. Cost check. It should be observed that in the above statement the total evaluation line must show the same figures as those shown on the cost line.

It may have been noticed by the reader that in each of the two previous examples process 1 was the process used for illustration. This was quite intentional, because this process allows a relatively easy introduction to the equivalent units technique. The problem in process 2 and subsequent processes is more involved, because not only does process 2 require direct materials, direct labour, and production overheads but its input includes the output from process 1; similarly, process 3 input includes process 2 output and so on. It is therefore necessary to distinguish between input from a previous process and input added in the current process. The input from the previous process must be 100% complete, or otherwise it should not have been transferred; input in the current process may vary from 0 to 100%, depending on the stage reached in the process when evaluation is to be made. The next illustration concerns process 2, and the same type of layout of the statements as that shown in the previous example will be used.

Example 3

The following information is available in respect of process 2 for the month of March.

Opening stock 1,200 units

Degree of completion:	Direct materials	60%
	Direct wages	50%
	Production overheads	40%

Process 2 transfer 7,600 units at   £2,824
Process 3 transfer 6,380 units
Direct materials added in process   £1,404
Direct wages incurred   £696
Production overheads incurred   £2,076
Units scrapped   820

Degree of completion:	Direct materials	80%
	Direct wages	60%
	Production overheads	60%

Closing stock   1,600 units

Degree of completion:	Direct materials	80%
	Direct wages	70%
	Production overheads	60%

Normal loss in process: 10% of throughput
Units scrapped realised: £0·1 per unit

Statements of Production, Cost, and Evaluation
Process 2   *March*

| Input | | Output | | Direct materials (1) | | Direct materials (2) | | Direct wages | | Production overhead | | Total £ |
Details	Units	Details	Units	Units	%	Units	%	Units	%	Units	%	
Opening stock	1,200	Opening stock	1,200	—	—	480	40	600	50	720	60	
Process 1	7,600	Normal loss	720	—	—	—	—	—	—	—	—	
		Abnormal loss	100	100	100	80	80	60	60	60	60	
		CPDP	5,180	5,180	100	5,180	100	5,180	100	5,180	100	
		Closing stock	1,600	1,600	100	1,280	80	1,120	70	960	60	
	8,800		8,800									
Equivalent units		£		6,880		7,020		6,960		6,920		

Cost	2,824	£	£	£	£
Less Scrap value	72				
		2,752	1,404	696	2,076	6,928
Per unit		0·4	0·2	0·1	0.3	1·0
Evaluation						
Opening stock		—	96	60	216	372
Normal loss		—	—	—	—	—
Abnormal loss		40	16	6	18	80
CPDP		2,072	1,036	518	1,554	5,180
Closing stock		640	256	112	288	1,296
		£2,752	£1,404	£696	£2,076	£6,928

NOTES

1. Normal loss is 10% of throughput

$\frac{10}{100} \times$ (Opening stock + Process 1 transfer − Closing stock)

$\frac{10}{100} \times$ (1,200   +   7,600   −   1,600)

2. Abnormal loss. Units scrapped − Normal loss
           820   −   720

3. Opening stock had reached the following stage of completion:
DM(1) 100%; DM(2) 60%; DW 50%; PO 40%

so DM(1) nil;   DM(2) 40%; DW 50%; PO 60% is required to complete.
It will be recalled that DM(1) is always 100% completed or it should not have been transferred to the next process.

4. Closing stock. DM(1) must be 100% completed, so the full charge is made to DM(1), the remaining equivalent units being as estimated.

5. Scrap value. The amount received as scrap value has been credited arbitrarily to DM(1). This item is invariably the largest element of cost, so it is convenient to credit this item rather than apportion the value over each element of cost.

The accounts in respect of the process will be as follows:

Process 2 Account

	Units	Amount £		Units	Amount £
Opening stock	1,200	828	Normal loss	720	72
Process 1	7,600	2,824	Abnormal loss	100	80
Direct materials		1,404	Process 3	6,380	6,380
Direct wages		696	Closing stock c/d	1,600	1,296
Production overheads		2,076			
	8,800	£7,828		8,800	£7,828
Balance b/d	1,600	1,296			

Process 3 Account

	Units	Amount £			
Process 2	6,380	6,380			

Abnormal Loss Account

	Units	Amount £		Units	Amount £
Process 2	100	80	Debtors	100	10
			Profit and loss		70
	100	£80		100	£80

NOTES

1. Opening stock is valued as follows:

Cost of 1,200 units at £1	£1,200
Cost of completion during March	372
Cost incurred in February	£828

Unless given the value of the opening stock, to calculate the figure one must assume that costs per unit are similar each month, as in a standard costing system.

2. Process 3 transfer is composed of opening stock plus units completely processed during the month:

$$(£828 + £372 + £5,180)$$

3. Scrap value. As in the earlier example, scrap value of normal loss is credited to the process, and scrap value of abnormal loss is credited to the abnormal loss account.

Example 4

This example is adapted from an examination question set in an accountancy paper by the Institute of Chartered Secretaries and Administrators. It is a simplified illustration of the method used in the previous example.

Process 2 account for the month of January is as follows:

Process 2

	£		£
WIP b/d	650	Finished goods	
Process 1 transfer	4,500	WIP c/d	
Direct materials	2,900		
Direct wages	2,175		
Production overheads	5,075		
	£		£

You are given the following information:

WIP at January 1 consisted of 500 units, half completed as regards materials, labour, and overheads.

Process 1 transfer represented 7,500 units.

Finished goods transfer represented 7,000 units.

WIP at January 31 consisted of 1,000 units, half complete as regards material, labour, and overheads.

There was no scrap during January.

You are required to complete the account for process 2.

Statements of Production, Cost, and Evaluation
Process 2   January

Input		Output		Element of Cost								Total
				Direct materials (1)		Direct materials (2)		Direct wages		Production overheads		£
Details	Units	Details	Units	Units	%	Units	%	Units	%	Units	%	
Opening stock	500	Opening stock	500	—	—	250	50	250	50	250	50	
Process 1	7,500	CPDP	6,500	6,500	100	6,500	100	6,500	100	6,500	100	
		Closing stock	1,000	1,000	100	500	50	500	50	500	50	
	8,000		8,000									
Equivalent units				7,500		7,250		7,250		7,250		

	£	£	£	£	
Cost	4,500	2,900	2,175	5,075	14,650
per unit	0·6	0.4	0.3	0.7	2.0
Evaluation					
Opening stock	—	100	75	175	350
CPDP	3,900	2,600	1,950	4,550	13,000
Closing stock	600	200	150	350	1,300
	£4,500	£2,900	£2,175	£5,075	£14,650

It may have been observed that in both this example and in example 2 the columns for each element of cost incurred in the process were the same. This occurs because the stage of completion reached in each element of cost was the same. When this occurs, it is not really necessary to show each element of cost separately; they could be shown together in one column at a cost per unit of ($£0·40 + £0·30 + £0·70$) = $£1·40$. This would save a little time in preparation, but it is considered by the authors that it is better to adopt a standard layout such as that shown above and master it.

The process account for process 2 would be as follows:

Process 2

	£		£
WIP b/d	650	Finished goods	14,000
Process 1	4,500	WIP c/d	1,300
Direct materials	2,900		
Direct wages	2,175		
Production overheads	5,075		
	£15,300		£15,300
Balance b/d	1,300		

By-products

In the process of producing the main product it frequently occurs that materials or other products emerge which are of less value than the main product. These are the by-products, and even if subsequent processing enhances their value, the resulting profit will be less than that from the main product, otherwise, of course, the by-product would become the main product, and vice versa. A typical example of by-products is in an oil refinery, where the crude oil is processed and refined oil might be the main product, with sulphur, bitumen, and chemical fertiliser among the many by-products.

The accounting treatment of by-products depends on two main considerations, whether:

    (*a*) the by-product is of little value; or
    (*b*) the by-product is of considerable value.

Where the By-product is of Little Value

In this case it is usually considered uneconomic to incur the expense of calculating the price of each unit produced. It is usually very difficult to ascertain the costs of producing a by-product up to the separation point from the main product. Where this is so the amount realised on the sale of the by-product may be treated as a profit and shown in the profit and loss account. Alternatively, and this is considered to be better, the amount realised may be credited to the main product, thus reducing the cost of the product.

Where the By-product is of Considerable Value

Here it is important that costs of the by-product are as accurate as possible, owing to possible large amounts being involved. A separate account should be kept for each by-product, to which is debited the estimated cost up to separation point. Usually these costs are determined by estimating or averaging costs over a period, or alternatively, by comparison with the market value of the by-product. The main product account is credited with the amount realised on transfer of the by-product.

Specimen Question

In the manufacture of Mart during period 3, the following output is obtained from process 1.

Main product Mart   360 units.
By-product Marart   90 units.
Normal process loss is 10%.
500 units at £10 per unit were issued to the process.
Direct materials amounted to £1,900.
Direct labour amounted to £700.
Production overhead incurred £1,400.

Show the accounts in respect of process 1.

Answer

Process 1

Description: Period: No. 3
                                                                       Output: 360 units

	Units	Cost per unit	Amount		Units	Cost per unit	Amount
		£	£			£	£
Units introduced	500	10	5,000	Normal loss	50	—	—
Direct material			1,900	By-product a/c	90	20	1,800
Direct labour			700	Process 2–output			
Production overhead			1,400	transferred	360	20	7,200
	500		£9,000		500		£9,000

Process 2

	Units	Cost per unit	Amount		Units	Cost per unit	Amount
		£	£			£	£
Process 1—output	360	20	£7,200				

By-product

	Units	Cost per unit	Amount		Units	Cost per unit	Amount
		£	£			£	£
Process 1	90	20	£1,800				

NOTE

The cost per unit of the by-product and the main product in this simple example is calculated as follows.

Cost to separation point £9,000.
Normal combined output 450 units.
Therefore cost per unit is £20.

Alternatively,

$$\text{Cost of by-product} = \frac{90}{450} \times 9,000 = £1,800.$$

$$\text{Cost of main product} = \frac{360}{450} \times 9,000 = £7,200.$$

Where further processing of a by-product is required it is essential that a separate account should be kept for the by-product, in which can be recorded all further costs in addition to the pre-separation point costs.

Joint Products

In a process where two or more products are inevitably produced, and each one earns approximately the same profit as another, the products would be considered joint products. The main costing problem concerned with joint products is to determine the cost of each product before the separation point, i.e. before reaching the point at which each product becomes separately identifiable and remains distinct from the other joint product. A number of methods may be used to estimate the cost up to the point of separation, among which are the following.

1. *Market value at point of separation*

The market value of the joint products at the separation point is ascertained, and the total cost incurred at that point is allocated to the products in the ratio of these values.

2. *Market value after further processing*

This method is rather similar to the previous one, except that selling prices of the finished products are used as the basis for calculation.

3. *Market value after further processing less further processing costs*

This method is considered to be the most satisfactory.

Inter-process Profits

Inter-process profits are sometimes provided for by transferring output to later processes at cost plus a percentage, to cover profit. The purpose is intended to make each head of a process responsible for producing at a cost competitive with open-market prices, which naturally includes profit. The complications introduced by this procedure make it undesirable, if only for the reason that for balance sheet purposes the profit so introduced must be eliminated from the book values of process and finished stocks. Interested readers are referred to *Wheldon's Cost Accounting.* *

*Macdonald & Evans Ltd, 1984.

Examination Questions

1. What do you regard as the special features of process costs? To what classes of manufacture are they generally applied? (*RSA*)

2. A manufacturing firm has two departments. Department No. 1 produces a waste product for which, until recently, no method has been known whereby it could be utilised or made saleable otherwise than as waste. During the past year a secret process has been discovered by which Department No. 2 has been enabled to treat this waste and convert it into a valuable commodity.

How would you suggest that the waste supplied by Department No. 1 to Department No. 2 should be dealt with in the departmental cost accounts? (*CAA*)

3. You are asked to advise the directors of a firm whose factory operates through several processes as to the basis to be adopted for transferring the output from one process to the next. Prepare a report outlining the methods that are available and state which method you recommend. (*IAADP*)

4. How would you deal with (*a*) losses of raw materials in manufacturing and (*b*) storage losses of raw materials in the cost accounts of a chemical manufacturing company? (*CAA*)

5. Explain what is meant by the terms "by-products," "joint-products," and "scrap." Give a cost accounting treatment of the first-named item. (*LCCI*)

6. Discuss the treatment of by-products in the cost accounts when:

(*a*) the by-product has a considerable market value;

(*b*) the by-product is subjected to further processes before utilisation as the raw material of a new product;

(*c*) the by-product is unsaleable and expense is incurred in its disposal. (*CAA*)

7. Define: (*a*) joint products; (*b*) by-products; (*c*) scrap. Illustrate the different cost accounting procedures required. (*RSA*)

8. After the main operations of a soap factory have been performed the resultant products (known as "bases") are transferred to a Toilet Department, where further operations of drying, milling, perfume mixing, wrapping, stamping and boxing are necessary. Each of these operations has its own "work centre cost account" by means of which the costs of these particular centres are ascertained. But it is still necessary to absorb these operational costs into a "pack cost," which is used for various price-list procedures.

Describe generally the different methods of absorption that could be used. (*RSA*)

9. (a) A company produces joint products and by-products from a common process. Discuss the problems of cost ascertainment and allocation that arise and the methods that can be used to assign costs to products. Give an example of each.

(b) One of the joint products can be further processed or sold at split-off point. By means of a simple example show how differential analysis can be of assistance to decision-making in such cases.

(ICSA)

10. (a) The manufacture of product A, by the Alphega Processing Company Limited, is completed by means of three consecutive processes.

You are required to prepare, for the month of April using the following information:
   (i) the work-in-progress account for processes 1, 2 and 3; and
   (ii) the accounts for:
        abnormal loss;
        abnormal gain;
        finished goods stock.

During April the input to process 1 of basic raw material was 5,000 units at a cost of £0·2 per unit. Total production overhead of £3,200 was charged to the costs of each process for the month as a percentage of the direct wages incurred. There were no opening or closing work-in-progress stocks. There were however in the finished goods stock the following balances:

	£
1st April	1,200
30th April	1,500

Information for the month for the individual processes was as follows:

	Process 1	Process 2	Process 3
Normal loss, as percentage of input	5	10	5
Output, in units	4,700	4,300	4,050
	£	£	£
Scrap value, per unit	0·10	0·50	0·60
Additional direct materials consumed	700	800	1,300
Direct wages incurred	300	500	800
Direct expenses incurred	275	191	256

(b) Discuss briefly the principles to be observed and the various bases that are available for evaluating work-in-progress stock for balance sheet purposes.

(ICMA)

11. In the manufacture of product N raw material is put into process at the start of process 1. The output of this process is

transferred to process 2, the output of process 2 is transferred to process 3 where product N is completed ready to be sold.

Production and cost data for the four weeks ended 2nd April are as follows:

Process 1
Work in process at 7th March:
Raw material, 800 units costing £26 per unit.
Labour and overhead, 800 units, 25% completed which had cost £1,600.
Input:
Labour and overhead, £4,800.
Output transferred, 800 units.

Process 2
Input:
Labour and overhead, £4,560
Output transferred, 600 units
Work in process at 2nd April:
200 units, 80% completed.

Process 3
Work in process at 7th March:
400 units, 50% completed, which had cost of:
transferred cost of £16,000 and a labour and overhead cost of £800.
Input:
Labour and overhead, £3,040
Output transferred, 900 units
Work in process at 2nd April:
100 units, 60% completed.

You are required to prepare the accounts for each of the processes 1, 2 and 3 for the four weeks ended 2nd April to show:

(*a*) the unit cost;

(*b*) the value of work in process in each process at 2nd April;

(*c*) the total cost of production transferred to finished goods stock for the four weeks.   (*RSA*)

12. (*a*) Distinguish between job costing and process costing.

(*b*) Explain how you would treat the following items in the accounts of a process costing system:

(*i*) waste

(*ii*) scrap

(*c*) A chemical is produced by passing a basic ingredient through four processes, during each of which direct materials are added.

From the information given below for the month of March, you are required to prepare a statement in which each element of cost is analysed and the output evaluated, and to show the accounts of process 3 and abnormal loss.

Data for process 3 include:

Work in process:

	Opening stock	Closing stock
Units	400	1,000
Degree of completion	%	%
Material X	80	50
Material Y	80	45
Labour	50	30
Overhead	40	25

Costs incurred during the period:

		£
Transfer from process 2	5,400 units	6,240
Material X		2,862
Material Y		944
Labour		468
Overhead		1,398

Transfer to process 4 during the period: 4,550 units
Rejections during the period:

Normal	200 units
Abnormal	50 units

Units rejected had reached the following stages:

	%
Material X	80
Material Y	80
Labour	60
Overhead	40

Rejected units are considered as waste.
The cost per unit in February and March was the same.   (*ICMA*)

13. (*a*) A chemical, Exalete, passes through processes A and B before completion. In process B, a by-product Exaletent is produced which, after further processing in process C, is sold at a profit of 16⅔% of selling price.

You are required, from the data given for the month of April, to prepare accounts for:

(*i*) processes A, B and C;
(*ii*) abnormal loss;
(*iii*) abnormal gain.

	Process		
	A	B	C
Output in units	4,200	3,800	100
Normal loss in process:			
% of input	20	5	—
	£	£	£
Scrap value of any loss in process, per unit	1·5	5	—
Costs:			
Direct materials introduced (5,000 units)	30,000	—	—
Direct materials added	10,000	3,100	100
Direct wages incurred at £3 per hour	12,000	14,700	300
Direct expenses	7,500	1,170	—

Production overhead for the month, £72,000, is absorbed by a labour hour rate.

(b) Define and explain briefly the accounting treatment of:
(i) by-products;
(ii) joint products. (*ICMA*)

Chapter 18

Marginal Costing

Introduction

THIS subject is linked with that of economics, and is becoming increasingly important to all manufacturers, who may be faced with keen competition both at home and abroad.

It is not really a system of cost accounting as, for example, is job costing or process costing; rather it is a technique of presenting data to management in a way which is different from the familiar absorption costing. It may be recalled that in the previous chapter the absorption of overheads was discussed, where the appropriate cost is added to the prime cost of a product or service; this is called absorption costing or total costing. This method has been in use since the beginning of this century. However in 1936 Jonathan E. Harris challenged the credibility of absorbing overheads, and the proposed alternative system of marginal costing was introduced.

The difference between absorption costing and marginal costing is essentially one of the treatment of overheads. In an absorption costing system, overheads are classified as production, administration and selling and distribution overheads, and these overheads are absorbed into product costs according to a variety of methods discussed previously. However, with marginal costing, the overheads are classified as fixed or variable, the variable costs being charged directly to the product, while the fixed costs are charged against the total profit of the company for the specific period. Consequently it is not possible to calculate the total cost of a product, or the profit of a product. However, and this is considered by many accountants to be more important, it is possible to ascertain the marginal cost of manufacturing a product, and what it contributes towards the total fixed overheads and profit of a company.

The difference in the manner of presentation is founded on a consideration of the way various items of expense behave as and when production rises and falls.

241

Example

A company is making felt hats. In year 1 its production is 200,000, and in year 2 production rises to 250,000. In general terms the nature of the changes in income and expenditure which are likely to take place is as follows.

Sales. Provided the additional production is sold, and not put into stock, and provided the prices charged remain the same, the total sales value will increase by reason of the increased volume of sales.

Direct materials. As production increases, so is there a likelihood that larger purchases can be made at improved prices. Although the total cost of direct materials will increase, it will not do so in strict proportion to the larger volume of production.

Direct wages. In order to achieve the greater volume of production, rates of pay may have to be increased to improve productivity. In this case therefore, the total labour cost will grow larger:

(*a*) by reason of increased volume of work;
(*b*) by reason of increased rates of pay.

Overhead. Some items of overhead expense will vary with increased production, but some will remain unchanged. Thus, electrical power for machines varies with the operating times of the machines, but depreciation, when charged on an annual basis, will not vary, whether production is high or low, always provided that new machines are not introduced.

Fixed and Variable Overhead

Of particular interest and importance in marginal costing is the separation of overhead into its fixed and variable elements. This is not easily done, except by mathematics, and first attempts by simpler methods must be checked in the light of experience.

Example

In year 1 when the output was 10,000 units the amount of expense incurred was £5,600. In year 2, when the output increased to 12,000, the expense incurred also rose to £6,400.

We may hazard a guess that the change of expense is due to a change in the variable costs, but we shall check to make sure that known "fixed" costs have not changed. Then we shall make the following analysis.

$$\frac{\text{Change in expense level}}{\text{Change in output}} = \frac{£800}{2,000} = £0\cdot4$$

Assuming that 0·4 is the unit cost of change due to variable costs, we have

Year	Total £	Fixed £	Variable £
1	5,600	1,600	$10,000 \times 0·4 = 4,000$
2	6,400	1,600	$12,000 \times 0·4 = 4,800$

The advantage of making this separation between fixed and variable overhead can be seen quite clearly in the following comparison:

Absorption costing	Product A £	Product B £	Total £
Sales	50,000	80,000	130,000
Direct materials	15,000	20,000	35,000
Direct wages	10,000	30,000	40,000
Overhead, added by a blanket rate of 100% on wages	10,000	30,000	40,000
	35,000	80,000	115,000
Profit	£15,000	—	£15,000

Marginal costing			
Sales	50,000	80,000	130,000
Direct materials	15,000	20,000	35,000
Direct wages	10,000	30,000	40,000
Variable overhead	6,000	19,000	25,000
Marginal cost	31,000	69,000	100,000
Contribution = Sales − Variable cost	£19,000	£11,000	30,000
Fixed overhead			15,000
Profit			£15,000

By using the conventional method of presentation, it would appear that product B makes no profit at all. If on those grounds we ceased to make it, what would be the position? The marginal method shows very clearly what it would be. The contribution of £11,000 which product B makes towards the fixed overhead and profit would be entirely lost. Instead of making a profit of £15,000 we should make only £4,000. The fixed overhead of £15,000 would still be incurred, and would have to be covered solely by product A's contribution.

The behaviour of costs is important in decision making, and this is particularly true in a marginal costing system. It was mentioned above that overheads are classified as fixed or variable, these costs being defined in the ICMA *Terminology* thus.

(*a*) *Fixed overhead cost* — "The cost which accrues in relation to the passage of time and which, within certain output and turnover limits, tends to be unaffected by fluctuations in the levels of activity (output or turnover). Examples are rent, rates, insurance and executive salaries. Other terms include period costs, and policy costs."

(*b*) *Variable overhead cost* — "Overhead cost which tends to vary with changes in the level of activity."

A graphical illustration (see Fig. 35) of the behaviour of these costs will demonstrate the paradox of fixed and variable costs: a fixed cost is fixed in total but is variable per unit, while a variable cost is variable in total but fixed per unit.

Thus it can be seen from the graphs in Fig. 35 that, at least in the short run, it is assumed that fixed costs remain fixed while variable costs increase with volume. With regard to the unit cost graphs, the larger the increase in volume the smaller is the fixed cost per unit, while the variable cost per unit is constant over all volumes, at least in the short term.

In marginal costing systems it is essential to analyse costs into fixed and variable categories, but this is not always an easy task. Some costs may be classified as semi-variable, i.e. they have a fixed element and a variable element. For example, a salesman may be paid a salary plus a commission on sales. It is common practice to ascertain the fixed element and include it in the fixed overheads for the period, and include the variable element in the variable overheads.

There is a variety of techniques of analysing semi-variable costs; regression analysis is discussed in some detail in *Managerial Accounting and Finance.*[*] However, two simple methods are illustrated here, one mathematical and one graphical.

---

[*]*Managerial Accounting and Finance,* 4th edition, J. L. Brown and L. R. Howard, Macdonald & Evans Ltd, 1982.

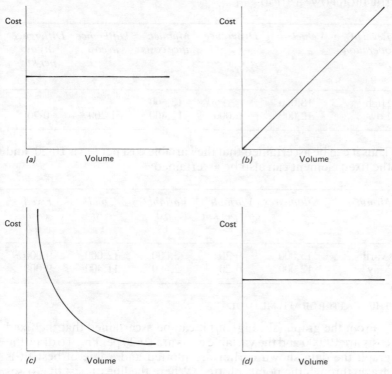

FIG. 35.—*Fixed and variable costs*

(*a*) Total cost, fixed. (*b*) Total cost, variable. (*c*) Unit cost, fixed. (*d*) Unit cost, variable

Example

Date	Vehicle-km	Maintenance costs £
April	15,000	12,000
May	12,000	11,400
June	14,000	11,800
July	16,000	12,200
August	18,000	12,600
September	17,000	12,400
	92,000	£72,400

THE HIGH/LOW METHOD

Level of operation	Vehicle-km	Difference	Mainten-ance costs £	Difference in cost £	Difference in cost per km £
High	18,000		12,600		
Low	12,000	6,000	11,400	1,200	0·20

Thus it can be ascertained that the variable cost per km is £0·20, and the fixed element can also be ascertained:

Month	Kilometres	Variable cost per km £	Variable cost £	Total cost £	Fixed cost £
April	15,000	0·20	3,000	12,000	9,000
May	12,000	0·20	2,400	11,400	9,000

THE SCATTERGRAPH METHOD

From the graph (*see* Fig. 36) it can be ascertained that the fixed costs are £9,000 and the variable costs are £0·20 per km. To draw the graph the data shown earlier are plotted and a line of best fit is drawn through the points plotted. Where the line of best fit crosses the axis is the point which determines the amount of fixed cost, while the slope of the line determines the behaviour of the variable costs above the crudely-estimated fixed costs.

The Marginal Equation

This equation is nothing more than a restatement in general terms of the illustration given above.

$$\text{Sales} - \text{Variable costs} = \text{Fixed overhead} + \text{Profit}$$
$$S - V = F + P$$

The expression $S - V$ is termed the "contribution" and it represents the contribution of a product or service towards the fixed overheads and profit of the organisation. A ratio has been developed from the use of contribution analysis and while it is often referred to as the P/V ratio (profit/volume ratio) it is now correctly referred to as the C/S% (contribution/sales percentage).

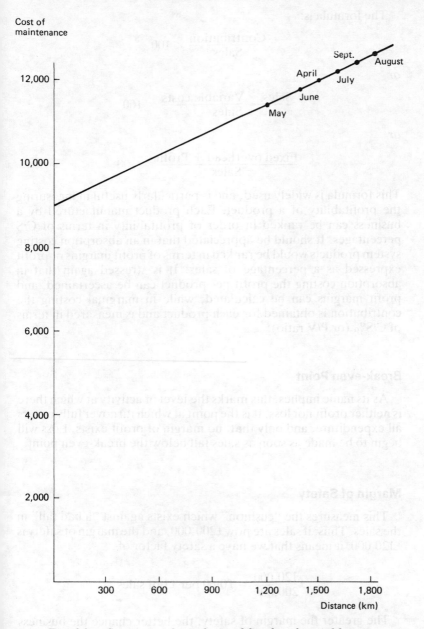

FIG. 36.—*Scattergraph analysis of fixed and variable costs*

The formula is:

$$\frac{\text{Contribution}}{\text{Sales}} \times 100$$

or

$$\frac{\text{Sales} - \text{Variable costs}}{\text{Sales}} \times 100$$

or

$$\frac{\text{Fixed overhead} + \text{Profit}}{\text{Sales}} \times 100$$

This formula is widely used, and is particularly useful in measuring the profitability of a product. Each product manufactured by a business can be ranked in order of profitability in terms of C/S percentages. It should be appreciated that in an absorption costing system products would be ranked in terms of profit margins or profit expressed as a percentage of sales. It is stressed again that in absorption costing the profit per product can be ascertained, and profit margins can be calculated, while in marginal costing the contribution is obtained for each product and is measured in terms of C/S% (or P/V ratio).

Break-even Point

As its name implies, this marks the level of activity at which there is neither profit nor loss. It is the point at which turnover fully covers all expenditure, and only that: no margin of profit exists. Loss will begin to be made as soon as sales fall below the break-even point.

Margin of Safety

This measures the "cushion" which exists against "a bad fall" in the sales. Thus, if sales are now £200,000, and the margin of safety is £120,000, it means that we have a safety factor of

$$£\frac{120,000}{200,000} = £0.60 \text{ per £1 of sales}$$

The greater the margin of safety, the better chance the business has of survival in times of depression. A good margin of safety would usually indicate relatively low fixed overheads.

Angle of Incidence

This shows the rate of the increase in profit, once the break-even point has been reached. The wider the angle, the greater is the rate of profit earning as sales increase. This is of considerable importance in times of expansion in the market. In general, a wide

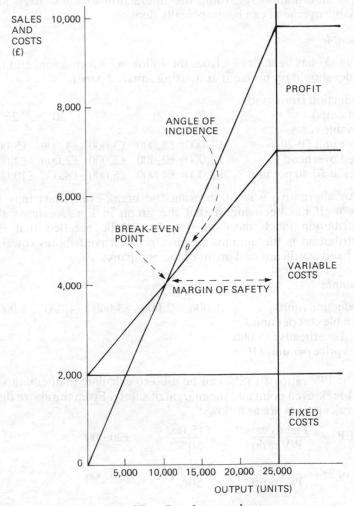

FIG. 37.—*Break-even chart*

The usual form of break-even chart, showing in this case a break-even point at £4,000 sales, and what appears to be a healthy position for the firm.

angle would suggest a low variable cost per unit of product. Once the fixed overheads have been absorbed, a good profit margin is obtained.

Break-even Charts

The information regarding the interaction of sales, fixed and variable overhead can be graphically depicted.

Example

Fig. 37 has been drawn from the following information, and the reader should try his hand at it, using squared paper.

Production (thousands of units)	5	10	15	20	25
Variable costs per unit £0·20	£1,000	£2,000	£3,000	£4,000	£5,000
Fixed overhead	£2,000	£2,000	£2,000	£2,000	£2,000
Sales at £0·40 per unit	£2,000	£4,000	£6,000	£8,000	£10,000

An alternative way of showing the break-even chart may be shown. It has been found that the graph in Fig. 38 shows the contribution much more clearly. It will be recalled that the contribution is the amount which a product contributes towards the fixed overheads and profit of the company.

Example

Production (units)	1,000	2,000	3,000	4,000	5,000

Variable cost per unit £5
Fixed overheads £15,000
Sales price per unit £10

The P/V ratio or C/S% can be used to calculate mathematically the break-even point and the margin of safety. From the above data the calculations are as follows:

$$\text{BEP} \quad \frac{\text{Fixed costs}}{\text{P/V ratio}} = \frac{£15,000}{50\%} = \underline{£30,000}$$

$$\text{M of S} \quad \frac{\text{Profit}}{\text{P/V ratio}} = \frac{£10,000}{50\%} = \underline{£20,000}$$

Note: P/V ratio or C/S% $= \dfrac{C}{S} \times 100$

$$= \frac{25,000}{50,000} \times 100 = 50\%$$

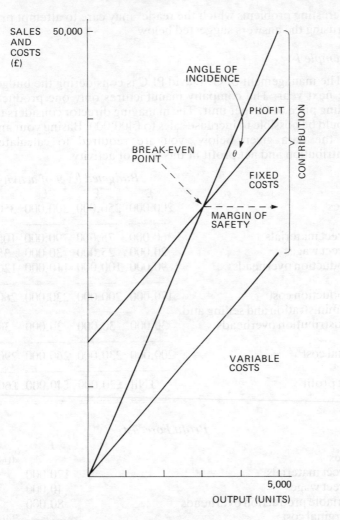

FIG. 38.—*Break-even chart*

The graph shows that the break-even point occurs at a sales volume of £30,000 and 3,000 units, and that the margin of safety is £20,000.

Applications of Marginal Costing

Two examples follow which are typical of examination questions in which an appreciation of marginal costing is required. They require a knowledge of basic concepts of marginal costing and are interesting problems which the reader may care to attempt prior to perusing the answers suggested below.

Example 1

The management of G. David PLC is considering the budget for the next year. The company manufactures only one product at a selling price of £10 per unit. The managing director considers that it should be possible to increase sales to £400,000. Basing your answer on the data given below, you are required to calculate the contribution and net profit at this level of activity.

	Budgeted level of activity			
	£	£	£	£
Sales	200,000	250,000	300,000	350,000
Direct materials	60,000	75,000	90,000	105,000
Direct wages	20,000	25,000	30,000	35,000
Production overheads	90,000	100,000	110,000	120,000
Production cost	170,000	200,000	230,000	260,000
Administration and selling and distribution overheads	30,000	30,000	30,000	30,000
Total cost	200,000	230,000	260,000	290,000
Net profit	£Nil	£20,000	£40,000	£60,000

Profit Forecast

	£	£
Sales		400,000
Direct materials	120,000	
Direct wages	40,000	
Variable production overheads	80,000	
Marginal cost		240,000
Contribution		160,000
Fixed overheads:		
Production	50,000	
Administration, selling	30,000	
		80,000
Net profit		£80,000

NOTE

Production overheads. You were required to calculate the contribution, and so this problem requires a marginal costing approach. It is therefore necessary to analyse production overheads into their fixed and variable element, so as to determine the marginal cost. This is calculated as follows:

Change in sales at each level of activity: 5,000 units
Change in production overheads at each level: £10,000

Therefore the variable element of production overhead must be £2 per unit.

Therefore the fixed element must be £50,000.

This can be checked as follows. Take, for example, sales of £300,000.

	£	£
Sales, 30,000 at £10		300,000
Direct materials	90,000	
Direct wages	30,000	
Variable production overheads	60,000	
		180,000
		120,000
Fixed overheads:		
Production	50,000	
Administration, selling	30,000	
		80,000
		£40,000

Example 2

The results of trading for year 1 of S. Paul PLC are as shown below. Owing to the unsatisfactory results, management decided to reorganise production methods and to increase the selling price of their product by 25%. These changes were effected from January 1 of year 2, the results for which year are also shown below. You are asked to analyse the change in contribution, so as to show the amount resulting from:

(a) the increase in sales price;
(b) the increase in sales volume;
(c) the decrease in production cost.

Profit and Loss Statement

	Year 1 £	Year 2 £
Sales	200,000	300,000
Cost of production	120,000	130,000
Contribution	80,000	170,000
Fixed overheads	100,000	120,000
Net profit	£(20,000)	£50,000

	£
Contribution in Year 2	170,000
Contribution in Year 1	80,000
Change in contribution	£90,000

Analysis of change in contribution

	£
(a) Increase in sales price	60,000
(b) Increase in sales volume	16,000
(c) Decrease in production costs	14,000
Change in contribution	£90,000

NOTES

1. The selling price is increased in year 2 by 25%, so one cannot compare the sales value for the two years, unless one converts the sales value of one year to a comparable value of the other year. It is probably easier to use the first year as a base and convert the second year's sales to the first year's prices. This is a similar exercise to the use of index numbers in statistics.

	£
Sales value of year 2 sales at year 1 price	240,000
Sales value of year 1 sales at year 1 price	200,000
Increase in sales volume	£40,000

(To convert year 2 sales to year 1 price is as follows: price increase was $1/4$; $4/5 \times 300,000 = £240,000$)

	£
Increase in sales volume	40,000
Marginal cost 60%	24,000
Contribution due to sales volume	£16,000

2.

	£
Sales value of year 2 sales at year 2 price	300,000
Sales value of year 2 sales at year 1 price	240,000
Contribution due to sales price	£60,000

3. Sales volume change as shown in (1) above was £40,000
   Sales in year 1 were £200,000
   The % change in volume was therefore 20%

Marginal cost in year 1 was	120,000
Marginal cost in year 2 should have been increased by 20%	144,000
Cost increase should have been	24,000
Cost increase was (£130,000 − £120,000)	10,000
Contribution due to change in production cost	£14,000

Business Decision Taking

The technique of marginal costing enables us to analyse a given situation, and may be of valuable assistance in formulating decisions such as:

(a) which product is the most or the least profitable;
(b) the effect of changing the selling price of a product;
(c) the sales required to earn a given profit;
(d) the profit which will be earned for a given volume of sales;
(e) which, of two machines, is the best to use from the point of view of profitability.

In the case of (e) we find that contribution/sales is not the only important relationship we can apply.

Key Factor or Limiting Factor

Sales is often the limiting factor in any situation, that is to say, the quantity of output is limited by the sales we can make. In other cases the availability of material or labour or machines is a limiting factor, and so in considering a case such as (e) above, we must seek for the key or limiting factor, and compare contribution/key factor for each machine. This might conceivably be the operating time of one machine as against that required by the other, so that contribution/ machine hours would give the contribution per machine hour. Similarly the contribution/labour hours would give the contribution per labour hour.

Example

The costs of manufacturing products Paulart and Jerart are as shown below:

| | Paulart | Jerart |
	£	£
Direct materials	20	48
Direct wages at £4 per hour	4	16
Overhead: variable	6	4
fixed	5	10
Total cost	35	78
Net profit	5	22
Sales price	£40	£100

Advise management on which product the company should concentrate its marketing activity, assuming that there is a shortage of labour and that total budgeted wages cost is £120,000 pa.

Using an absorption costing approach, it would appear that Jerart is a more profitable one than Paulart, with a profit of £22 as compared with £5, or with a 22% profit on sales as compared with a 12½% profit on sales.

Using a marginal costing approach, the contribution would be calculated as follows:

	Paulart		Jerart	
	£	£	£	£
Sales price		40		100
Direct materials	20		48	
Direct wages	4		16	
Variable overhead	6		4	
Marginal cost		30		68
Contribution		£10		£32
P/V ratio, $\dfrac{\text{Contribution}}{\text{Sales}} \times 100$		25%		32%
Contribution/Key factor		250%		200%
Contribution pa		£300,000		£240,000

NOTES

1. P/V ratios $\qquad\qquad \dfrac{10}{40} \times 100 \qquad \dfrac{32}{100} \times 100$

2. Contribution/Key factor $\qquad \dfrac{10}{4} \times 100 \qquad \dfrac{32}{16} \times 100$

3. Contribution pa $\qquad$ £120,000 × 250% £120,000 × 200%

This statement shows that with a marginal costing approach, the contribution of Jerart is £32 while that of Paulart is only £10. In terms of P/V ratios, Jerart shows 32% against 25% for Paulart. However the essential criterion is that of contribution/key factor, and, as can be seen above, it is 250% for Paulart and 200% for Jerart. Hence in management decision-making, the obvious choice would be Paulart.

To check this solution, let us assume that the key factor is direct wages and that the budgeted labour for a year is 30,000 hours at £4 per hour. This would mean that either 30,000 units of Paulart or 7,500 units of Jerart could be manufactured. Contribution at these levels of activity would be £300,000 (30,000 × £10) or £240,000 (7,500 × £32). Hence it would be profitable to concentrate on Paulart.

For a fuller consideration of the subject of marginal costing, the student is referred to *Managerial Accounting and Finance*.*

---

* *Managerial Accounting and Finance*, 4th edition, J. L. Brown and L. R. Howard, Macdonald & Evans, 1982.

Examination Questions

1. "The three factors of price, cost, and volume are fundamental to virtually every business activity, every business decision." Discuss this statement, explaining the inter-relation of the factors named.   (CAA)

2. Explain the significance of "break-even point." Illustrate your answer with a suitable chart, mentioning the conclusions which may be drawn from it.   (SCCA)

3. A company with many products finds that although the average profit on cost over all products is 20%, the profit on product "Z" is only 5%. The total demand exceeds supply. What facts would you take into account in reporting to the Board of Directors on the advisability or otherwise of discontinuing the product "Z"?   (SCCA)

4. In industry no costs remain static, and yet in determining comparatively short-term budgets we refer to a substantial portion of costs as being "fixed." Why is it reasonable to do this? (SCCA)

5. Assuming that the break-even point for a company occurs at the high level of 90% of its maximum possible output and that selling prices are competitive, what is the problem to be faced and what remedies are indicated?   (SCCA)

6. "Volume of Production has a significant effect on costs per unit of production." Discuss this statement.   (SCCA)

7. What is marginal costing?
Contrast its value to management when the business is working to
(a) normal capacity, and
(b) less than normal capacity.   (ACA)

8. Owing to a shortage of orders in certain industries at the present time, considerable competition is arising and prices quoted are becoming very keen. Some of the quotations appear to be below cost. With regard to these conditions you are asked what principles should be followed to ensure that in endeavouring to maintain prices at a level which covers cost plus a reasonable profit, the loss arising out of reduced output through orders lost in the face of this competition is not greater than it would have been if estimates had been tendered and orders secured at lower prices. What advice would you give?   (CAA)

9. Discuss the practical disadvantages which may be experienced in basing the export prices of goods on a system of marginal costing.   (SCCA)

10. (a) Give concise definitions of (i) fixed cost; (ii) variable cost; and (iii) contribution.

(b) It is estimated that the output of 1,000 units would cost £10,000 and that 1,100 units would cost £10,700.

(*i*)   What would be the estimated cost of 990 units?
(*ii*) What is the amount of fixed cost?
(*iii*) Taking the unit selling price as £11, calculate the break-even point.   (*SCCA*)

11. Report to Management on the relative profitability of the two products A and B:

	Production cost per unit	
	Product A	Product B
	(output 200	(output 100
	per week)	per week)
	£	£
Materials	20	15
Wages	10	20
Fixed overhead	35	10
Variable overhead	15	20
	—	—
	80	65
Gross profit	20	35
	—	—
	£100	£100

Explain the variations disclosed by your statement.   (*SCCA*)

12. A summary statement of the trading results of a manufacturing company for the year ended 31st March are given below:

	£	£
Cost of goods sold:		
direct materials	20,040	
direct labour	8,920	
	———	28,960
production overhead:		
variable	2,100	
fixed	13,200	
	———	15,300
Other costs:		
variable	3,800	
fixed	3,600	
	———	7,400
Total cost		51,660
Profit		6,440
Sales		£58,100

Number of units made and sold   830

You are required to:

(a) draw a break-even chart and to state the number of units to be sold to break-even;

(b) state the profit or the loss if the number of units sold were:

(i) 500;

(ii) 900;

(c) calculate the number of units to be sold to make a profit of £12,600 per annum.   (RSA)

13. The following information has been extracted from the accounts of G Limited, who makes a single product, for the year ended 31st March 19–2:

	£	£
Sales 50,000 units		1,200,000
Cost of goods made and delivered to finished goods stock 46,000 units:		
Variable	414,000	
Fixed	322,000	
		736,000
Cost of selling and distribution		
Variable	100,000	
Fixed	125,000	
		225,000

Valuation of units in finished goods stock at both 1st April 19–1 and 31st March 19–2 are to be based on the following information:

	£
Costs: Variable	9·00
Fixed	7·00

At 1st April 19–1 there were 7,500 units in finished goods stock.

You are required to:

(a) prepare:

(i) a statement showing the profit on a marginal costing basis;

(ii) a statement showing the profit on an absorption costing basis;

(b) state, with supporting figures, the reason for any difference of profit shown in the two statements you have prepared in answer to (a) above.   (RSA)

14. Two businesses Y Ltd. and Z Ltd. sell the same type of product in the same type of market.

Their budgeted profit and loss accounts for a month are as follows

	£	Y Ltd. £	£	Z Ltd. £
Sales		150,000		150,000
Less				
Variable costs	120,000		100,000	
Fixed costs	15,000		35,000	
		135,000		135,000
Budgeted net profit		£15,000		£15,000

You are required to:
(*a*) calculate the break-even point of each business;
(*b*) calculate the sales volume at which each of the businesses will earn £5,000 profit;
(*c*) state which business is likely to earn greater profits in conditions of:
(*i*) heavy demand for the product;
(*ii*) low demand for the product;
and briefly give your reasons. (*ICMA*)
15. The summarised trading and profit and loss accounts of a company are as follows:

Year ending December 31	19–1 £	19–2 £
Sales	125,000	225,000
Cost of production	100,000	120,000
Gross profit	25,000	105,000
General overheads	55,000	60,000
Net profit or loss	£(30,000)	£45,000

In view of the adverse results in 19–1 the selling prices of all the company's products were increased by 25% as from January 1 19–2 and the production methods were reorganised.

You are required to compute how much of the increase in gross profit may be said to result from: (*a*) increase in selling price; (*b*) increase in volume (as distinct from value), of sales; and (*c*) decrease in production costs. (*LCCI*)

Chapter 19

Uniform Costing

UNIFORM costing is not a system of costing which is different from those discussed in Chapters 14 to 17; it is a system which can be applied in connection with one or other of those systems. The chief characteristic of uniform costing is that there is uniformity of application of principles, e.g. allocation and recovery of overheads and determining cost and selling prices; this is found to be advantageous for comparing efficiencies and as a means of controlling costs in different undertakings. In this way, reliable cost comparisons between similar production units may be made.

Applications of Uniform Costing

Uniform costing may be introduced in two different types of organisation.

(a) *A business which operates numerous factories, each of which is controlled by the main firm.* If the products manufactured by each factory are identical, then the costs per unit can be readily compared. However, if products are not comparable, then it may be possible to compare costs of similar operations, processes, or services.

(b) *A trade association which advises its members, each of which may operate quite independently of the other.* A number of trade associations have been formed to help member firms with costing problems; this is done by arranging to exchange costs between the firms concerned. In such cases the term used is "inter-firm comparisons" rather than "uniform costing".

It was mentioned in *Target,* December 1956, that:

Forty years ago, the British Federation of Master Printers realised the advantage of a uniform costing system which could be adopted throughout the industry. It had to be a system sufficiently simple, accurate and flexible to meet the requirements of the varying types of business which go to make up the printing industry. It had to embrace a number of basic principles. The fundamentals are much the same now as they were then, only the emphasis has changed. What started out as

262

simply a method of cost finding has been widened to embrace both the control and the reduction of costs.

A great many firms have used the system throughout a period of widely changing conditions, and today it is used by most of the Federation's 5,000 members. Many printers overseas have either adopted it or modelled their own system on it.

The use of uniform costing methods does not mean that costs in different businesses will be the same. It does mean, however, that a comparison of the costs of different firms will be logical if they have been completed on similar lines. Uniform costing makes possible the exchange or comparison of cost figures prepared on a similar basis in each business, and this provides a means of improving efficiency throughout the industry. By profiting from the experience of the most efficient firms, others are able to reduce costs. It facilitates investigations into specific cost problems of the industry.

Where a system of inter-firm comparison is adopted there is a voluntary exchange of information regarding such matters as performances, prices, costs, and profits. Usually the information is collected from the firms concerned by a third party, e.g. a trade association cost department; it is then recorded under code numbers given to each of the participants, and then final results are presented in a way which offers members the most useful information. One of the purposes of this system is to render competition less destructive, by ensuring that all the members know what is included in cost and how to arrive at it. Another purpose is to standardise a method of collecting figures in order to fix selling prices on a basis acceptable to those engaged in the industry.

Requirements of Uniform Costing

Before a system of uniform costing can be adopted it will be necessary to determine what type of costing is desirable for that industry, e.g. job or process costing. When this has been determined it will then be necessary to suggest a procedure to be adopted in relation to the following.

(a) The basis for the apportionment and allocation of overhead.

(b) The departments or production centres to be used for analysis and comparison of costs.

(c) What items shall be regarded as production, as distinct from administration overhead.

(d) How overheads shall be recovered.

(e) How expenses in connection with the buying, storing, handling, and issuing of stores materials shall be treated.

(*f*) What rates of depreciation shall be applied to plant and machinery.

(*g*) Whether interest on capital is to be included in cost, and if so, how and on what basis.

(*h*) What rental charge is to be made for the building, if freehold or leasehold.

(*i*) How service departmental costs shall be computed.

(*j*) The demarcation between direct and indirect wages.

The Purposes and Value of Uniform Costing

In a group of amalgamated manufacturers, or in the case of a firm controlling a number of factories, actual detailed costs can be compared, standard costs may be set up, and controls by comparisons secured. The most economical and suitable distribution of orders received can be made. Actual and relative efficiencies can be compared, and through effective management, costs may be reduced.

Where manufacturers are only associated, or where the system is organised by a manufacturer's federation, less precise cost comparisons may be provided, as, for example:

(*a*) the cost value of production on some common basis, e.g. per £ of direct wages, or other factor;

(*b*) the ratio of indirect labour to direct labour, say by processes;

(*c*) the number of plant-hours worked, and the output per hour for similar operations;

(*d*) the ratio of each kind of expense to prime cost;

(*e*) an index-number as a guide to the degree of utilisation of capacity—by this means, suitable comparison can be made.

It will be obvious that greater advantage is obtained by those actually controlling a group of factories than by individual manufacturers operating a system organised for their particular industry, owing to the reluctance of some manufacturers to disclose pertinent facts to competitors.

The British Institute of Management has for some time operated a department for carrying out inter-firm comparisons, and information of great value to the participants has come to light. Much more of this kind of interchange of information is done in the USA than in Great Britain, and it has not been found to harm the interests of those taking part. On the contrary, "spreading the light" has benefited the industry. This topic is discussed more fully in *Managerial Accounting and Finance.* *

Examination Questions

1. A group of manufacturers of a specific type of product decide to consider the formulation of a uniform system of costing. Mention the main points and difficulties which are likely to arise.   (*CAA*)

2. What is meant by "uniform costing"? What advantages would you expect from its adoption in an industry?   (*AIA*)

3. Certain industries have evolved a uniform system of costing for adoption by all firms in the industry. What are the requirements for uniform costing and what are the advantages and disadvantages of such a system?   (*IAADP*)

4. A holding company controls three factories, all of which make similar products. It is desired to introduce a system of uniform costing in the three factories. Describe briefly the principles on which you would base the system you would propose to install.
   (*RSA*)

5. State concisely your opinion as to the possibility of standardising costing systems in particular industries. Give reasons showing whether it is or is not desirable to attempt this task.   (*AIA*)

6. State as fully as possible what you consider are the advantages and disadvantages of uniform costing to: (*a*) an individual firm; (*b*) an industry; (*c*) the public.   (*ICMA*)

7. State the essential principles of a uniform costing system and the advantages which may be derived therefrom, applied:

   (*a*) to a large undertaking controlling subsidiaries;

   (*b*) to a whole industry.   (*ICMA*)

8. A trade association proposes to introduce a system of uniform costing and to publish periodical reports on costs, based on information supplied by members.

List three important features concerning overheads which you consider the uniform costing system should include, and give a brief justification for your inclusion of each feature.   (*CAA*)

9. Design a form of Cost Statement suitable for a number of concerns engaged in the manufacture of the same standard product, adding a note as to the factors which you would consider in order to

---

* *Managerial Accounting and Finance*, 4th edition, J. L. Brown and L. R. Howard, Macdonald & Evans Ltd, 1982.

ensure that the results of the various concerns are strictly comparable. (*CAA*)

10. What steps would you take to establish a system of uniform costing for fixing price standards in an industry controlled by a combine? (*ICMA*)

11. The Chief Accountant of a group of companies in the same industry wishes to introduce uniformity of costing methods—and you are charged with investigating this objective. Tabulate the fundamental costing principles which need agreement, and in respect of each give an example. (*ICMA*)

12. Set out (in skeleton form) the advantages that can accrue from the adoption of a scheme of Uniform Costing by:

(*a*) a concern with a number of associated or wholly owned subsidiary companies;

(*b*) individual concerns in the same class of industry. (*RSA*)

Chapter 20

Budgetary Control

Introduction

Definitions of Budgets and Budgetary Control

THE Institute of Cost and Management Accountants' *Terminology* gives the following definitions.

A Budget

> A plan quantified in monetary terms and approved prior to a defined period of time, usually showing planned income to be generated and for expenditure to be incurred during that period, and the capital to be employed to attain a given objective.

Budgetary Control

> The establishment of budgets relating the responsibilities of executives to the requirements of a policy and the continuous comparison of actual with budgeted results, either to secure by individual action the objective of that policy or to provide a basis for its revision.

Today, modern management must plan its operations with great care. Managers must consider possible developments and conditions which are likely to affect their sphere of business. In addition to planning ahead, procedures must be introduced which will enable management to compare actual results with expected results, so that any differences can be investigated without delay, and appropriate action taken.

The principles involved in budgeting have been likened to those adopted by the captain of a ship. Before setting out on a voyage he studies the course, ascertains local conditions, tides, hazards, etc. He then plans his route and sails. During the journey he must record details of progress and frequently check actual progress with that planned, making allowances for any unexpected hazards but trying to keep to his plan. When the journey is completed he can assess his success, which will be a valuable contribution to future voyages.

This analogy is similar to the steps taken in preparing a budget. These steps may be briefly stated as follows.

(*a*) Prepare a plan which it is possible to attain, considering all pertinent factors.

(*b*) Record actual achievements.

(*c*) Compare regularly actual results with those planned.

(*d*) Act without delay to initiate investigations into differences and, when required, take necessary steps to remedy the situation.

Budgetary control has now been widely adopted in the USA and in the UK, as more and more firms realise the contribution which an efficient system can give. Every year thousands of businesses fail, frequently due to the fact that there was no efficient forward planning which would have revealed that:

(*a*) the business should not have been started; or

(*b*) there were dangers ahead which would have to be faced in good time.

Investigations have shown that of the many businesses which fail, only a small number used budgets.

The Objectives of Budgetary Control

The general objectives of a system of budgetary control are:

(*a*) to plan the policy of a business;

(*b*) to co-ordinate the activities of a business so that each is part of an integral whole;

(*c*) to control each function so that the best possible results may be obtained.

Preparation of the Budget

An effective system of budgetary control requires the active co-operation of all executives. The chief executive normally establishes the guiding principles, but the actual operation of the system is usually delegated to a budget committee. This committee is usually composed of executives from the main departments of the business, e.g. the sales manager, production manager; the chairman of the committee may be the chief executive, while the responsibility for operating the system is undertaken by the budget officer, who may act as secretary of the committee.

The budget committee will formulate a general programme for the preparation of the budget, and the budget officer will be responsible for such functions as:

(a) issuing instructions to departments regarding requirements, dates of submission of data, etc.;

(b) providing historical information to departmental managers to help them in their forecasting;

(c) receiving and checking budget estimates;

(d) suggesting possible revisions;

(e) discussing difficulties with managers;

(f) ensuring that budgets are received in agreed time;

(g) preparing budget summaries;

(h) charting the departmental estimates on a master plan;

(i) submitting budgets to the committee and furnishing explanations on particular points;

(j) informing the departmental managers of any revisions made in their budgets by the committee;

(k) preparing the final master plan approved by the committee;

(l) co-ordinating all budget work.

The Budget Period

Budget periods vary greatly between different industries, some firms using periods of three, six, or twelve months or even much longer. However, the period of a year is usually regarded as being a natural period for budgeting. The determining of the budget period is usually related to two factors.

1. The type of business

In businesses in which capital expenditure is high and long-term planning is necessary, e.g. airlines and shipping, budget periods must cover years in advance. However, in businesses which experience seasonal demand, e.g. ladies' clothing and meat products, budget periods usually cover one seasonal cycle.

2. The control aspect

Controlling a business is one of the main objectives of budgetary control, so it is essential that regular short-term reports should be available.

The budget period adopted is usually a combination of these two factors, in that budgets are prepared for long-term periods, but are subdivided into monthly periods, thus allowing for efficient control.

The Key Factor

In the preparation of budgets it is essential to consider the key factor, or as it is sometimes termed in budgeting, the principal budget factor. This is the factor the extent of whose influence must first be assessed in order to ensure that the functional budgets are reasonably capable of fulfilment. It was mentioned on page 268 that one of the objectives of budgetary control was to co-ordinate the activities of a business. One of the main steps taken is to see that the production and sales budgets are in general agreement. Thus if the sales estimate is greatly in excess of the production capacity, then capacity will be a key factor.

The ICMA *Terminology* defines a key factor as:

A factor which at any time or over a period may limit the activity of an entity, often one where there is a shortage or difficulty of supply.

The limiting factor may change from time to time for the same entity or product. Thus, when raw materials are in short supply, performance or profit may be expressed as per kg of material, or, in a restricted skilled labour market, as per skilled labour hour. Alternatively, the limiting factor may be one critical process in a chain.

Steps may be taken to reduce the influences of a key factor. For example, if insufficient capacity is available long-term plans for expansion may be implemented, and/or short-term plans for overtime working, shift working, and subcontracting work, or improved control procedures, may be adopted.

Functional Budgets

A functional budget is one which relates to any of the functions of an undertaking. Functional budgets are subsidiary to the *master budget,* which is the summary budget, incorporating its component functional budgets, which is finally approved, adopted, and employed.

There are many types of functional budgets, of which the following are frequently used:

(*a*) sales budget;
(*b*) production budget;
(*c*) production cost budget;
(*d*) plant utilisation budget;

(e) capital expenditure budget;
(f) selling and distribution budget;
(g) purchasing budget;
(h) cash budget.

Budgetary control relates expenditure to the person who incurs the expenditure, so that actual expenses can be compared with those budgeted, thus affording a convenient method of control. It is an important principle of budgeting that no executive is held responsible for expenditure which is beyond his control.

Sales Budget

This is the most difficult functional budget to prepare. It is not easy to estimate consumers' future demands, especially when a new product is being introduced. It is possibly the most important subsidiary budget, because if the sales figure is incorrect, then practically all the other budgets will be affected, especially the master budget.

The sales manager must ascertain what his customers can be expected to buy, while the production manager must ascertain whether or not he can produce that output. Occasionally the production manager will state the output he can produce, and the sales manager must then decide whether or not he can sell that output. It is the responsibility of the budget committee to see that the plans are co-ordinated.

The sales budget is usually prepared in terms of quantities, then is evaluated at budgeted prices. In preparing the budget the sales manager has many aids, such as reports by salesmen, market research, and historical analysis of sales. The budget will show sales classified according to products, salesmen, customers, territories, and periods.

Production Budget

This subsidiary budget is prepared by the production manager, and shows production in terms of products, manufacturing departments, and periods. It is based upon the following factors:

(a) the sales budget;
(b) the production capacity;
(c) the budgeted finished goods stock requirements.

Example

	Units
Budgeted sales for the year	8,000
Budgeted opening stock of finished goods	300
Budgeted closing stock of finished goods	500

Production Budget

Balance required in stock at the end of the budgeted period	500
Budgeted sales during forthcoming year	8,000
	8,500
Balance estimated to be in stock at beginning of the budgeted period	300
Production required	8,200

Production Cost Budget

This budget expresses the information contained in the production budget in terms of cost of production. Each element of production cost—direct materials, direct wages and production overhead—would be calculated in terms of budgeted production requirements. Thus, if required, it should be relatively easy to build up direct wages and production overhead budgets as subsidiary budgets to the main production cost budget. However in the case of direct materials, if a direct materials budget was required, it would be necessary to make adjustments in respect of stock, in rather a similar manner to the finished goods stock adjustments which were shown in the production budget above.

Direct Materials Budget

This subsidiary budget is based upon the following factors:

(*a*) the production budget;
(*b*) the budgeted raw materials stock requirements.

Example

Production budgeted for the year is as shown above, viz. 8,200 units

Budgeted opening stock of raw materials   1,300 units
Budgeted closing stock of raw materials   1,600 units

Direct Materials Budget

	units
Closing stock budgeted	1,600
Budgeted production	8,200
	9,800
Opening stock budgeted	1,300
	8,500

Plant Utilisation Budget

This budget expresses the plant capacity required to meet the production budget. This may be very useful because:

(*a*) it details the machine load in every manufacturing department;

(*b*) it draws attention to any overloading in time for any corrective action to be taken, e.g. shift working, overtime working;

(*c*) it draws attention to any underloading, so that the sales manager can be requested to investigate possible increased sales.

Capital Expenditure Budget

This budget shows the estimated expenditure on fixed assets during the period concerned. It is based on information supplied by the executives of the various functions in the business, such as requests by the production manager for new machinery. It shows each project to be undertaken during a budget period, with an analysis of balances outstanding at the beginning of the period, amount to be appropriated during the period and the balances which are expected to be outstanding at the end of the period.

Selling and Distribution Cost Budget

This budget represents the cost of selling and distributing the quantities shown in the sales budget.

Cash Budget

This budget reveals the estimated cash balances each month, together with the estimated receipts and payments during the period. It has two very important functions.

(a) It ensures that sufficient cash is available when required.

(b) It may reveal an unexpected shortage of cash, so that the necessary action may be taken, e.g. a bank overdraft may be arranged. Alternatively, it may reveal a surplus of cash which the company may wish to invest for a short period.

Specimen Question

From the following budgeted figures prepare a cash budget in respect of the three months to June 30.

Month	Sales	Materials	Wages	Overheads
	£	£	£	£
January	30,000	20,000	5,500	3,100
February	28,000	24,000	5,800	3,300
March	32,000	25,000	6,000	3,400
April	40,000	28,000	6,200	3,600
May	42,000	31,000	6,500	4,300
June	38,000	25,000	7,000	4,000

Estimated cash balance on April 1: £10,000.

Accounts for materials and overheads are paid during the month following the month of supply. Wages are paid during the month in which they are earned.

Credit terms of sale are payment by the end of the month following the month of sale; it is estimated that one-half of sales are paid when due, the other half being paid during the next month.

A sales commission of 5% on sales is to be paid within the month following actual sales.

Preference share dividend of 10% on capital of £300,000 is to be paid on May 1.

Plant and machinery to be installed in May at a cost of £10,000 will be payable on June 1.

10% calls on ordinary share capital of £250,000 are due on April 1 and on June 1.

Cash Budget
Period: 3 months ending June 30

Details	Month		
	April	May	June
RECEIPTS	£	£	£
Balance brought down	10,000	28,800	(5,300)
Sales*	30,000	36,000	41,000
Capital	25,000	—	25,000
Total	£65,000	£64,800	£60,700
PAYMENTS			
Materials	25,000	28,000	31,000
Wages	6,200	6,500	7,000
Overheads	3,400	3,600	4,300
Sales Commission	1,600	2,000	2,100
Preference Share Dividend	—	30,000	—
Plant and Machinery	—	—	10,000
Total	£36,200	£70,100	£54,400
Balance carried down	£28,800	£(5,300)	£6,300

* ½ March	16,000	½ April	20,000	½ May	21,000
½ February	14,000	½ March	16,000	½ April	20,000
	£30,000		£36,000		£41,000

NOTE

From the cash budget, it can be readily observed that the cash balance is expected to fall severely due to the payment of dividend in May, so much so that there will not be enough cash to meet requirements. This appears to be a very serious situation, so management's attention would be drawn to this fact in good time to consider the advisability of arranging for a bank overdraft, or for taking some alternative action.

The Master Budget

On completion of the subsidiary budgets, the budget officer will prepare a master budget as shown on page 276. This contains the total budgeted sales and costs which were detailed in the subsidiary budgets. It shows the total picture of the projected results of the business for the next period.

The budget committee will consider the master budget and, if they approve it, it will be submitted to the board of directors for final approval. Amendments may be requested at this stage, and frequent alterations may be necessary. However, when the budget is finally approved it represents a standard which should be achieved by each department in the business.

When the budget is submitted to the board for approval it is usual practice to supply suitable notes to explain why any major differences from previous periods have occurred. For example, in the illustration given, a note would explain why the sales were expected to be higher than those last year.

Budgeted Profit and Loss Account
Year Ending 31 December 19–2

Details	19–2		19–1	
	Amount	%	Amount	%
Net sales	£880,000	100·0	£820,000	100·0
Production cost	510,000	58·0	485,000	59·1
GROSS PROFIT	370,000	42·0	335,000	40·9
Less Operating expenses:				
Administration	82,000	9·3	80,000	9·8
Selling and distribution	143,000	16·2	126,000	15·4
Research and development	20,000	2·3	20,000	2·4
Financial	15,000	1·7	14,000	1·7
TOTAL	260,000	29·5	240,000	29·3
OPERATING PROFIT	110,000	12·5	95,000	11·6
Add Other income	5,000	0·6	5,000	0·6
NET PROFIT before taxation	115,000	13·1	100,000	12·2
Less Provision for taxation	50,000	5·7	45,000	5·5
NET PROFIT	65,000	7.4	55,000	6·7
Dividend	15,000	1·7	10,000	1·2
BALANCE	£50,000	5·7	£45,000	5·5

Budgeted Balance Sheet as at 31 December 19–2

	£	19–2 £	£	19–1 £
Freehold property		500,000		500,000
Plant and machinery	500,000		400,000	
Less Depreciation	100,000		80,000	
		400,000		320,000
Motor vehicles	200,000		200,000	
Less Depreciation	80,000		40,000	
		120,000		160,000
Stock		180,000		200,000
Debtors		170,000		120,000
Bank		25,000		20,000
		£1,395,000		£1,320,000
Ordinary share capital		1,000,000		1,000,000
Reserves		95,000		45,000
Debentures		200,000		200,000
Creditors		100,000		75,000
		£1,395,000		£1,320,000

The Operation of Budgetary Control

The budget officer will ensure that the head of each department receives a copy of the budget relating to his department. It might be prudent if the budget officer discusses with the head concerned any important points or amendments which may have been made to the original budget. Each month a copy of the departmental budget report, a simple illustration of which is given in Fig. 39, will be sent to the head of each department.

On receipt of the report, the departmental head concerned (in this illustration the northern sales manager) can see immediately where he has over-spent and/or under-spent his budgeted allowance. From the performance percentage figure he can see that as far as expenditure is concerned his department has been inefficient this month (93%) and cumulatively inefficient (97%). It must be pointed out, however, that even though the department has spent more money than was budgeted, it does not necessarily follow that this was not money well spent, e.g. sales may have risen considerably, more than covering the increased cost. Nevertheless,

BUDGET REPORT ON CONTROLLABLE EXPENSES

Date Issued: 5th April

Prepared by: Q.N.H.
Checked by: A.C.G.

Budget Centre: 32
Department: Sales (Northern)

		MARCH	
		Month	Cumulative
		93	97

Performance %

Code	Element of Cost — Description	Month Expense Budget	Month Expense Actual	Month Expense Variance	Cumulative Expense Budget	Cumulative Expense Actual	Cumulative Expense Variance
	INDIRECT MATERIAL						
01	Printing and stationery	200	180	20	600	550	50
02	Photographic supplies	100	90	10	300	280	20
03	Cleaning materials	300	320	(20)	900	840	60
04	General	150	180	(30)	450	410	40
	INDIRECT LABOUR						
11	Clerical salaries	3,500	3,400	100	10,000	9,800	200
12	Salesmen's salaries	10,000	11,000	(1,000)	28,000	29,000	(1,000)
13	Executives' salaries	3,000	3,000	—	9,000	9,000	—
14	Commission	5,000	5,200	(200)	16,000	16,800	(800)
15	Overtime	200	150	50	300	200	100
16	Absence	150	250	(100)	500	300	200
17	National insurance	600	650	(50)	1,700	1,650	50
	MISCELLANEOUS						
21	Repairs: Buildings	200	200	—	200	200	—
22	Transport	3,000	3,580	(580)	10,000	11,260	(1,260)
23	Equipment	50	70	(20)	300	240	60
24	Depreciation: Buildings	100	100	—	300	300	—
25	Transport	5,000	5,500	(500)	14,000	14,500	(500)
26	Equipment	100	100	—	300	300	—
27	Heat, Light and Power	100	90	10	400	360	40
28	Personnel Service	200	50	150	600	800	(200)
29	Postage and Telephones	450	500	(50)	1,200	1,050	150
30	Staff expenses	3,400	3,960	(560)	10,000	10,940	(940)
31	General expenses	200	120	80	600	510	90
		£36,000	£38,690	£(2,690)	£105,650	£109,290	£(3,640)

FIG. 39.—*Budget report*

above-budget expenditure should not be allowed without the approval of management, otherwise a shortage of cash may result, to mention only one aspect.

The point to be observed is that any excess expenditure is highlighted, and it is the task of the person responsible for the department to justify the expenditure.

Management by Exception

One of the main advantages of budgetary control is that management is enabled to control the business by considering only the factors which do not work out according to plan; management concentrates on the exceptions. Thus, in Fig. 39 the northern sales manager would investigate those variances which are of significance. The main variances seem to be on codes 12, 14, 22, 25 and 30. The investigation might conceivably reveal the following details: due to increased consumer demand for the product in the northern area, two extra salesmen were engaged on March 1. This would result in increased salaries, depreciation of salesmen's cars, and staff expenses, also possibly increased commission and repairs to transport. However, in connection with commission and repairs, it will be noted that cumulatively these expenses are already considerably overspent, which may show that increased sales in the first two months had earned existing salesmen increased commission, while repairs were high because of increased wear and tear, unexpected increased cost of repairs, or possible accidents. It might be observed that cumulatively, personnel service expenses are high, probably due to recruiting costs of the extra salesmen.

It must be emphasised that in budgetary control relative speed is more important than relative accuracy. It is essential that management receives budget reports as soon as possible, so that corrective action can be taken where necessary. Any delay in reports makes investigation more difficult, and may mean that adverse costs may go undetected for some time.

Budget reports are issued for each department, and then summaries are prepared for each division of the business. A report of all significant variances may be given to management, with brief explanations of the causes of such variances.

The preparation of a cash budget and budgeted final accounts of a company is a useful exercise, both for accountants who are to be involved in planning a company's development and for students who are preparing for examinations. The following simple illustration is based on an examination question which was set by the Institute of Bankers.

Example

Susaeme PLC was incorporated in March and during the month 400,000 ordinary shares of £1 each were issued and fully paid up. Fixed assets amounting to £160,000 were purchased and paid for. It was proposed to commence business as from 1 April.

It was forecast that sales would amount to £48,000 in April, £80,000 in May and £160,000 per month thereafter. The gross profit margin was expected to be 25% of sales. Purchasing was so arranged that, at the end of each month, the stock of materials would be exactly sufficient to supply all the sales for the following month.

It was expected that every customer would pay for his goods before the last day of the second month after that in which the goods were sold. Trade creditors were to be paid on the last day of the month in which the goods were purchased. It was forecast that wages and salaries would amount to £8,000 each month, and would be paid on the last day of the month in which they were incurred. General expenses, estimated at £12,000 per month, were to be paid on the last day of the month after that in which they were incurred. Any temporary excess of payments over receipts were to be financed by a bank overdraft.

Prepare the cash budget and budgeted final accounts for the period ending 30 September. Ignore taxation and depreciation.

Cash Budget, six months ending 30 September (£000)

	April	May	June	July	August	September
Receipts:						
Balance b/d	240	196	116	24	(36)	(16)
Sales	—	—	48	80	160	160
	240	196	164	104	124	144
Payments:						
Purchases	36	60	120	120	120	120
Wages	8	8	8	8	8	8
Expenses	—	12	12	12	12	12
	44	80	140	140	140	140
Balance c/d	196	116	24	(36)	(16)	4

Budgeted Profit and Loss Account
for six months ending 30 September

	£000	£000		£000
Opening stock	36		Sales	768
Purchases	660			
	696			
Less Closing stock	120			
Cost of sales		576		
Gross profit c/d		192		
		768		768
			Gross profit b/d	192
Wages and salaries	48			
General expenses	72			
Net profit c/f	72			
		192		192

Budgeted Balance Sheet as at 30 September

	£000		£000
Ordinary share capital	400	Fixed assets	160
Reserves	72	Stock	120
Creditors	120	Debtors	320
Accruals	12	Bank	4
	604		604

The importance of preparing a cash budget can be seen from this simple illustration. Despite the fact that there was an apparent surplus of cash available when the company was formed, there was a need for a bank overdraft to finance the business during July and August. The preparation of a cash budget would facilitate the negotiation of a bank overdraft. Similarly any surplus funds could be used to earn short-term interest.

Continuous Budgeting

The introduction of continuous budgeting, or the use of a rolling budget, is an attempt to update budgets. The *Terminology* of the ICMA gives the following definitions.

Rolling Forecast

A continuously updated forecast covering one or more periods ahead, whereby each time actual results are reported a further forecast period is added, and intermediate period forecasts are updated. Often used to isolate underlying trends from seasonal or cyclical effects, so that both trends and effects are properly incorporated in the new forecast.

Rolling Budget

The continuous updating of a short term budget by adding, say, a further month or quarter, and deducting the earliest month or quarter, so that the budget can reflect current conditions.

It will be appreciated that in the normal fixed budget the company's forecast is limited to the end of a specific budget period. Thus, if in November the management accountant finalises budgets for the year 19–3, then the company's plans and objectives are established for 19–3. However, if the 19–4 budgets are prepared in November 19–3, then in October 19–3 the company's future plans are constrained to December 19–3. The idea of continuous budgeting is to ensure that not only is the budget updated as the environment changes, but also that the company's plans for twelve months ahead are established, so that there is always a full year planned ahead.

If one assumes that the normal budget is January to December 19–3, and each month during that period is scheduled separately, then as January 19–3 passes so January 19–4 is forecast; similarly with February, etc.

Zero Base Budgeting (ZBB)

The concept of zero base budgeting was introduced in 1969 and has been adopted in a number of large organisations, particularly in local government. Traditionally, many accountants have prepared their budgets based essentially on the previous year's budget, and the actual results for that period, which inherently assumes that this constituted an acceptable norm. With ZBB, budgets are prepared from zero: in other words previous results are ignored, and each budget is prepared from the beginning.

Peter Pyhrr of Texas Instruments is credited with the development of this system of budgeting. The adoption of ZBB by the then Governor of Georgia (later the President of the USA) Jimmy Carter, ensured a great interest in the system, and it would appear to have been successfully introduced in the public sector. It has been defined in the ICMA *Terminology* thus.

A method of budgeting whereby all activities are re-evaluated each time a budget is formulated. Each functional budget starts with the assumption that the function does not exist and is a zero cost. Increments of cost are compared with increments of benefits culminating in the planned maximum benefits for a given budgeted cost.

ZBB is simple in concept but is difficult to undertake in practice, because, while it is easy to talk of re-evaluating each activity, it is often a major operation to do so. Many managers do not like having their departmental functions investigated, analysed and compared, so opposition is frequently encountered when introducing ZBB.

Of course, it creates work and it takes time, but hopefully the benefits which can be obtained are considerable. The basic steps in implementing a ZBB system are:

(a) identify each function and activity of the organisation—this is referred to as a "decision package";

(b) evaluate each decision package so as to ensure that it is cost effective;

(c) compare each activity with possible alternatives;

(d) rank each activity—in some cases decision packages can be evaluated in terms of profitability, but in most cases it will be necessary to rank in subjective terms using cost–benefit analysis;

(e) allocate resources in accordance with the ranking of activities, and with resources available to the organisation.

In practice, ZBB is particularly relevant to non-manufacturing activities such as administration and selling functions. Usually, manufacturing activities are controlled by such techniques as standard costing, inventory control etc., and it may be found difficult to undertake a complete evaluation of every activity each year. It is therefore sometimes desirable to select activities in rotation, so that over a period of time each activity in the organisation is reviewed. Nevertheless, it is a salutary experience for functions to be reviewed as rigorously as is required by ZBB.

Flexible Budgetary Control

In recent times a number of firms have developed a system of flexible budgetary control, particularly those engaged in industries whose output depends on sales which are difficult to forecast, e.g. the soft drinks trade, which is affected by changes in weather. This system allows for a budget which provides estimates for different levels of production and sales. A flexible budget is defined in the ICMA *Terminology* as:

A budget which, by recognising the difference in behaviour between fixed and variable costs in relations to fluctuations in output, turnover, or other variable factors such as number of employees, is designed to change appropriately with such fluctuations.

For a full consideration of flexible budgetary control, the student is referred to *Managerial Accounting and Finance.* *

Behavioural Aspects of Budgeting

The impression may have been created that budgets, and indeed cost data in general, are concerned only with figures—profit, sales, etc. It is probably true to say that until relatively recently this was the situation, but certainly in the 1960s and 1970s, management accountants became more aware of the importance of considering people and the environment. The idea of participative budgeting is much more prevalent now than it was, allowing staff to be actively involved in budget preparation.

Much research has been undertaken into the effect on managers of being constrained by budgets, of their being held responsible for budgets produced without their participation, and of their being responsible for variances which are outside their control. It is generally agreed now that it is essential to motivate staff at varying levels in budget preparation, to invite the co-operation of managers in the setting of their budgets, and to co-ordinate the various functions of the organisation so that each is aware of its involvement in the plans for the organisation as a whole.

An organisation may establish objectives, but unless the various functions work together it cannot expect to achieve "goal congruence". Goal congruence can only be achieved where

Managerial Accounting and Finance, 4th edition, J. L. Brown and L. R. Howard, Macdonald & Evans, 1982.

managers of each function are working for the general benefit of the company and not only for the benefit of their particular function. In setting budgets, key factors are of prime importance; for example, it is of limited use for the sales manager to budget for the sale of 50,000 units of a product if the production manager can produce only 40,000 units.

The ICMA *Terminology* defines goal congruence as follows.

The state that exists in a control system when it leads individuals and/or groups to take actions which are both in their self-interest and also in the best interest of the entity.

If managers are to be held responsible for their budgets they must be actively engaged in the preparation of their budgets. "Responsibility accounting", as defined in the *Terminology* is:

A system of accounting that segregates revenues and costs into areas of personal responsibility in order to assess the performance attained by persons to whom authority has been assigned.

This is an important aspect of budgetary control. Not only must managers be actively involved, but they should receive frequent reports on their performance. This feedback of information forms the link between planning and control.

Examination Questions

1. What do you understand by "budgetary control"? In this connection, explain a "budget" and outline the steps to be taken in the compilation of a comprehensive one for a manufacturing business. (*CAA*)

2. Define the costing terms "budget" and "standard cost". It has been said, "You can have a budget without standard costs, but for standard costs a budget is essential." Discuss this statement. (*RSA*)

3. State the basic factors which must be taken into account in building up an administration budget. To the best of your ability show also further considerations which would have a bearing on the building up of this budget. (*SCCA*)

4. An organisation comprising several companies and a number of factories situated in different parts of the country has decided to adopt a system of control which involves the preparation and use of a budget. Explain the system to be adopted and prepare detailed instructions for the staff, bearing in mind the necessity for uniformity throughout the organisation. You may assume the business of the group to be of any kind with which you are familiar. (*LCCI*)

5. In connection with budgetary control, enumerate and describe briefly the usual subsidiary budgets which make up the master budget.   (*SCCA*)

6. State the basic factors to be considered when building up a sales budget. Have in mind that production and sales budgets must balance apart from variation in stocks.   (*SCCA*)

7. (*a*) Describe what is meant by the term "master budget" and state the items it contains.

(*b*) Name the functional budgets that are incorporated into the master budget and outline briefly the contents of each.

(*c*) Describe briefly or by a diagram how the various functional budgets are inter-related.   (*RSA*)

8. A company selling consumer products by means of representatives to both retailers and wholesalers wishes to prepare a budget for the year for selling and distribution expenses. As this has never been undertaken by them before, you are asked to give them your advice.

State:

(*a*) the items of expenditure you would expect to include in such a budget;

(*b*) the methods you would adopt to build up the budget.   (*RSA*)

9. Using the under-mentioned data formulated by a company prepare a cash forecast for the three months ended 30 June. Comment on any findings from such forecast which appear to be significant.

Budgeted Sales

Month ended March 31	£48,000
April 30	£58,200
May 31	£60,240
June 30	£70,856

Note: Sales income is expected to be received in the following month.

Ancillary Income

Rentals receivable June 30	£1,000

Budgeted Expenditure

Month	Wages	Salaries	Overheads	Materials	Proposed Dividends
April	£12,500	£3,000	£14,000	£25,000	—
May	£14,900	£3,000	£12,000	£20,000	—
June	£14,400	£3,200	£11,500	£21,000	£10,000

Note: Each month includes £1,000 for depreciation.

Opening Cash Balances April 1. At bank £2,500. In hand £400.

     (*AIA*)

10. MNO Ltd manufactures a product for which peak demand is in the summer. The company's policy is to maintain its labour force by providing steady employment throughout the year. This involves building up large stocks of product during the winter, during which time the company's bankers provide overdraft accommodation.

The following budget figures relate to five months:

	Sales £	Purchases £	Wages and Expenses £
November	60,000	41,500	9,000
December	50,000	48,000	7,600
January	40,000	50,000	8,000
February	50,000	50,000	8,000
March	60,000	46,000	8,000

Credit terms of sale are payment by the end of the month following the month of supply. On average, one half of sales are paid for on the due date, whilst the other half are paid for during the following month. Creditors are paid during the month following the month of purchase. One quarter of wages and expenses are paid in the month following that in which they were incurred. The budgeted bank overdraft as at January 1 is £1,100.

You are required to prepare a cash budget for the quarter commencing on January 1, showing the budgeted amount of bank overdraft required at each month end. (*SCCA*)

11. Norman Berman is a trader whose draft balance sheet as at 30 June 19–2 is as follows:

Balance Sheet at 30 June 19–2

Capital	£000s		£000s	£000s
Balance at 1 July 19–1	120	Fixed assets at cost		89
Add: Net profit	24	Less: Depreciation		31
Less: Drawings	(18)			—
	—			58
Balance at 30 June 19–2	126	Current Assets		
		Stock-in-trade	64	
Current Liabilities		Trade debtors	35	
Trade creditors	32	Bank	1	100
	—			—
	158			158

There is a buoyant demand for Berman's products, and sales have increased steadily over the years. The following forecasts and estimates are made for the year ending 30 June 19–3.

1. Forecast monthly sales are as follows:
       19–2 July–December £40,000 per month

19–3 January–June £45,000 per month
July–December £50,000 per month.

2. The gross profit margin will be 20% on sales.

3. It is Berman's policy to maintain stocks, at the end of each month, sufficient to cover the expected sales for the following *two* months.

4. The period of credit allowed to customers and obtained from suppliers is expected to remain the same as for the year ended 30 June 19–2, i.e. one month.

5. Berman has sufficient accommodation for the planned increase in sales, but vehicles and equipment costing £20,000 will need to be purchased and paid for in December 19–2.

6. Wages and general expenses (including an allowance for bank interest) are paid for in the month that they are incurred and will amount to £5,000 per month.

7. The depreciation charge for the year is to be £12,000.

8. Berman will withdraw £2,000 each month for personal use.

9. Berman's bank has agreed to provide any overdraft facilities required during the year ended 30 June 19–3.

Required:

(*a*) A forecast cash statement, showing the bank balance or overdraft at the end of each month, for the year ending 30 June 19–3.

(*b*) Berman's forecast profit and loss account for the year ending 30 June 19–3.

(*c*) Berman's forecast balance sheet at 30 June 19–3.

Notes:

Ignore taxation. Assume for the purpose of the question that your calculations are being made on 1 July 19–2 and that the year to 30 June 19–3 consists of twelve months of equal length.   (*IAADP*)

12. Product P is manufactured from 10 lb of raw material M at a cost of £0·2 per lb. The selling price of P is £5 per unit and the sales budget for 19–1 was:

Month 19–1	Sales value £000	Month 19–1	Sales value £000
January	10	July	40
February	10	August	40
March	15	September	30
April	20	October	20
May	30	November	15
June	40	December	10

In preparation for the budget for the coming year the sales manager has forecast the following increases in sales for 19–2 over the budgeted figures given above:

19–2	%
January to April, inclusive	10
May to August, inclusive	20
September to December, inclusive	10

It is estimated that the stock at December 31 19–1 will be:

Product P	500 units
Material M	4,000 lb

The monthly average stock levels for 19–2 have been forecast to be as given below:

Month 19–2	Product P Units	Material M lb	Month 19–2	Product P Units	Material M lb
January	400	3,000	July	1,600	15,000
February	400	4,000	August	1,600	16,000
March	600	6,000	September	1,100	12,000
April	800	7,000	October	700	10,000
May	1,200	13,000	November	500	8,500
June	1,600	16,000	December	400	5,000

It may be assumed that stocks increase or decrease evenly throughout each month.

You are required, in preparation for the 19–2 budget, to prepare the purchases budget for material M for 19–2 in total and for each month. (*ICMA*)

13. DC Limited manufactures two products, X and Y, whose selling prices and costs are stated below.

	Product X per unit £	Product Y per unit £
Selling price	50	45
Direct material	18	15
Direct labour	6	4
Variable production overhead	6	5

Budgeted sales for four months next year are:

	X units	Y units
January	900	1,400
February	1,100	1,600
March	1,200	1,800
April	1,300	1,500

Management policy is to hold in stock at the end of each month finished units equal to one half of the budgeted sales for the next month. Assume that this requirement will be met on 1st January.

Work-in-progress may be ignored.

Fixed production overhead is budgeted at £15,000 per month and this is treated as a period cost. The budgeted selling and administration costs (all fixed) are £6,000 and £5,000 per month respectively.

You are required to:

(a) prepare a production budget on a unit basis for each product in respect of each of the first three months of next year;

(b) convert this production budget into a variable production cost budget showing costs for each of the first three months by element of cost for each product and in total;

(c) prepare a statement for the first quarter showing the budgeted results for each product and in total (monthly figures are not required and the selling and administration costs are not to be apportioned to the products);

(d) list any *two* factors which might have influenced the management policy to have stock on hand at the end of each month equal to one half of the following month's budgeted sales;

(e) explain what is meant by "period cost" and suggest an alternative way of accounting for the budgeted fixed production overhead of £15,000 per month.   (*ICMA*)

Chapter 21

Standard Costing

IN previous chapters on methods of costing (Chapters 14–19) the historical nature of costing was discussed; information was presented of actual costs incurred during a past period. Such information is, of course, useful to management, but not as valuable as it might be because:

(*a*) management receives the data after the period is ended, so that corrective action is not possible before considerable delay has occurred;

(*b*) there is no suitable yardstick by which performance can be satisfactorily measured.

To rectify these deficiencies in costing, a technique has been developed in recent years known as standard costing, the aim of which is to present to management cost data, which will be most useful in controlling the business.

Standard costing is a natural development from budgetary control: budgetary control compares actual results of operating a department with planned results; standard costing compares actual results of producing and selling a product with planned results.

Standard costs are predetermined estimates of cost of a single unit, or of a number of units of a product or service, to be used as a measure with which actual costs may be compared as the work proceeds. The standard costs set up are usually planned costs for current or anticipated conditions. Sometimes they are the costs which are assumed for normal or ideal conditions of efficiency, based on an assumed output, having regard to current conditions.

The setting up of standards for costing is an operation requiring careful investigation and calculation; consequently, standards are not altered except when conditions undergo considerable change. Thus, when standards have been adopted using expected prices of material and rates for labour, changes of the standards used would be made only when persisting alterations of material prices or rates of wages occur.

Standard costing is a method of ascertaining costs whereby statistics are prepared to show:

291

(*a*) the standard cost;
(*b*) the actual cost;
(*c*) the difference between these costs, which is termed the *variance*.

Advantages of Standard Costs

(*a*) Standard costs provide a yardstick by which actual performance can be compared with standard.

(*b*) Standard costs are a valuable aid to management in determining prices and formulating policies.

(*c*) Variances can be analysed in detail, enabling management to investigate the causes.

(*d*) The principle of "management by exception" can be applied. Management does not spend time and effort searching through unnecessary information, but can concentrate attention on important matters.

(*e*) The costing procedure is simplified.

(*f*) Setting up standards requires careful investigation into procedures, which often result in improved methods being developed.

(*g*) Management is encouraged to look and plan ahead.

The Level of Attainment

In preparing standard costs it is important to consider at which level of production the business will be expecting to operate. There are normally three levels to be considered.

1. *That which past performance suggests is capable of attainment*
This level may be considered satisfactory in that the standard achievement should be easily attained, but may lead management into complacency.

2. *That which would necessitate maximum possible efficiency*
This level can seldom be attained, and certainly never sustained for long periods. It is unrealistic and will almost invariably result in adverse variances due to the high standard demanded. Variances revealed may stimulate management to greater effort, but generally will have the effect of discouraging staff.

3. *That which is possible by efficient working and management*
This level is usually the most satisfactory because it is realistic, and yet provides a challenge to better effort. Any adverse variances revealed may point the way to economies.

The Establishment of Standard Costs

It is essential that the standards set are as accurate and reliable as possible; the success of a standard costing system rests on setting the standards. Usually the cost accountant is responsible for the task, but he will be required to co-operate with many personnel, e.g. time-and-motion-study engineers, production engineers, and buyers. It is necessary to consider standards of performance, usage of material, cost rates, and many other factors before establishing standards.

Standard costs must be set for each of the following elements of cost.

1. DIRECT MATERIAL

A standard price is settled, having regard to the current rates and those expected in the immediate future. Quantities and qualities of materials as shown on the specification for production are considered and allowance is made for normal scrap or waste.

2. DIRECT WAGES

The different grades of labour required in production will be assessed and evaluated at standard rates per hour, and standards of performance will be established.

3. VARIABLE OVERHEAD

It is assumed that variable overhead costs are proportionate to output achieved, therefore a standard cost per unit or per hour will be set. In other words, the cost per unit will remain the same, irrespective of the production level.

4. FIXED OVERHEAD

It is assumed that fixed overhead costs are more or less constant, within reasonable limits, irrespective of the level of output. In setting a standard cost it is necessary to consider:

(a) the total fixed overhead costs for the period;
(b) the budgeted production for the period;
(c) the expected number of working hours during the period.

The Standard Cost of a Product

After the standard cost for each element of cost of a product has been established, a standard cost per unit can be set, a simple illustration of which follows.

Example

Standard cost of product Eyrfix

	Mix	£	£
Direct material:	30 kg of X20 at £3 per kg	90	
	70 kg of Y7 at £2 per kg	140	
	100		230
	20 Normal loss 20%		
	80 kg		230
	Scrap value		30
			200
Direct labour:	Process 1—10 hours at £4·00 per hour	40	
	Process 2—5 hours at £4·80 per hour	24	
			64
Variable overhead:	Process 1—£6 per mix	6	
	Process 2—£4 per mix	4	
			10
Fixed overhead:	Production:		
	Process 1—10 hours at £4·40 per direct labour hour	44	
	Process 2—5 hours at £6·40 per direct labour hour	32	
			76
			350
	Administration: 20% of production cost		70
			420
	Selling and Distribution: 25% of production and administration cost		105
	TOTAL COST		525
Profit			75
Selling Price			£600

The above statement shows the standard price of the product,

£600 per mix or £7·50 per kg, and also the standard cost of each element of cost.

A standard costing system shows what the cost *ought to be*, which is most useful to management. It is the yardstick by which actual costs can be compared.

Before the introduction of standard costing it was common practice to compare actual costs of the current period with those of a previous period. This was not a very useful comparison when one considers that:

(*a*) the costs incurred in the previous year may have been abnormally high or low;

(*b*) conditions may change from year to year;

(*c*) improved methods of production and introduction of machinery will necessarily affect costs.

However, in a standard costing system, where possible, allowances are made for changing conditions, improved methods of production, and so on. Thus, any variations from what the cost ought to be are readily revealed.

The Standard Hour

Production is usually expressed in terms of units, pounds, gallons, etc. This may be satisfactory in many cases, but, as will be appreciated, it may be inconvenient when considering different types of products, especially when the products are measured in different units, e.g. gases and liquids.

When a system of standard costing is in use production can be expressed in terms of a measure common to all production, viz. the "standard hour." The standard hour is the quantity of output or amount of work which should be produced in one hour.

Example

A company manufacturing detergents markets three brands: Soapy, Sudsy and Washy. It is estimated that in one hour production can be attained of 2,000, 2,500 and 3,000 packets respectively. During the month of August, output was 80,000, 175,000 and 270,000 packets respectively.

Production could be measured in terms of standard hours as follows:

Production   *August*

Product	Actual production (packets)	Standard output per hour (packets)	Production in standard hours
Soapy	80,000	2,000	40
Sudsy	175,000	2,500	70
Washy	270,000	3,000	90
TOTAL			200

Variances

The idea of "management by exception" has been mentioned more than once in this book; variances contribute a vital part to this aspect of control. There are many kinds of variances which can be calculated, each of which may be important in its particular field. Thus, for instance, a direct material usage variance would reveal that the actual material consumed was greater or less than the standard set; a direct labour rate variance would show that the actual labour employed was paid more or less per hour than the standard rate. Thus variances reveal where actual costs have differed from standards. It is therefore easy to ascertain who is responsible for variances, so that possible action may be taken when required.

Many different variances are calculated in practice, some of them peculiar to a certain industry, e.g. job cost variance, but there are a number of variances common to many industries, among which the following are important.

1. Direct Materials

(*a*) *Total variance*. The difference between the standard cost of direct materials specified for the output achieved and the actual cost of direct materials used.

(*b*) *Price variance*. That portion of the direct materials cost variance which is due to the difference between the standard price specified and the actual price paid.

(*c*) *Usage variance*. That portion of the direct materials cost variance which is due to the difference between the standard quantity specified and the actual quantity used.

2. Direct Labour

(a) *Total variance.* The difference between the standard direct wages specified for the activity achieved and the actual direct wages paid.

(b) *Rate variance.* That portion of the direct wages variance which is due to the difference between the standard rate of pay specified and the actual rate paid.

(c) *Efficiency variance.* That portion of the direct wages variance which is due to the difference between the standard labour hours specified for the activity achieved and the actual labour hours expended.

(d) *Idle-time variance.* The standard cost of the actual hours employees were idle due to abnormal circumstances.

3. Variable Overhead

Expenditure variance. The difference between the standard cost of the overhead absorbed in the output achieved and the actual overhead cost.

4. Fixed Overhead

(a) *Total variance.* The difference between the standard cost of overhead absorbed in the output achieved and the actual overhead cost.

(b) *Expenditure variance.* In the case of fixed overhead it is the difference between the budgeted fixed overhead and the actual cost incurred.

(c) *Volume variance.* That portion of the fixed overhead variance which is the difference between the standard cost of the overhead absorbed in actual output and the standard allowance for that output. (In this definition it should be noted that the standard allowance means, in effect, the budgeted overhead. This is because it is well understood that volume variance represents the over- or under-absorption of fixed costs in the period concerned.)

(d) *Efficiency variance.* That portion of the volume variance which reflects the increased or reduced output arising from efficiency above or below the standard which is expected.

(e) *Capacity variance.* That portion of the volume variance which is due to working at higher or lower capacity usage than standard.

The Cost Accounts

There are a number of methods which have been adopted for recording standard costs in the accounts, but it is proposed to illustrate only one method. In this method all expenses incurred are charged at actual cost to the accounts concerned, but are recovered at standard cost in the work-in-progress account; finished output is then transferred at standard cost to finished goods account.

The result of this method is that the work-in-progress account is maintained at standard cost, which means that any balance at the end of the period will be valued at standard cost. Finished goods account will be similarly affected. Consequently, if market prices fall so that the standard cost is greater than the actual cost it will be necessary to revalue the stocks so as to conform to the theory of the lower of cost or replacement price.

Definitions

Before illustrating a standard cost system it will be expedient to define six of the terms to be used in this chapter.

(*a*) *Actual production*. The actual quantity produced during the actual hours worked.

(*b*) *Budgeted production*. The budgeted quantity to be produced during the budgeted hours to be worked.

(*c*) *Standard production*. The quantity which should have been produced during the actual hours worked.

(*d*) *Actual cost*. The actual quantity produced at the actual cost per unit.

(*e*) *Budgeted cost*. The budgeted quantity to be produced at the standard cost per unit.

(*f*) *Standard cost*. The actual quantity produced at the standard cost per unit.

Example 1

1. Direct Materials

Eyress is the only product manufactured by Eyre Engineering PLC. Production engineers have estimated that 400 units should be produced from each tonne of material consumed, the standard price of which is £720 per tonne. During the first week of January 20 tonnes of raw materials were issued to production, the purchase price of which was £729 per tonne. Actual production for the week was 7,750 units.

(a) Direct Material Total Variance

Formula: Standard cost − Actual cost

$$SC - AC$$
$$£13,950 - £14,580 = \underline{£630\,(A)}$$

NOTES

1. (F) signifies a favourable variance.
(A) signifies an adverse variance.
2. SC is the actual quantity produced at the standard cost per unit.

$$AQ \times SC/unit$$
$$7,750 \times £1 \cdot 80 = £13,950$$

3. SC/unit. Each tonne of material should produce 400 units

Each tonne of material should cost £720

Therefore each unit should cost $\dfrac{£720}{400} = £1 \cdot 80$

This variance shows that the actual material costs were in excess of what they should have been. This variance will have been the result of a difference in the price of raw material and/or material usage, being different from the standard set. The sub-variances, viz. price variance and usage variance, will show the position in detail.

(b) Direct Material Price Variance

Formula: Actual quantity (Standard price − Actual price)

$$AQ\,(SP - AP)$$
$$20\,(£720 - £729) = \underline{£180\,(A)}$$

This variance compares the price which was paid for the material with that which should have been paid; in this case the price actually paid was in excess of standard price. Price variance allocates responsibility to the buyer, who must explain why prices were unfavourable.

(c) Direct Material Usage Variance

Formula: Standard price (Standard quantity − Actual quantity)

$$SP\,(SQ - AQ)$$
$$£720\,(19\tfrac{3}{8} - 20) = \underline{£450\,(A)}$$

NOTES

1. In **(b)** above the variance due to a change in price was eliminated, so that in calculating the usage variance only the standard price should be considered.

2. SQ: actual output was 7,750 units, so that, at a standard consumption rate of 400 units per tonne, this output should have required 19·375 tonnes of direct materials.

This variance compares the actual quantity which was produced with that which should have been produced from the actual input of materials. In this case it reveals that actual output was not up to the standard expected. Usage variance allocates responsibility to the production manager, who will be asked to explain the reason for the reduced output.

Check

(*a*) Direct materials cost variance =
$$SC - AC$$
$$£13,950 - £14,580 = £630\,(A)$$

(*b*) Direct materials cost variance =
$$Price\ V + Usage\ V$$
$$£180\,(A) + £450\,(A) = £630\,(A)$$

Accounting entries

	£	£
Dr Work in progress	14,400	
Direct material price variance	180	
Cr Stores ledger		14,580
Dr Finished goods ledger	13,950	
Direct material usage variance	450	
Cr Work in progress		14,400

2. Direct Labour

Fifty employees are engaged in the manufacture of Eyress. The standard rate per employee is £4·80 per hour; a 40-hour week is in operation. The standard performance is set at 200 articles per hour. Abnormal idle time due to a power failure amounted to 4 hours for each employee. During the first week in January three employees were paid at the rate of £4·40 per hour, and two employees were paid at the rate of £5·00 per hour; the remainder were paid at standard rate.

(a) Direct Labour Total Variance

Formula: Standard cost − Actual cost

$$SC - AC$$
$$£9,300 - £9,568 = \underline{£268\,(A)}$$

1. SC = AQ × SC/unit
   7,750 × £1·20 = £9,300

2. SC/unit: Each hour the factory operates costs £240 (50 employees at £4·80 per hour)
   Each hour of work should produce 200 units
   Therefore each unit should cost £1·20

$$\frac{\text{Cost per hour}}{\text{Standard output per hour}} \quad \frac{£240}{200}$$

	£
3. AC: 45 employees at 40 hours at £4·80 per hour	8,640
3 employees at 40 hours at £4·40 per hour	528
2 employees at 40 hours at £5·00 per hour	400
	£9,568

This variance is similar to the direct material total variance, in that it is a total variance. It shows that the wage payments were in excess of what the cost should have been. This variance will have been the result of a difference in the rate of pay and/or the efficiency of labour. The sub-variances, viz. rate variance and efficiency variance, will show the position in detail.

(b) Direct Labour Rate Variance

Formula: Actual hours (Standard rate − Actual rate)

AH (SR − AR)
120 (£4·80 − £4·40)   £48 (F)
80 (£4·80 − £5·00)   £16 (A) = £32 (F)

A rate variance can occur only where the actual rate differs from standard, and so only those hours worked at non-standard rates are considered, e.g. 3 employees × 40 hours = 120 hours at £4·40. This reveals that rates were paid which differed from those set as standard. It should be noted that idle hours must be paid for, unless, exceptionally, the employee is at fault. The personnel department should be able to explain why these rates were paid.

(c) Direct Labour Efficiency Variance

Formula: Standard rate (Standard hours − Actual hours)

SR (SH − AH)
£4·80 (1,937½ − 1,800) = £660 (F)

NOTES

1. In **(b)** above the variance due to changes in rates was eliminated, so that in calculating the efficiency variance only the standard rate should be considered.

2. $SH = \dfrac{\text{Actual production}}{\text{Standard production per hour}} \times \text{Number of employees}$

$$\frac{7{,}750 \text{ units}}{200 \text{ units}} \times 50 = 1{,}937\tfrac{1}{2}$$

3. AH: 50 employees worked 36 hours = 1,800

In this calculation, the actual hours worked, not the actual hours paid, is shown. This is because it would be unreasonable to measure efficiency of employees when they were unemployed owing to a power failure. We are trying to measure how efficiently the employees worked while the production facilities were operating. The hours which are idle are best segregated to show an idle-time variance; obviously, if the actual hours paid for were used in this calculation there would be no place for such a variance. The authors consider it to be prudent to show the idle-time variance, and so it is calculated in **(d)** below.

The direct labour efficiency variance compares the hours worked with those which should have been required to produce the actual output recorded. In this case it reveals that in 1,800 hours worked the equivalent of 1,937½ hours' output was achieved; thus actual performance was better than the standard set. The production manager should be able to explain why this occurred. It should be noted that favourable variances as well as adverse variances should be investigated, even if perhaps less vigorously.

(d) Direct Labour Idle-time Variance

Formula: Hours idle × Standard hourly rate

50 employees × 4 hours × £4·80 per hour = £960 (A)

This variance reveals the cost of production time lost owing to abnormal conditions, such as a power failure or machine breakdown or material shortage.

Check

(a) Direct wages variance = SC − AC

£9,300 − £9,568 = £268 (A)

(b) Direct wages variance = Rate V + Efficiency V + Idle time V

£32 (F) + £660 (F) + £960 (A)

= £268 (A)

Accounting entries

	£	£
Dr Work in progress	9,600	
Cr Direct labour rate V		32
Wages		9,568
Dr Finished goods ledger	9,300	
Direct labour idle time V	960	
Cr Direct labour efficiency V		660
Work in progress		9,600

3. Variable Overhead

The term variable overhead implies that this element of cost varies directly with production. It is therefore relatively easy to calculate the standard variable overhead for any period. For example, if budgeted output for period 1 is 10,000 units and for period 2 is 12,000 units, and the variable overhead rate per unit is £0·10, then the total variable overheads will be £1,000 and £1,200 respectively. Irrespective of the number of units produced, the variable overhead cost *per unit* will not change, at least in the short run.

However, it is possible that the cost of variable overheads may change, owing, for example, to a price increase by the supplier. Where this occurs, the result will give rise to an expenditure variance.

Thus, if one assumes that variable overheads vary strictly with production only an expenditure variance can result. As with direct materials, direct wages, and, as will be shown later, fixed overheads, a total or cost variance can be calculated, which is the total of the sub-variances; with variable overheads the total variance is therefore the same as the one sub-variance: expenditure variance.

In the manufacture of Eyress the standard variable overhead cost per unit is £0·50. Actual expenditure on variable overheads was £3,975 during the first week in January.

(a) Variable Overhead Total Variance

Formula: Standard cost − Actual cost

$$SC - AC$$
$$£3,875 - £3,975 = \underline{£100 \, (A)}$$

NOTE: SC =   AQ × SC/unit
            7,750 units × £0·50/unit

(b) Variable Overhead Expenditure Variance

Formula: SC − AC
$$£3,875 - £3,975 = \underline{£100\,(A)}$$

This variance reveals that the price change for some item of variable overhead was more than the standard cost set; the buyer should be able to explain the reason for this difference. As explained above, the expenditure variance must be the same as the total variance, if one assumes that variable overheads vary directly with output.

Accounting entries

	£	£
Dr Work in progress	3,875	
Variable overhead expenditure V	100	
Cr Variable overhead		3,975
Dr Finished goods	3,875	
Cr Work in progress		3,875

4. Fixed Overhead

The term fixed overhead implies that this element of cost does not vary directly with production; in theory, within limits it does not change, at least in the short run, i.e. the total is fixed. In Chapter 9 the recovery of overheads was discussed, from a study of which the reader should realise that recovery depends on two factors, viz. the output of units and expenses incurred. Thus, if either of these factors differs from the standards set, recovery of overheads will be affected; these differences are referred to as volume variance and expenditure variance respectively.

There are many reasons why the actual volume of production differs from standard, e.g. inefficient utilisation of machines, plant breakdown, and shortage of materials. Overhead variances show up where inefficiencies occur, so that, where possible, management may take the necessary action to remedy the situation.

Production of Eyress has been budgeted at 400,000 units per annum. Fixed overheads are expected to amount to £600,000 for the year. Actual expenditure during the first week in January was £12,300. There are two weeks' holiday during the year, during which time no production is undertaken.

(a) Fixed Overhead Total Variance

Formula: Standard cost − Actual cost

$$SC - AC$$
$$£11,625 - £12,300 = £675\,(A)$$

NOTES

1. SC = $\quad AQ \times SC/\text{unit}$
   $7,750 \text{ units} \times £1·50 = £11,625$

2. SC/unit = $\dfrac{\text{Budgeted fixed overhead pa}}{\text{Budgeted output pa}}$

$$\dfrac{£600,000}{400,000}$$

This variance shows that the actual expenditure on fixed overheads was greater than the amount of overhead recovered in actual production, so the result is unfavourable. This difference may have been due to a difference in the expenditure expected and that incurred, or to a difference in the volume of output expected and that incurred.

(b) Fixed Overhead Expenditure Variance

Formula: Budgeted cost − Actual cost

$$BC - AC$$
$$£12,000 - £12,300 = £300\,(A)$$

NOTE: BC = $\dfrac{\text{Budgeted fixed overhead pa}}{\text{Weeks to be worked pa}}$

$$\dfrac{£600,000}{50}$$

This variance is in effect a price variance, rather similar to the direct material price variance, direct labour rate variance, and variable overhead expenditure variance. It reveals that the cost of fixed overhead was greater than expected, and so the buyer should be asked to give an explanation.

(c) Volume Variance

Formula: Standard cost − Budgeted cost

$$SC - BC$$
$$£11,625 - £12,000 = £375\,(A)$$

This reveals that the output of the factory (actual output at standard cost) was less than budgeted, which may be due to a number of reasons. The following two variances, which are sub-variances of the volume variance, help to explain the reasons for changes in volume. However, before calculating the two sub-variances it may be of interest to the reader to show an alternative method of calculating the volume variance. This method is based on output in terms of units produced.

Formula: Standard cost (Actual quantity − Budgeted quantity) per unit

$$SC(AQ - BQ)$$
$$£1·50 (7,750 - 8,000) = \underline{£375 (A)}$$

NOTE: BQ = $\dfrac{\text{Budgeted output pa}}{\text{No. of weeks pa}}$

$$\dfrac{400,000 \text{ units}}{50 \text{ weeks}}$$

Based on the same technique used to calculate the volume variance above, viz. output in units, the sub-variances of the volume variance may be calculated as follows:

(d) Efficiency Variance

Formula: Standard cost (Actual quantity − Standard quantity) per unit

$$SC(AQ - SQ)$$
$$£1·50 (7,750 - 7,200) = \underline{£825 (F)}$$

NOTE: SQ = Actual hours worked × Standard output per hour
36 hours × 200 units

This reveals that the manufacturing process was carried out more efficiently than was expected. The production manager would probably be asked to explain how this had occurred. It may be remembered that the direct labour efficiency variance was also favourable, which is as would be expected.

(e) Capacity Variance

Formula: Standard cost (Standard quantity − Budgeted quantity) per unit

$$SC(SQ - BQ)$$
$$£1·50 (7,200 - 8,000) = \underline{£1,200 (A)}$$

This reveals that the available plant capacity was not utilised as much as had been expected; it was budgeted to produce 8,000 units during the week, but owing to idle time the machine utilisation was reduced, so that in the time which was available an output of only 7,200 units could be expected.

It should be noted that:

$$\text{Volume V} = \text{Efficiency V} + \text{Capacity V}$$
$$£375\,(A) = £825\,(F) + £1,200\,(A)$$

It follows, therefore, that when preparing the accounting entries for fixed overheads the volume variance or the efficiency variance and the capacity variance should be shown, but not all three variances. It is preferable to show the two sub-variances, which give an analysis of volume variance.

Check I

(a) Overhead total variance =   Standard cost − Actual cost
                                   £11,625 − £12,300 = £675 (A)

(b) Overhead total variance =   Expenditure + Volume + Capacity
                                variance   variance variance
                           £300 (A) + £825 (F) +£1,200 (A)
                                         = £675 (A)

Check II

(a) Charge to finished goods =
                    AQ × SC/unit
          7,750 units × £1·50 = £11,625
(b) Accounting entries in finished goods account = £11,625
                     (see below)

Accounting entries

	£	£
Dr Work in progress	12,000	
Overhead expenditure variance	300	
Cr Fixed overhead		12,300
Dr Finished goods	11,625	
Capacity variance	1,200	
Cr Efficiency variance		825
Work in progress		12,000

Standard Cost of Production

Actual output: 7,750 units

Element of cost	Per unit £	Total cost £
Direct materials	1·80	13,950
Direct wages	1·20	9,300
Variable overheads	0·50	3,875
Fixed overheads	1·50	11,625
Total cost	£5·00	£38,750

The cost ledger control accounts in a cost control accounting system would be as shown below. It is assumed that the total output for the week was sold for £50,000 and that there were no stocks of any kind.

Cost Control Account

	£		£
Sales	50,000	Stores control	14,580
		Wages control	9,568
		Variable overheads	3,975
		Fixed overheads	12,300
		Costing profit and loss	9,577
	£50,000		£50,000

Stores Ledger Control Account

	£		£
Purchases	14,580	Direct material price variance	180
		Work in progress	14,400
	£14,580		£14,580

Direct Wages Account

	£		£
Wages	9,568	Work in progress	9,600
Direct labour rate variance	32		
	£9,600		£9,600

Variable Overhead Account

	£		£
Overheads	3,975	Variable overhead expenditure variance	100
		Work in progress	3,875
	£3,975		£3,975

Fixed Overhead Account

	£		£
Overheads	12,300	Fixed overhead expenditure variance	300
		Work in progress	12,000
	£12,300		£12,300

Work-in-Progress Ledger Control Account

	£		£
Stores ledger control	14,400	Direct material usage variance	450
Direct wages control	9,600	Direct idle time variance	960
Variable overhead	3,875	Fixed overhead capacity variance	1,200
Fixed overhead	12,000		

	£	Finished goods ledger	38,750
Direct wages efficiency variance	660		
Fixed overhead efficiency variance	825		
	£41,360		£41,360

Finished Goods Ledger Control Account

Work in progress	£38,750	Cost of sales	£38,750

Cost of Sales Account

Finished goods ledger	£38,750	Profit and loss	£38,750

Direct Material Price Variance Account

Stores ledger control	£180	Profit and loss	£180

Direct Material Usage Variance Account

Work in progress	£450	Profit and loss	£450

Direct Labour Rate Variance Account

Profit and loss	£32	Direct wages	£32

Direct Labour Efficiency Variance Account

Profit and loss	£660	Work in progress	£660

Direct Labour Idle-time Variance Account

Work in progress	£960	Profit and loss	£960

Variable Overhead Expenditure Variance Account

Variable overhead	£100	Profit and loss	£100

Fixed Overhead Expenditure Variance Account

Fixed overhead	£300	Profit and loss	£300

Fixed Overhead Efficiency Variance Account

Profit and loss	£825	Work in progress	£825

Fixed Overhead Capacity Variance Account

Work in progress	£1,200	Profit and loss	£1,200

Costing Profit and Loss Account Week Ending January 9

	£		£
Cost of sales	38,750	Sales	50,000
Direct material price		Direct labour rate	
variance	180	variance	32
Direct material usage		Direct labour efficiency	
variance	450	variance	660
Direct labour idle-time		Fixed overhead	
variance	960	efficiency variance	825
Variable overhead			
expenditure variance	100		
Fixed overhead			
expenditure variance	300		
Fixed overhead capacity			
variance	1,200		
Profit	9,577		
	£51,517		£51,517

It should be noted that the cost control account is recorded at actual cost, so there will be no problem involving use of standards when reconciling the cost accounts with the financial accounts.

The "price variances", i.e. direct material price, direct labour rate, variable overhead expenditure and fixed overhead expenditure variances, are shown in the respective expense accounts, viz. stores, direct wages, variable overheads, and fixed overheads. The "quantity" variances, i.e. direct material usage, direct labour efficiency and direct labour idle-time, fixed overhead efficiency, and capacity variances, are shown in the work-in-progress ledger control account. This procedure is followed because amounts spent on the different elements of cost (direct materials, direct wages, variable and fixed overheads) are charged at actual cost to the account concerned, but are transferred at standard cost to work in progress; this reveals the "price" variances. When the manufacturing process is carried out the "quantity" variances are calculated, and so are shown in work-in-progress ledger control account.

Presentation to Management

Quick and effective presentation of information to management is essential if the standard costing system is to justify itself. Furthermore, it is essential that management should act speedily to investigate variances and, where possible, make decisions to prevent recurrences of adverse variances.

Information presented to management should be as concise as possible, yet revealing all pertinent data. It has been mentioned already that one of the great advantages of both budgetary control and standard costing is that "management by exception" is facilitated. This principle is illustrated below, in the form of a profit and loss statement showing clearly where differences from standard have occurred, which enables management to concentrate on the major variances.

In Eyre Engineering PLC if a standard costing system had not been introduced information concerning the transactions discussed in this chapter may have been presented as follows:

Trading and Profit and Loss Account
for the week ending January 9

	£		£
Direct materials	14,580	Sales	50,000
Direct wages	9,568		
Variable expenses	3,975		
Fixed expenses	12,300		
Net profit	9,577		
	£50,000		£50,000

This simple account reveals that during the period concerned the company obtained a profit of £9,577, which represents about 20% of turnover. This figure appears to be satisfactory, but management have no yardstick by which to determine whether or not this figure could be improved upon.

However, a standard costing system is in use in Eyre Engineering PLC so that the information could be presented to management as follows:

Profit and Loss Statement
Week ending January 9

		£	£
Sales			50,000
Less Standard cost of sales:			
Direct materials		13,950	
Direct wages		9,300	
Variable overheads		3,875	
Fixed overheads		11,625	
			38,750
STANDARD NET PROFIT			11,250

Variances	F	A	F	A
	£	£	£	£
Direct material:				
Price		180		
Usage		450		
Total		—		630
Direct labour:				
Rate	32			
Efficiency	660			
Idle time		960		
Total		—		268
Variable overhead:				
Expenditure		100		
Total		—		100
Fixed overhead:				
Expenditure	300			
Efficiency	825			
Capacity	1,200			
Total		—		675
			—	1,673
Actual profit				£9,577

This statement reveals to management that the net profit expected during the period was £11,250, compared with that actually achieved of £9,577; this represents a very unfavourable reduction of £1,673. Investigations would be initiated into the major variances, particularly those which are adverse. It can be readily observed that idle time was an important factor, resulting in an adverse direct labour idle time variance and a consequent adverse overhead capacity variance; in addition, expenditure on overheads was greater than expected.

With regard to the favourable variances, it is encouraging to note that direct labour efficiency is high, with a resulting favourable overhead efficiency variance. It rather appears that management should concentrate their enquiries into ascertaining why idle time is so predominant, even though the labour force is so efficient. Investigations may reveal frequent plant breakdowns, power failures, or shortages of materials, so that possibly remedial action may be taken very quickly.

Example 2

This example is based on an examination question set by the Institute of Chartered Secretaries and Administrators. It is a general question involving most of the basic variances, and should provide a very useful revision of the variances discussed in the previous example.

Paulart PLC manufactures only one product.

The standard cost of one unit of product is made up as follows.

Direct materials: 20 units at £0·50 per unit
Direct wages: 3 hours at £4·00 per hour
Fixed overheads: 4 machine hours at £2·00 per machine hour

Budgeted output for the month of July is 10,000 units.
Budgeted fixed overheads for the month are £80,000.
Actual output for the month was 10,500 units.
There were no stocks of any kind.
Actual machine hours worked were 41,800.
Actual costs for the month were:

Purchases 215,000 units at £0·45 per unit
Wages   28,000 hours at £4·10 per hour

Fixed overheads were £84,500.

Prepare an operating statement for July, showing standard and actual costs, and an analysis of variances.

Details	Budgeted Cost			Actual Cost			Standard Cost		
	£		£		£		£		£
Direct materials	200,000	0·50	100,000	215,000	0·45	96,750	210,000	0·50	105,000
Direct wages	30,000	4·00	120,000	28,000	4·10	114,800	31,500	4·00	126,000
Fixed overheads	40,000	2·00	80,000	41,800		84,500	42,000	2·00	84,000
			£300,000			£296,050			£315,000

Operating Statement

Elements of Cost		Standard Cost £	Actual Cost £	Variance £	(F) £	(A) £
Direct materials		105,000	96,750	8,250		
	Price				10,750	
	Usage					2,500
Direct labour		126,000	114,800	11,200		
	Rate					2,800
	Efficiency				14,000	
Fixed overheads		84,000	84,500	500		
	Expenditure					4,500
	Efficiency				400	
	Capacity				3,600	
		£315,000	£296,050	£19,950		

NOTE: Standard cost
    Actual quantity produced × Standard cost per unit,
 e.g. Direct materials
   10,500 units required 20 units each at £0·50 per unit

Direct materials total variance
$$SC - AC$$
$$£105,000 - £96,750 = \underline{£8,250\,(F)}$$
Price variance
$$AQ\,(SP - AP)$$
$$215,000\,(£0·50 - £0·45) = \underline{£10,750\,(F)}$$
Usage variance
$$SP\,(SQ - AQ)$$
$$£0·50\,(210,000 - 215,000) = \underline{£2,500\,(A)}$$
Direct labour total variance
$$SC - AC$$
$$£126,000 - £114,800 = \underline{£11,200\,(F)}$$
Rate variance
$$AH\,(SR - AR)$$
$$28,000\,(£4·00 - £4·10) = \underline{£2,800\,(A)}$$
Efficiency variance
$$SR\,(SH - AH)$$
$$£4\,(31,500 - 28,000) = \underline{£14,000\,(F)}$$
Fixed overhead total variance
$$SC - AC$$
$$£84,000 - £84,500 = \underline{£500\,(A)}$$
Expenditure variance
$$BC - AC$$
$$£80,000 - £84,500 = \underline{£4,500\,(A)}$$

Volume variance

$$SC(AQ - BQ)$$
$$£8\,(10,500 - 10,000) = \underline{£4,000\,(F)}$$

Efficiency variance

$$SC(AQ - SQ)$$
$$£8\,(10,500 - 10,450) = \underline{£400\,(F)}$$

Capacity variance

$$SC(BQ - SQ)$$
$$£8\,(10,000 - 10,450) = \underline{£3,600\,(F)}$$

NOTE: SQ The quantity which should have been produced in the actual hours worked.

Hours which machines worked   41,800
Standard machine hours per unit   4
Therefore 10,450 units should have been produced.

Example 3

This example is a specific overhead variance problem. It is a relatively simple example and illustrates an easy approach to the calculation of basic overhead variances.

Budgeted overheads   £20,000
Budgeted output   10,000 units
Standard performance is 1 unit per hour
Actual overheads incurred   £21,500
Actual hours worked   11,000
Actual output   12,000 units

Calculate the overhead variances.

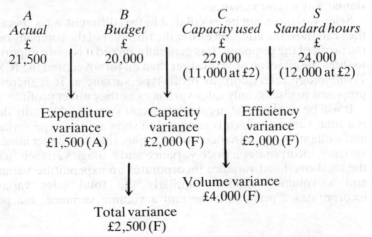

A Actual £	B Budget £	C Capacity used £	S Standard hours £
21,500	20,000	22,000 (11,000 at £2)	24,000 (12,000 at £2)

Expenditure variance £1,500 (A)   Capacity variance £2,000 (F)   Efficiency variance £2,000 (F)

Volume variance £4,000 (F)

Total variance £2,500 (F)

Check by formula

Total variance

$$SC - AC$$
$$£24,000 - £21,500 = \underline{£2,500\,(F)}$$

Expenditure variance

$$BC - AC$$
$$£20,000 - £21,500 = \underline{£1,500\,(A)}$$

Volume variance

$$SC\,(AQ - BQ)$$
$$£2\,(12,000 - 10,000) = \underline{£4,000\,(F)}$$

Efficiency variance

$$SC\,(AQ - SQ)$$
$$£2\,(12,000 - 11,000) = \underline{£2,000\,(F)}$$

Capacity variance

$$SC\,(SQ - BQ)$$
$$£2\,(11,000 - 10,000) = \underline{£2,000\,(F)}$$

Sales Variance

The basic variances discussed earlier have been concerned with the various elements of cost, viz. direct materials, direct labour, variable and fixed overhead. However, important though the effects of cost variances are on profits, there is another important influence on profits, namely, sales. Clearly, a change in sales price or a change in quantity of products sold will have an effect on a company's profit. Consequently sales variances can be analysed in a similar way to cost variances.

Sales variances can be calculated in two different ways, because they can show the effect on either the turnover of the company or on the profit of the company. It is generally agreed it is more important to show the effect on profits rather than on turnover, and the ICMA *Terminology* refers only to profit-type variances. It is therefore proposed to discuss only sales variances as they affect profit.

It will be recalled that in calculating cost variances basically there is a total variance which is analysed to show a price-type variance and a quantity-type variance; for example, the total direct material variance incorporates a price variance and a usage variance, while the total overhead variance incorporates an expenditure variance and a volume variance. Similarly the total sales variance incorporates a price variance and a volume variance, the price variance showing any change in actual price from that budgeted, and the volume variance showing any change in the quantity of sales.

Example

The budgeted sales for Jeraul PLC for the month of May are as follows.

Product	Quan-tity	Sales price per unit	Amount	Cost per unit	Amount	Profit per unit	Amount
		£	£	£	£	£	£
Jer	5,000	6·00	30,000	4·50	22,500	1·50	7,500
Aul	5,000	4·00	20,000	3·00	15,000	1·00	5,000
			£50,000		£37,500		£12,500

Actual sales for May were:

Jer	7,000	5·00	35,000	4·50	31,500	0·50	3,500
Aul	6,000	3·50	21,000	3·00	18,000	0·50	3,000
			£56,000		£49,500		£6,500

These results show that the actual quantities sold are different from those budgeted and the prices obtained are also different from those budgeted. In order to calculate the sales variances we need to know the standard sales which represent what the value of sales should have been in relation to the actual quantity sold—in other words actual quantity at standard prices. Hence the standard sales for May were:

		£	£	£	£	£	£
Jer	7,000	6·00	42,000	4·50	31,500	1·50	10,500
Aul	6,000	4·00	24,000	3·00	18,000	1·00	6,000
			£66,000		£49,500		£16,500

(a) Profit variance due to sales

Formula: Budgeted profit −   Actual profit

	BP	−	AP	£
	£		£	
Jer	7,500	−	3,500	4,000 (A)
Aul	5,000	−	3,000	2,000 (A)
	£12,500	−	£6,500	£6,000 (A)

(b) *Profit variance due to selling prices*
Formula   Standard profit   −   Actual profit
                SP   −   AP

	£		£	£
Jer	10,500	−	3,500	7,000 (A)
Aul	6,000	−	3,000	3,000 (A)
	£16,500	−	£6,500	£10,000 (A)

(c) *Profit variance due to sales volume*
Formula: Budgeted profit −   Standard profit
                BP   −   SP

	£		£	£
Jer	7,500	−	10,500	3,000 (F)
Aul	5,000	−	6,000	1,000 (F)
	£12,500	−	£16,500	£4,000 (F)

These variances show that while sales prices were lower than expected and so attracted a higher volume of sales than expected, the overall result was bad, reflected in the total variance of £6,000 adverse.

Investigation of Variances

On page 313 it was mentioned that in the presentation of data to management, variances highlight where specific action is needed to rectify differences from the budget. However, the question arises as to how significant is the variance, and is it worth investigation. Such an investigation costs money, in terms of time and effort of staff involved, so it is important to realise that the possible cost of an investigation should be balanced against the benefits likely to be obtained from such an action.

Frequently it is difficult to evaluate the cost of an investigation, and it is even more difficult to evaluate the benefits of such an investigation. Consequently some companies may adopt a "rule of thumb" attitude, such as to investigate only those variances which are adverse or those which exceed £100 or those which are greater than 5% of the standard. On the other hand some companies adopt refined statistical models which incorporate control limits, probability theory, tolerances, normal distribution curves, etc.

The importance of variance investigation must be stressed; variance analysis is of no value to management unless action results. It is essential that management is made aware of variances, that major variances are investigated, and that corrective action is taken.

Examination Questions

1. What is meant by standard costs; in what circumstances may they be safely employed; what advantages do they offer? (*ICMA*)

2. Give the main bases used in building up a standard cost within the divisions of material, labour and overhead costs.   (*SCCA*)

3. Distinguish between standard costs and actual costs, and explain the functions and values of each.   (*LCCI*)

4. What are the more important variances you would expect to appear in the operating statement of a manufacturing business using standard costs? What is the main reason for each, and what remedial action, if any, would you consider appropriate?   (*CAA*)

5. Give instances where efficiencies are indicated in costing information.   (*RSA*)

6. The comment is sometimes made that actual costs are better than standard costs. How does a proper standard costing system give both standard cost and actual cost and consequently give the benefit of comparison?   (*SCA*)

7. Illustrate by means of example the significance of "variances" in relation to standard costing technique and discuss the interpretation of such variances.   (*CAA*)

8. What are the most important variances you would expect to find in an operating statement of a manufacturing business using standard costs? Discuss the reasons for three types of variances and indicate any action you suggest should be taken to minimise such variances in future.   (*AIA*)

9. To assist factory management it is usual to analyse labour total variances as to cause. Give two instances each of the causes of:

   (*a*) labour rate variance;

   (*b*) labour efficiency variance.

In each case show how the amount of the variance would be obtained and what corrective action factory management might take.   (*ICMA*)

10. Give the main bases used in building up a standard cost within the divisions of material, labour and overhead costs.

                                                          (*SCCA*)

11. Wages variances cover wage-rate variance and labour efficiency variance.

What methods would you adopt to ascertain these variances?

(*LCCI*)

12. It sometimes happens that a favourable variance from one standard is directly related to an adverse variance from another, e.g. the purchase of processed materials may cause an adverse material price variance but a favourable labour efficiency variance. Give two examples other than the one given above, and explain how you would present and interpret the analysis of variances in such cases.

(*ICMA*)

13. Define the term "standard time". Of what factors is it made up? Give examples of its use.

(*RSA*)

14. A company using standard costs prepares a monthly profit and loss statement. What variances would you expect to find under the following headings: (*a*) material cost; (*b*) labour cost; and (*c*) head office expenses? Write a short note indicating the nature of each variance.

(*CAA*)

15. What are standard costs? Explain why their use is considered to be preferable to a comparison of actual costs with costs incurred in the past.

(*LCC*)

16. A manufacturer of electric irons is to introduce a standard costing system into his business and has asked you to assist him to compile reliable standard product costs and to advise him of their use.

You are required to:

(*a*) set out in the form of brief notes particulars of the information that would be required and of the steps to be taken to build the information obtained into the standard costs of the products being manufactured;

(*b*) state the use that could be made of the standard product costs by management in the running of the business and by the accountant in the accounting system

(*RSA*)

17. B Limited makes two products: C and D. Data on which the standard direct material costs per unit are based are as follows:

	Material E	Material F
Standard price per kilogram	£0·80	£0·50
Standard quantity, in kilogram		
Product C	4	5
Product D	3	6

During week ended 10th April in producing the following:

Product C	1,200
Product D	900

the materials consumed were:

	Quantity in kilogram	Actual price per kilogram £
Material E	7,400	0·84
Material F	11,400	0·49

You are required for week ended 10th April to:

(a) calculate the total standard direct material cost of the products made;

(b) calculate the total direct material cost variance;

(c) analyse (b) above into:

    (i) direct material price variance;

    (ii) direct material usage variance;

(d) state whether the variance you have calculated in answer to (c) (ii) above is consistent or inconsistent with the following comment:

"material losses in production were less than had been allowed for in the standard".   (RSA)

18. A lawn mower manufactured by PQR Limited consists of several components, three of which are made in the company's own machine shop. Production details of these are (per component):

Component	Metal cost	Hours
A	£12·00	4
B	£ 8·00	2
C	£10·00	3

The components which are purchased from outside suppliers cost £30·00 per lawn mower. Machining hourly rates are—wages £3·00, overhead £2·50.

Assembly details are:

Manufactured components:
    One component A at cost
    Two components B at cost
    One component C at cost

Purchased components £30·00
Direct wages: 8 hours at £2·80 per hour
Overhead: 8 hours at £1·40 per hour

Compile a standard cost sheet in two sections:
(a) showing the cost of each internally made component;
(b) showing the cost of one fully assembled lawn mower.

(LCCI)

19. From the information given below relating to SLM Limited, you are required to:
    (a) calculate and present the following variances:
        (i)   direct labour total;
        (ii)   direct labour rate;
        (iii) direct labour efficiency;
        (iv) direct labour idle time;
    (b) show the following accounts in the cost ledger, which is not integrated:
        (i)   direct wages:
        (ii) work-in-progress, direct labour.

The standard wage rate for the 500 employees in department X is £4·00 per hour. SLM Limited operates a 40-hour week, without any overtime, and the standard performance for the department for one hour is 1,000 units.

During a given period of four weeks, the actual output for the department was 158,000 units, all of which was transferred to finished stock. Due to a power failure four hours of idle time were incurred. Fifteen employees were actually paid at a rate of £4·25 per hour, five employees were paid at £3·75 per hour and the remainder were paid at the standard rate.

(ICMA)

20. BS Limited manufactures one standard product and operates a system of variance accounting using a fixed budget. As assistant management accountant you are responsible for preparing the monthly operating statements. Data from the budget, the standard product cost and for the month ended 31st October are given below.

Using the data given you are required to prepare the operating statement for the month ended 31st October to show the budgeted profit; the variances for direct materials, direct wages, overhead and sales, each analysed into causes; and actual profit.

Budgeted and standard cost data:
    Budgeted sales and production for the month 10,000 units
    Standard cost for each unit of product:
        Direct material: *X* 10 kilograms at £1 per kilogram
                        Y 5 kilograms at £5 per kilogram
        Direct wages   5 hours   at £3 per hour
        Fixed production overhead is absorbed at 200% of direct wages

Budgeted sales price has been calculated to give a profit of 20% of sales price.

Actual data for month ended 31st October:

Production, 9,500 units sold at a price of 10% higher than that budgeted.

Direct materials consumed:

    X 96,000 kilograms at £1·20 per kilogram

    Y 48,000 kilograms at £4·70 per kilogram

Direct wages incurred 46,000 hours at £3·20 per hour

Fixed production overhead incurred   £290,000   (*ICMA*)

Answers

Chapter 6

48. Reorder level

$$\begin{array}{ccc} \text{Max. C} & \times & \text{Max. RP} \\ 100 & \times & 7 \end{array} = \underline{700}$$

Minimum stock level

$$\begin{array}{ccc} \text{RL} & - & (\text{NC} \times \text{NRP}) \\ 700 & - & (60 \times 5) \end{array} = \underline{400}$$

Maximum stock level

$$\begin{array}{ccc} \text{RL} & - & (\text{Min C} \times \text{Min RP}) + \text{RQ} \\ 700 & - & (20 \times 3) + 400 = \underline{£1,040} \end{array}$$

Average stock level*

$$\frac{\text{Min. SL} + \text{Max. SL}}{2}$$

$$\frac{400 + 1,040}{2} = \underline{720}$$

		A		B
49. Reorder level	Max. C	×	Max. RP	
	75	×	6	75×4
		$\underline{450}$		$\underline{300}$

Minimum stock level

$$\begin{array}{cccc} \text{RL} & - & (\text{NC} \times \text{NRP}) & \\ 450 & - & (50 \times 5) & 300 - (50 \times 3) \\ & & \underline{200} & \underline{150} \end{array}$$

Maximum stock level

$$\begin{array}{cccc} \text{RL} & - & (\text{Min. C} \times \text{Min. RP}) + \text{RQ} & \\ 450 & - & (25 \times 4) + 300 & 300 - (25 \times 2) + 500 \\ & & \underline{650} & \underline{750} \end{array}$$

Average stock level*

$$\text{Min. SL} + \frac{\text{RQ}}{2}$$

$$200 + \frac{300}{2} \qquad 150 + \frac{500}{2}$$

$$\underline{350} \qquad\qquad \underline{400}$$

50. (a)   *Stores Ledger Account*

Material ....   Maximum level ....

Code ....   Minimum level ....

                                         Reorder level ....

*These two alternative formulae may be used according to preference.

Date	GRN	Receipts Q	P	A	SRN	Issues Q	P	A	Stock Q	P	A
Mar 1		180		720					180	4·0	720
4						120	4	480	60	4·0	240
8		120		552					180	4·4	792
11						90	4·4	396	90		396
14		90		432					180	4·6	828
17						72	4·6	331	108		497
21						48	4·6	221	60		276
24		120		624					180	5·0	900
28						46	5·0	230	134		670

(b) (i) Stock loss is 4 units at £5·2   £20·8
    FIFO system—last price is £624 ÷ 120 units
(ii) Physical stock is 130 units

60 of March 1 receipts at £4·00	240
70 of March 28 receipts at £5·20	364
	£604

51. (a) First method used is FIFO.

Receipts			Issues		
600	1·25	750			
200	1·20	240			
			400	1·25	500
500	1·15	575	200	1·25	250 }
			200	1·20	240 } 490
600	1·10	660			
			400	1·15	460

and so on

(b) Second method used is LIFO.

Receipts			Issues				Stock	
600	1·25	750					600	750
200	1·20	240					800	990
			400	200	1·20	240		
				200	1·25	250	400	500
500	1·15	575					900	1,075
			400	400	1·15	460	500	615
600	1·10	660					1,100	1,275
			400	400	1·10	440	700	835
500	1·20	600					1,200	1,435
			400	400	1·25	480	800	955
			300	100	1·20			
				200	1·10	220	500	615
500	1·15	575					1,000	1,190
			600	600	1·15	690	400	500
400	1·20	480					800	980
			300	300	1·20	360	500	620

It should be noted that the contracted method of showing the stock as one figure, e.g. 1,100 £1,275 (half way down), is not practical. One would have to show its makeup:

400	1·25	500
100	1·15	115
600	1·10	660
		1,275

and a means would have to be devised to keep these details of the composition of the stock readily available for use on each and every occasion, preferably on the face of the account.

52. Cost of stores loss: 40 at £1·25   £50

Receipts	2,420
Issues	2,000
Stock	420
Inventory	380
Loss	40

(i)   LIFO price

200 at £1·35	270	
200 at £1·30	260	530

(ii)   HIFO price

200 at £1·30	260	
100 at £1·20	120	380

(iii)   NIFO price

200 at £1·30		260

(iv)   Simple average price:

Receipts			Issues	
420	420	1·20	200	200
300	720	1·25	400	600
200	920	1·25	200	800
400	1,320	1·20	300	1,100
100	1,420	1·20	300	1,400
200	1,620	1·30	400	
300	1,920	1·30		
200	2,120	1·35		

The cumulative issues prior to 27th October are 1,400 which is greater than the cumulative receipts to 16th October. Therefore there are as yet four prices which have not been exhausted, so the average price of the remaining receipts is (1·20 + 1·30 + 1·30 + 1·35) ÷ 4 = £1·2875

(v)   Weighted average price

Receipts			Issues			Stock		
						420	1·2	506
			200	1·2	240	220		264
300	1·25	375				520	1·229	639
							£1·229	

(vi)   Periodic simple average price
(1·25 + 1·25 + 1·20 + 1·20 + 1·30 + 1·30 + 1·35 + 1·35) ÷ 8 = £1·275

(*vii*) Periodic weighted average price

	Receipts	
300	1·25	375
200	1·25	250
400	1·20	480
100	1·20	120
200	1·30	260
300	1·30	390
200	1·35	270
300	1·35	405
2,000		2,550 £1·275

Chapter 8

36. Skilled operators:

4 workers × 40 hour week	160 hours
Units produced per hour ×	12
	1,920 units

Actual output	2,400
Expected output	1,920
Bonus output	480

$$\% \frac{480}{2,400} \times 100 = \underline{20\%}$$

Unskilled operator:

Basic pay	40 hours at £2·50	100
Bonus 20%		20
Gross pay		£120

37. (*a*) *Rowan system*

	Job 123	*Job 345*
Time allowed	24	40
Time taken	18	25
Time saved	6	15
% Bonus	25%	37·5%

A's remuneration

Job 123	Pay 18 hours at £4	72	
	Bonus 25%	18	90
Job 345	Pay 25 hours at £4	100	
	Bonus 37·5%	37·5	137·5
			£227·5

Effective hourly rate

$$\frac{227 \cdot 5}{43} = \underline{£5 \cdot 3}$$

(b) *Halsey 50/50 system*

Job 123 Pay 18 hours at £4	72	
Bonus 3 hours at £4	12	84
Job 345 Pay 25 hours at £4	100	
Bonus 7·5 hours	30	130
		£214

38.

Time allowed	50 hours		
Time taken	40 hours		
Time saved	10 hours		
Pay 40 hours at £3		120	
Bonus 5 hours at £3		15	£135

39.

Time allowed	40 hours	
Time taken	32 hours	
Time saved	8 hours	

Halsey 50% scheme:

Pay 32 hours at £4	128	
Bonus—half time saved	16	
	£144	

Rowan scheme:

Pay 32 hours at £4	128	
Bonus—time saved/allowed		
8/40 = 20%	25·6	
	£153.6	

40. (a) Daywork system:

	A	B	C	D	E
Hours	170	146	162	164	183
Per hour	£2·20	£2·20	£2·20	£2·20	£2·20
Earnings	£374·00	£321·20	£356·40	£360·80	£402·60

(b) Piecework system:

	A	B	C	D	E
Production:					
H	97	38	—	188	2
	£2·20	£2·20		£2·20	£2·20
	£213·40	£83·60		£413·60	£4·40

	A	B	C	D	E
J	80	12	54	10	134
	£3·20	£3·20	£3·20	£3·20	£3·20
	£256·00	£38·40	£172·80	£32·00	£428·80
K		120	156		44
		£1·50	£1·50		£1·50
		£180·00	£234·00		£66·00
Total	£469·40	£302·00	£466·80	£445·60	£499·20

(c) Bonus system:

	A	B	C	D	E
Hours	170	146	162	166	183
Rate	£2·00	£2·00	£2·00	£2·00	£2·00
(i)	£340·00	£292·00	£324·00	£328·00	£366·00

Bonus:

	A	B	C	D	E
H units	97	38		188	2
S hours	1	1		1	1
	97	38		188	2
J units	80	12	54	10	134
S hours	1½	1½	1½	1½	1½
	120	18	81	15	201
K units		120	156		44
S hours		¾	¾		¾
		90	117		33

Total S hours for bonus calculation	217	146	198	203	236
Actual hours	170	146	162	164	183
Bonus hours	47	—	36	39	53
Rate	£3·00		£3·00	£3·00	£3·00
(i) Bonus payable	£141·00		£108·00	£117·00	£159·00
Total pay (i) + (ii)	£481·00	£292·00	£432·00	£445·00	£525·00

Chapter 11

32. *Machine costs per annum*

Depreciation	2,600	
Maintenance	480	
Power	2,000	
Rent and rates	440	$8,800 \times \frac{1}{20}$
Supervision	240	$7,200 \times \frac{1}{30}$
	£5,760	

$$\text{Hourly rate} \quad \frac{5,760}{1,800} = \underline{£3.20}$$

33.

Month	Overhead incurred	Overhead absorbed	Over/under absorption	Cumulative
Jan	2,800	2,400	− £400	− £400
Feb	2,700	2,300	− £400	− £800
Mar	2,900	2,500	− £400	− £1,200
Apr	2,700	2,350	− £350	− £1,550
May	2,300	2,700	+ £400	− £1,150
June	2,250	2,800	+ £550	− £600
July	3,400	1,200	− £2,200	− £2,800
Aug	2,300	2,450	+ £150	− £2,650
Sep	2,250	2,700	+ £450	− £2,200
Oct	2,900	4,200	+ £1,300	− £900
Nov	2,600	4,050	+ £1,450	+ £550
Dec	2,900	2,350	− £550	0
	£32,000	£32,000		

Note:

$$\text{Overhead absorption rate} = \frac{\text{Production overhead}}{\text{DLH}}$$

$$= \frac{£32,000}{192,000}$$

$$= £\frac{1}{6}$$

34. (*a*) Three methods of overhead absorption:

(*i*)   % of direct materials
(*ii*) labour hour rate
(*iii*) machine hour rate

Overhead rates:

(*i*) $\dfrac{\text{Overhead}}{\text{Direct materials}} \times 100 = \dfrac{45,000}{90,000} \times 100 = \underline{50\%}$

(*ii*) $\dfrac{\text{Overhead}}{\text{Labour hours}} = \dfrac{45,000}{30,000} = £1.50 \text{ per DLH}$

(*iii*) $\dfrac{\text{Overhead}}{\text{Machine hours}} = \dfrac{45,000}{10,000} = £4.50 \text{ per MH}$

Cost per unit:

Direct materials	90,000	
Direct labour	15,000	
		105,000
Overhead		45,000
		£150,000

The cost per unit will be the same under each method when based on the above data.

35. (a) Overhead absorption rates.

$$\begin{array}{cc}
\textit{Department P} & \textit{Department Q} \\
\dfrac{\text{Production overhead}}{\text{Direct labour}} \times 100 & \dfrac{\text{Production overhead}}{\text{Machine hours}} \\
\dfrac{517,500}{450,000} \times 100 & \dfrac{922,500}{180,000} \\
115\% & £5{\cdot}125
\end{array}$$

(b) Production overhead to be absorbed by Job 186.

Direct labour cost	£360	Machine hours	260
Absorption rate 115%		Absorption rate £5·125 per h.	
115% of £360 =	£416	260 × £5·125 =	£1,332·5

Hence total = £1,746·5

(c) Over/under absorbed overhead.

Direct labour cost	450,000	Machine hours	180,000
Rate	1·15		5·125
	517,500		922,500
Incurred	555,000		900,000
	£(37,500)		£22,500

£(15,000)

This analysis shows that £15,000 has been under-absorbed.

(d) The use of an overhead absorption rate which is based on a direct labour cost is not recommended, because labour rates can change, and/or there may be different rates of pay within the department, either of which would distort the absorption. Essentially overheads are incurred as a function of time, so a time-based absorption rate such as direct labour hour rate would reflect more effectively the time spent in production.

36. (a) The costs of the service departments H and J are to be absorbed by the production departments F and G. The absorption of service department costs is discussed briefly in the text, but is fully discussed in *Wheldon's Cost Accounting*, L. W. J. Owler and J. L. Brown (Macdonald & Evans, 1984).

	F	G	H	J
Overhead cost	380	240	160	180
H 70% 30%	112	48	(160)	
J 60% 40%	108	72	—	(180)
	£600	£360		

(b) Overhead absorption rate.

			F	G
(i)	Direct wages %:			
		$\dfrac{\text{Production overhead}}{\text{Direct wages}}$	$\dfrac{600}{500} \times 100$	$\dfrac{360}{450} \times 100$
			120%	80%
(ii)	Direct labour hour rate:			
		$\dfrac{\text{Production overhead}}{\text{Direct labour hours}}$	$\dfrac{600}{200}$	$\dfrac{360}{180}$
			£3	£2
(iii)	Direct materials %:			
		$\dfrac{\text{Production overhead}}{\text{Direct materials}}$	$\dfrac{600}{1,000} \times 100$	$\dfrac{360}{750} \times 100$
			60%	48%
(iv)	Prime cost %:			
		$\dfrac{\text{Production overhead}}{\text{Prime cost}}$	$\dfrac{600}{1,500} \times 100$	$\dfrac{360}{1,200} \times 100$
			40%	30%
(v)	Units of production:			
		$\dfrac{\text{Production overhead}}{\text{Units}}$	$\dfrac{600,000}{3,600,000}$	$\dfrac{360,000}{3,600,000}$
			£⅙th	£⅒th

NOTE:

Direct labour hours:	F	G
$\dfrac{\text{Direct labour cost}}{\text{Rate per hour}}$	$\dfrac{£500,000}{2\cdot5}$	$\dfrac{£450,000}{2\cdot5}$
	200,000	180,000
Units produced:		
Direct labour hours × Units per hour	200,000	180,000
	× 18	× 20
	3,600,000	3,600,000

Prime cost = Direct materials + Direct wages

(c) This answer is similar to that shown in the suggested answer to question 35 above.

Chapter 12

6. (a)   *Raw material stock*

Balance b/d	£190	Work in progress	£320
Purchases	350	Balance c/d	220
	£540		£540
Balance b/d	£220		

Work in progress

Balance b/d	£200	Finished goods	£864
Raw materials	320	Balance c/d	178
Wages	232		
Overhead	290		
	£1,042		£1,042
Balance b/d	£178		

Finished goods

Balance b/d	£260	Cost of sales	£904
Work in progress	864	Balance c/d	220
	£1,124		£1,124
Balance b/d	£220		

Production overhead

Purchases	£28	Work in progress	
Wages	114	$£232 \times \dfrac{125}{100}$	£290
Expenses	88		
Depreciation	50		
Profit & loss	10		
	£290		£290

Selling and distribution overhead

Wages	£52	Profit and loss	£96
Expenses	24		
Depreciation	20		
	£96		£96

(b)   *Profit and loss account*

Cost of sales	£904	Production overhead over	
Selling overhead	96	absorbed	£10
Profit	210	Sales	1,200
	£1,210		£1,210

7.

Cost ledger control

Sales	£148,800	Balance b/d	£22,410
Balance c/d	28,590	Purchases	43,200
		Wages	61,200
		Production expenses	36,216
		Selling expenses	5,760
		Net profit	8,604
	£177,390		£177,390
		Balance c/d	£28,590

Stores ledger control

Balance b/d	£7,560	Work in progress	£42,480
Purchases	43,200	Balance c/d	8,280
	£50,760		£50,760
Balance b/d	£8,280		

Work in progress

Balance b/d	£12,600	Finished goods	£135,060
Stores	42,480	Balance c/d	16,920
Wages	61,200		
Production overhead	35,700		
	£151,980		£151,980
Balance b/d	£16,920		

Finished goods

Balance b/d	£2,250	Cost of sales	£133,920
Work in progress	135,060	Balance c/d	3,390
	£137,310		£137,310
Balance b/d	£3,390		

Production overhead

Expenses	£36,216	Work in progress	£35,700
		Overhead under absorbed	516
	£36,216		£36,216

Selling and distribution overhead

Expenses	£5,760	Cost of sales	£5,610
		Overhead under absorbed	150
	£5,760		£5,760

Overhead under/over absorbed

Production overhead	£516	Profit and Loss	£666
Selling overhead	150		
	£666		£666

Cost of sales

Finished goods	£133,920	Profit and Loss	£139,530
Selling expenses	5,610		
	£139,530		£139,530

Profit and loss account for the year ending 31st December

Overhead under absorbed	£666	Sales	£148,800
Cost of sales	139,530		
Net profit	8,604		
	£148,800		£148,000

Trial balance as at 31st December

Stores ledger control	£8,280	
Work in progress	16,920	
Finished goods	3,390	
Cost ledger control		£28,590
	£28,590	£28,590

8.

Raw materials

Balance b/d	£15,832	Returns	£6,324
Purchases	98,746	Work in progress	93,247
		Balance c/d	15,007
	£114,578		£114,578
Balance b/d	£15,007		

Work in progress

Balance b/d	£8,110	Finished goods	£262,988
Raw materials	93,247	Balance c/d	7,815
Direct wages	84,723		
Overheads	84,723		
	£270,803		£270,803
Balance b/d	£7,815		

Finished goods

Balance b/d	£24,005	Cost of sales	£262,417
Work in progress	262,988	Balance c/d	24,576
	£286,993		£286,993
Balance b/d	£24,576		

Check:

Cost accounting profit and loss

Finished goods:			
Cost of sales	£262,417	Sales	£417,548
Overheads under absorbed	2,808		
Profit	152,323		
	£417,548		£417,548

9. (a)   General ledger control

Stores ledger control	£780	Balance b/d	£110,700
Sales	210,000	Stores ledger	21,250
Balance c/d	32,670	Wages	31,400
		Production salaries	24,100
		Production expenses	56,000
	£243,450		£243,450
		Balance b/d	£32,670

Stores ledger control

Balance b/d	£45,200	Returns	£780
General ledger	21,250	Work in progress 1	10,600
		Work in progress 2	5,200
		Work in progress 3	3,400
		Production overhead	640
		Balance c/d	45,830
	£66,450		£66,450
Balance b/d	£45,830		

Work in progress 1

Debit side of the account

	DM	DW	PO	Total
Balance b/d	£4,100	£3,200	£11,200	£18,500
Stores	10,600			10,600
Wages		8,400		8,400
Production overhead			29,400	29,400
	£14,700	£11,600	£40,600	66,900
Balance b/d	£2,160	£1,600	£5,600	£9,360

	DM	DW	PO	Total
Credit side of the account:				
A Loss	£240	£200	£700	£1,140
WiP 2	12,300	9,800	34,300	56,400
Balance c/d	2,160	1,600	5,600	9,360
	£14,700	£11,600	£40,600	£66,900

Work in progress 2

	DM	DW	PO	Total
Debit side of the account:				
Balance b/d	£15,600	£4,400	£11,000	£31,000
WiP 1	56,400			56,400
Stores	5,200			5,200
Wages		10,800		10,800
Prod. overhead			27,000	27,000
	£77,200	£15,200	£38,000	£130,400
Balance b/d	£21,500	£4,800	£12,000	£38,300
Credit side of the account:				
A Loss	£700	£140	£350	£1,190
WiP 3	55,000	10,260	26,650	90,910
Balance c/d	21,500	4,800	12,000	38,300
	£77,200	£15,200	£38,000	£130,400

Work in progress 3

	DM	DW	PO	Total
Debit side of the account:				
Balance b/d	£28,800	£6,400	£9,600	£44,800
WiP 2	90,910			90,910
Stores	3,400			3,400
Wages		12,200		12,200
Prod. overhead			18,300	18,300
	£123,110	£18,600	£27,900	£169,610
Balance b/d	£37,400	£5,600	£8,400	£51,400
Credit side of the account:				
A Loss	£1,450	£220	£330	£2,000
Finished goods	84,260	12,780	19,170	116,210
Balance c/d	37,400	5,600	8,400	51,400
	£123,110	£186,000	£27,900	£169,610

Finished goods

Balance b/d	£44,500	Cost of sales		£111,610
WiP 3	116,210	Balance c/d		49,100
	£160,710			£160,710
Balance b/d	£49,100			

Production overhead

Stores	£640	WiP1	£29,400
Salaries	24,100	WiP2	27,000
Expenses	56,000	WiP3	18,300
		Overhead under recovered	6,040
	£80,740		£80,740

Production overhead under/over recovered

Production overhead	£6,040	Balance b/d	£2,400
		Balance c/d	3,640
	£6,040		£6,040
Balance b/d	£3,640		

Wages

Direct wages	£31,400	WiP1	£8,400
		WiP2	10,800
		WiP3	12,200
	£31,400		£31,400

Abnormal loss

Balance b/d	£4,500	Balance c/d	£8,830
WiP1	1,140		
WiP2	1,190		
WiP3	2,000		
	£8,830		£8,830
Balance b/d	£8,830		

Cost of sales

Balance b/d	£264,600	Balance c/d	£376,210
Finished goods	111,610		
	£376,210		£376,210
Balance	£376,210		

Sales

Balance c/d	£550,000	Balance b/d	£340,000
		Sales	210,000
	£550,000		£550,000
		Balance b/d	£550,000

(b)   *Trial balance as at 30th April*

General ledger control		£32,670
Stores ledger	£45,830	
WiP1	9,360	
WiP2	38,300	

WiP3	51,400	
Finished goods	49,100	
Production overhead underabsorbed	3,640	
Abnormal loss	8,830	
Cost of sales	376,210	
Sales		550,000
	£582,670	£582,670

Chapter 13

10.   *Reconciliation statement*

Profit as per financial books	£16,624	Profit as per cost accounts	£23,063
Stock difference	3,076	Wages	1,734
Overhead	1,112	Administration exs.	550
Selling expenses	4,851	Sundry income	316
	£25,663		£25,663

NOTES:

Stock:

Cost books	£78,197
Fin. books	75,121
	£3,076

Direct wages:

Cost books	£24,867
Fin. books	23,133
	£1,734

Factory overhead:

Fin. books	£20,826
Cost books	19,714
	£1,112

Administration:

Cost books	£10,395
Fin. books	9,845
	£550

Selling expenses:

Fin. books	£22,176
Cost books	17,325
	£4,851

11. (*a*) Interest on capital is debited to production overhead and credited to interest on capital. The overhead charge is absorbed into work in progress and

eventually into cost of sales, thus reducing the profit, while the credit is transferred to profit and loss account, thus increasing the profit. The real effect on profit is zero because it is purely a nominal charge. However it has reflected the cost of investing capital in stocks, which is the object of the exercise.

(*b*) Underabsorption of overheads can occur because production is lower than expected or expenditure is greater than expected. Any under absorption of overheads should be written off to the cost accounting profit and loss account.

(*c*) Profit shown in cost accounts.

Sales		£747,800	
Costs:			
Materials	£205,600		
Wages	71,400		
Overhead	154,200		
	431,200		
WiP:			
Opening £10,200			
Closing 10,600	400		
	430,800		
F goods:			
Opening 22,100			
Closing 22,000	100	430,900	
		316,900	
Production overhead under absorbed	2,200		
Interest on capital	5,000	2,800	
Profit		£319,700	

Reconciliation account

Profit per financial accounts		£319,500	Profit per cost accounts		£319,700
Differences in stock			Differences in stock		
R M closing	£1,000		R M opening	£1,300	
WiP opening	800		WiP closing	700	2,000
F G opening	300				
F G closing	100	2,200			
		£321,700			£321,700

12. (*a*)

Raw materials

Balance b/d	£25,648		Work in progress		£101,573
Difference	160	£25,808	Balance c/d	£23,691	
			Difference	211	23,902
Purchases	102,346				
Returns	2,679	99,667			
		£125,475			£125,475
Balance b/d	23,691				
Difference	211	£23,902			

Work in progress

Balance b/d	£12,248		Finished goods		£241,762
Difference	175	£12,073	Balance c/d	£11,862	
			Difference	148	
Direct materials		101,573			
Direct wages		40,036			12,010
Production overhead					
250% of direct wages		100,090			
		£253,772			£253,772

Finished goods

Balance b/d	£31,945		Cost of sales		£240,871
Difference	326	£31,615	Balance c/d	£32,851	
			Difference	341	32,510
Work in progress		241,762			
		£273,381			£273,381

(b)   Production overhead

Actual	£95,340
Absorbed	100,090
Over-absorbed	£4,750

13. (a)   Raw materials

Balance b/d	£110		Work in progress		£678
Difference	7	103	Balance c/d	£130	
			Difference	15	145
Purchases	640				
Returns	20	620			
		£723			£723
Balance b/d	130				
Difference	15	145			

Work in progress

Balance b/d	£25		Finished goods		£984
Difference	3	£28	Balance c/d	£27	
			Difference	5	22
Direct materials		578			
Direct wages		240			
Production overhead		160			
		£1,006			£1,006
Balance b/d	27				
Difference	5	22			

Finished goods

Balance b/d	£82		Cost of sales		£989
Difference	9	£73	Balance c/d	£72	
			Difference	4	68
Work in progress		984			
		£1,157			£1,157
Balance b/d		£68			

Profit and loss

Cost of sales	£989	Sales	£1,500
Production overhead	2		
Administration	200		
Profit	309		
	£1,500		£1,500

(*b*) As discussed in 11 (*a*) above, notional interest on capital locked up in stock may be included in the cost accounts. Brief reasons for this are that interest is the reward of capital, and that this interest would have to be paid to someone if the capital was borrowed. If interest has been treated as discussed in 11 (*a*) then there will be no need to reconcile the accounts, because the cost accountant will have eliminated the effect of the interest charged, and the financial accountant will ignore completely any notional charge.

Chapter 14

4.

			Job 171		*Job 172*		*Job 173*
Contract price			£3,550		£3,475		—
Costs:							
Materials	£900 + £216			£864		£1,243	
Wages	288 + 720			1,080		630	
Overhead	258 + 648			972		567	
	£1,446 + £1,584	3,030		2,916		£2,439	
		£520		£559		—	

Profit earned in April:		
Job 171	£520	
Job 172	559	
Job 173	—	(assumed no profit taken)
	£1,079	
Overhead under absorbed	63	(£2,250 − £2,187)
	£1,016	

5.

Contract account

Direct materials	£340	Returns to store	£8
Direct wages	220	Returns to suppliers	7
Direct wages accrued c/d	10	Transfers	15
Direct expenses	25	Materials on site c/d	20
Direct expenses accrued c/d	5	Plant c/d	75
Plant	100	Cost c/d	720
Overhead	85		
Establishment charges	60		
	£845		£845

Cost b/d	720	Value of work certified	800
Profit and loss	84	Cost of work c/d	60
Profit provision c/d	56		
	£860		£860
Materials b/d	20	Wages b/d	20
Plant b/d	75	Expenses b/d	5
Cost b/d	60	Profit provision b/d	56

NOTE:

$$\text{Profit and Loss} = 2/3 \times \frac{\text{Cash received}}{\text{Work certified}} \times \text{Notional profit}$$
$$= 2/3 \times \frac{720,000}{800,000} \times 140,000$$

Work in progress

Cost to date	£720,000
Profit	84,000
	804,000
Cash	720,000
	£84,000

6. Contract 320

Materials	£38,000	Returns	£600
Materials	4,000	Plant returned	600
Wages	15,000	Materials c/d	1,300
Expenses	2,000	Plant c/d	3,000
Plant	5,000	Cost c/d	71,500
Fees	2,000		
Sub-contract	7,000		
Head office overhead	4,000		
	£77,000		£77,000

Cost b/d	71,500	Value of work certified	82,500
Profit and loss	10,000	Work not certified c/d	4,000
Profit provision a/c	5,000		
	£86,500		£86,500

Materials b/d	1,300	Profit provision b/d	5,000
Plant b/d	3,000		
Cost b/d	4,000		

Work in progress

This may be shown as:

	Value of retention	£8,250
	Work not certified	4,000
		12,250
	Profit provision	5,000
		£7,250

or as:

	Cost	£71,500
	Profit	10,000
		81,500
	Cash received	74,250
		£7,250

Balance Sheet (Extract)

Plant	£3,000
Materials on site	1,300
Work in progress	7,250

7. (*a*)   *Selling price*

Direct materials	£100	
Direct wages	120	
Variable overhead	20	
	240	
Production overhead	120	(30 h × £4/h)
	360	
Administration overhead	90	
	450	
Selling overhead	180	
	630	
Profit 33⅓% on cost		
or 25% on SP	210	
	£840	

NOTE:
(1)   Administration overhead (charged as a % of production cost) =

$$\frac{\text{Administration overhead}}{\text{Production cost}} \times 100$$

$$= \frac{350,000}{1,400,000} \times 100$$

$$= \underline{25\%}$$

(2)   Selling overhead = $\dfrac{\text{Selling overhead}}{\text{Production cost}} \times 100$

$$= \frac{700,000}{1,400,000} \times 100$$

$$= \underline{50\%}$$

8. (a)   *Contract M101*

Direct materials	£2,560	Returns	£25
Direct wages	1,320	Insurance	30
Direct wages accrued c/d	30	Stock c/d	355
Direct expenses	240	Plant c/d	1,500
Direct expenses accrued c/d	10	Cost c/d	4,800
Plant	2,000		
Site overhead	370		
Allocated charge	180		
	£6,710		£6,710

Cost b/d	4,800	Value of work certified	5,000
Profit and loss	540	Cost not certified c/d	700
Profit provision c/d	360		
	£5,700		£5,700

Stock b/d	355	Wages accrued b/d	30
Plant b/d	1,500	Expenses accrued b/d	10
Cost of work not certified	700	Profit provision b/d	360

(b)   *Work in progress*
As in question 6, this may be shown in one of the following ways:

Value of retention	£500
Work not certified	700
	1,200
Profit provision	360
	£840

or as:

Cost	£4,800
Profit	540
	5,340
Cash received	4,500
	£840

348   ANSWERS

Chapter 15

6. February is the least productive: £886 ÷ 636 = £1·39
   March is the most productive: £2,266 ÷ 1,584 = £1·43
   Average monthly production: £9,200 ÷ 6,738 = £1·36

This seems to be an illogical method of charging cost to the machine operations, e.g. March operations are considerably less than for April, yet the labour cost is higher. Similarly the other overheads charged to each of these two months is the same.

7.

Materials	£18,000 + 20% + 20%	£25,920
Wages	£27,000 + 20% + 5%	34,020
Overheads	£11,250 + 33⅓%	15,000
		74,940
Management salaries		13,500
Rent		2,250
Selling expenses		6,750
General expenses		4,500
		101,940
Profit		25,485
		£127,425

Selling price $\frac{£127,425}{2,700}$ £47·20

Chapter 16

7. (a)

	1	2	3	4	
Annual mileage	150	160	60	70	
Average passengers	16	15	8	12	
Passenger miles	2,100	2,400	480	840	
Revenue	£105	£120	£24	£42	
Variable costs	£45	£48	£18	£21	
Fixed costs	18	24	12	12	
	£63	£72	£30	£33	
Revenue less costs	42	48	(6)	9	93
General admin.					74
					£19

(b)

Annual mileage	60	
Average passengers	16	
Passenger miles	960	
Revenue	£36	
Variable costs	30	
Contribution	£6	

8. (a) Analysis of fixed and variable costs—see graph. Fixed costs are approximately £7,200, variable costs are approximately £3 per hour, e.g.:

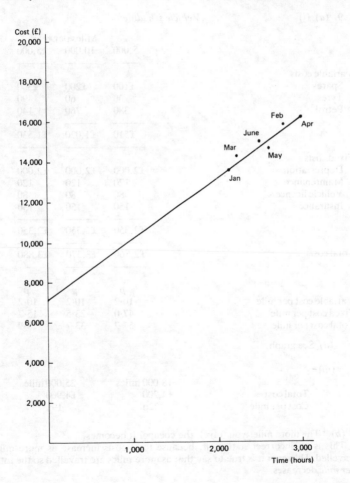

April

Total costs	£16,200	
Fixed costs	7,200	
Variable costs	£9,000	for 3,000 hours

(*b*) Charging out of costs would be briefly as follows.

(*i*) Transport costs would be analysed into fixed and variable costs.
(*ii*) A rate for each type of vehicle would be calculated, say per ton/mile.
(*iii*) Each department using a vehicle would be charged at this standard rate.
(*iv*) Results would be monitored to ensure that the rates were viable.

9. (*a*) (*i*)

Vehicle schedule

	Miles per year			
	5,000	10,000	15,000	30,000
Variable costs				
Spares	£100	£200	£300	£600
Tyres	30	60	90	180
Petrol	380	760	1,140	2,280
	£510	£1,020	£1,530	£3,060
Fixed costs				
Depreciation	£2,000	£2,000	£2,000	£2,000
Maintenance	120	120	120	120
Vehicle licence	80	80	80	80
Insurance	150	150	150	150
	£2,350	£2,350	£2,350	£2,350
Total costs	£2,860	£3,370	£3,880	£5,210
	p	*p*	*p*	*p*
Variable cost per mile	10·2	10·2	10·2	10·2
Fixed cost per mile	47·0	23·5	15·7	7·8
Total cost per mile	57·2	33·7	25·9	18·0

(*ii*) See graph.

(*iii*)

	18,000 miles	25,000 miles
Total cost	£4,200	£4,900
Cost per mile	22p	19p

(*b*) "The more miles you travel, the cheaper it becomes."

This is an incorrect statement, because total costs increase as more miles are travelled. However it is true to say that as more miles are travelled so the total cost *per mile* decreases.

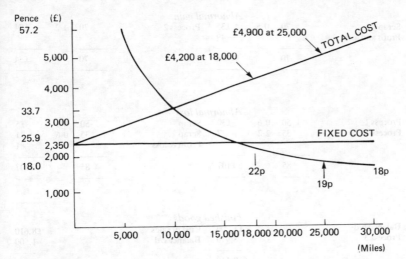

Chapter 17

10.

Process 1

Direct materials	5,000	0·2	£1,000	Normal loss	250	0·1	£25
Direct materials			700	Abnormal loss	50	0·6	30
Direct wages			300	Process 2	4,700	0·6	2,820
Direct expenses			275				
Production overhead			600				
	5,000		£2,875		5,000		£2,875

Process 2

Process 1	4,700	0·6	£2,820	Normal loss	470	0·5	£235
Direct materials			800	Process 3	4,300	1·2	5,160
Direct wages			500				
Direct expenses			191				
Production overhead			1,000				
Abnormal gain	70	1·2	84				
	4,770		£5,395		4,770		£5,395

Process 3

Process 2	4,300	1·2	£5,160	Normal loss	215	0·6	£129
Direct materials			1,300	Abnormal loss	35	2·2	77
Direct wages			800	Finished goods	4,050	2·2	8,910
Direct expenses			256				
Production overhead			1,600				
	4,300		£9,116		4,300		£9,116

Abnormal gain

Scrap	70	0·5	£35	Process 2	70	1·2	£84
Profit and loss			49				
	70		£84		70		£84

Abnormal loss

Process 1	50	0·6	£30	Scrap	50	0·1	£5
Process 3	35	2·2	77	Scrap	35	0·6	21
				Profit & loss			81
	85		£107		85		£107

Finished goods

Balance b/d	£1,200	Cost of sales	£8,610
Process 3	8,910	Balance c/d	1,500
	£10,110		£10,110
Balance b/d	£1,500		

11.

Process 1

Opening stock							
DM	800	26	£20,800	Process 2	800	34	£27,200
DL & O		8	1,600				
Labour & overhead			4,800				
	800		£27,200		800		£27,200

Process 2

Process 1	800	34	£27,200	Process 3	600	40	£24,000
Labour & overhead		6	4,560	Closing stock			
				DM	200	34	6,800
				DL & O		6	960
	800		£31,760		800		£31,760

Process 3

Opening stock							
DM	400	40	£16,000	Finished goods	900	44	£39,600
DL & O		4	800	Closing stock	100	40	4,000
Process 2	600	40	24,000			6	240
Labour & overhead			3,040				
	1,000		£43,840		1,000		£43,840

12. *Equivalent units evaluation*

Input		Output		DM1	DM2	DM3	DW	PO	Total
Opening stock	400	Opening stock	400	—	80	80	200	240	
Process 2	5,400	NL	200	—	—	—	—	—	
		AL	50	50	40	40	30	20	
		CPDP	4,150	4,150	4,150	4,150	4,150	4,150	
		CS	1,000	1,000	500	450	300	250	
Equiv. units	5,000		5,800	5,200	4,770	4,720	4,680	4,660	
Cost (£)				6,240	2,862	944	468	1,398	£11,912
Cost per unit (£)				1·20	0·60	0·20	0·10	0·30	£2·40

Evaluation

		DM1	DM2	DM3	DW	PO	Total
Opening stock	—	£48	£16	£20		£72	£156
Abnormal loss	£60	24	8	3		6	101
Finished goods	4,980	2,490	830	415		1,245	9,960
Closing stock	1,200	300	90	30		75	1,695
	£6,240	£2,862	£944	£468		£1,398	£11,912

Process 3

Opening stock	400	£804	Normal loss	200	—
Process 2	5,400	6,240	Abnormal loss	50	£101
Material			Process 4	4,550	10,920
X		2,862	Closing stock	1,000	1,695
Y		944			
Direct wages		468			
Production overhead		1,398			
	5,800	£12,716		5,800	£12,716

Abnormal loss

Process 3	£101	Profit and loss	£101

13. *Process A*

Direct material	5,000	£30,000	Normal loss	1,000	£1,500
Direct material	10,000		Process B	4,200	94,500
Direct wages		12,000			
Direct expenses		7,500			
Production overhead		32,000			
Abnormal gain	200	4,500			
	5,200	£96,000		5,200	£96,000

Process B

Process A	4,200	£94,500	Normal loss	210	£1,050
Direct materials		3,100	Abnormal loss	90	3,420
Direct wages		14,700	Byproduct	100	3,800
Direct expenses		1,170	Finished goods	3,800	144,400
Production overhead		39,200			
	4,200	£152,670		4,200	£152,670

Byproduct Process B

Process B	100	£3,800	Sales	100	£6,000
Direct materials		100			
Direct wages		300			
Production overhead		800			
Profit and loss		1,000			
	100	£6,000		100	£6,000

Abnormal loss

Process B	90	£3,420	Scrap	90	£450
			Profit and loss		2,970
	90	£3,420		90	£3,420

Abnormal gain

Scrap	200	£300	Process A	200	£4,500
Profit and loss		4,200			
	200	£4,500		200	£4,500

Chapter 18

10. (b)

1,000 units cost	£10,000
1,100 units cost	10,700
100 units cost	£700 (incremental cost)

Hence variable cost per unit is £7.

    (i) Cost of 990 units:

Marginal cost £990 × 7	£6,930
Fixed cost	3,000
	£9,930

  (ii) Fixed cost:

1,000 units cost	£10,000
Marginal cost 1,000 × 7	7,000
Hence fixed cost	£3,000

  (iii) Breakeven point:

$$\text{Fixed cost} \div \text{C/S\%}$$
$$\text{or Fixed cost} \times \text{C/S\%}$$
$$£3,000 \times \frac{11}{4} = \underline{£8,250}$$

Check:

Sales 750 × 11	£8,250	
Marginal cost × 7	5,250	
Contribution	3,000	
Fixed cost	3,000	
Profit	nil	

11.

		A		B
Sales price		£100		£100
Materials	£20		£15	
Wages	10		20	
Overhead (variable)	15	45	20	55
Contribution		£55		£45
Per week		£11,000		£4,500

The most profitable product is A.

Marginal costing shows the contribution which each product makes towards the total fixed overhead and profit. Absorption costing shows the fixed overhead absorbed by each product and, as shown in the question, has distorted the profit figure.

12.

Sales			£58,100
Direct materials		£20,040	
Direct labour		8,920	
Variable production overhead		2,100	
Variable overhead		3,800	34,860
Contribution			23,240
Fixed overhead: production		13,200	
other		3,600	16,800
Profit			£6,440

(*a*) See graph.
(*b*) See graph.
(*c*)

$$\frac{\text{Fixed cost} + \text{profit}}{\text{C/S\%}} = \frac{£29,400}{40\%}$$

$$= \frac{£29,400 \times 100}{40}$$

$$= £73,500$$

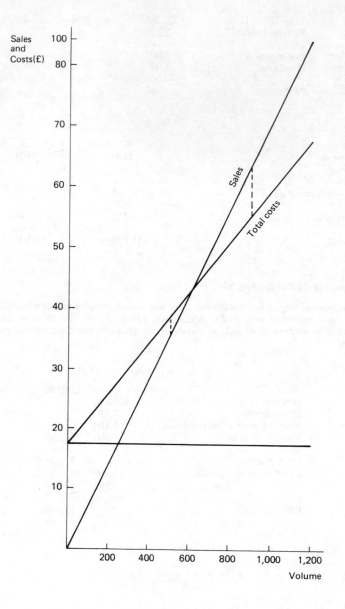

Check:

Sales 1,250 at £70	£73,500	
Marginal cost at £42	44,100	
Contribution	29,400	
Fixed cost	16,800	
Profit	£12,600	

In (b) above it can be seen from the graph that the profit at an output of 500 units is approximately (£3,000) and at an output of 900 units is approximately £8,000. This can be checked:

	5,000 units	9,000 units
Sales at £70	£35,000	£63,000
Marginal cost at £42	21,000	37,800
Contribution	14,000	25,200
Fixed cost	16,800	16,800
	£(2,800)	£8,400

13. (a) (i) Marginal costing basis:

Sales	£1,200,000
Marginal cost	450,000
Contribution	750,000
Fixed overhead	447,000
Profit	£303,000

(ii) Absorption costing basis:

Sales		£1,200,000
Marginal cost of sales		450,000
		750,000
Fixed overhead:		
Production	£322,000	
Opening stock	52,500	
	374,500	
Closing stock	24,500	
	350,000	
Selling	125,000	475,000
Profit		£275,000

(b) Difference in profit:

Marginal costing	£303,000
Absorption costing	275,000
	£28,000

This difference is due to the fact that in marginal costing, the overhead for a period is carried by the production *in that period,* whereas in absorption costing overhead is *absorbed* at a rate, and therefore the amount is affected by opening and closing stocks. Hence

Opening stock	7,500 × £7	£52,500
Closing stock	3,500 × £7	24,500
		£28,000

14.

	Y	Z
Sales	£150,000	£150,000
Variable costs	120,000	100,000
Contribution	30,000	50,000
Fixed costs	15,000	35,000
Profit	£15,000	£15,000

(a) Break-even point:

$$\frac{F}{C/S\%}$$

	Y	Z
	15,000	35,000
	20%	33⅓%
	£75,000	£105,000

A break-even chart could be drawn to show these points and to indicate the margin of safety.

(b) To earn a profit of £5,000 it is necessary to add the profit to the break-even point. Thus the formula is

$$\frac{F+P}{C/S\%} =$$

	Y	Z
	$\dfrac{15,000 + 5,000}{20\%}$	$\dfrac{35,000 + 5,000}{33⅓\%}$
	£100,000	£120,000

(c) In conditions of heavy demand, Company Z, which has low variable costs, will be likely to earn greater profits, while in conditions of low demand, Company Y, which has low fixed costs, will be likely to earn greater profits. If a break-even chart is drawn for each business, it will be apparent that the above remarks will be shown to be relevant.

15. Where a change in price occurs, as in the question, it is essential to compare results which are based on the same price levels. Here, prices for 19–2 should be converted to those of 19–1. (It may be recalled that in statistics, price indices are used for this purpose.)

Thus 19–2 sales are converted thus:

Sales at 19–2 prices	£225,000	
Price change 25% 100/125 × 225	180,000	
	£45,000	
19–2 sales at 19–1 prices	180,000	
19–1 sales at 19–1 prices	125,000	
Favourable volume change	£55,000	
Increase in selling price		£45,000
Favourable volume change	55,000	

Gross profit margin

$$\frac{\text{Gross profit}}{\text{Sales}} \times 100 = \frac{25,000}{125,000} \times 100 = \underline{20\%}$$

Hence profit is increased by volume change:

£55,000 × 20%		11,000

Decrease in production costs:

19–1 cost of production	£100,000	
Volume change $\frac{55,000}{125,000} \times 100 = 44\%$	44,000	
Expected costs 19–2	144,000	
Actual costs 19–2	120,000	24,000
Change in gross profit		£80,000
Year 2 gross profit	£105,000	
Year 1 gross profit	25,000	
	£80,000	

Chapter 20

9.

Cash forecast

	April	May	June
Balance b/d	£2,900	£(2,600)	£6,700
Sales	48,000	58,200	60,240
Ancillary income	—	—	1,000
Total	£50,900	£55,600	£67,940

Payments:	*April*	*May*	*June*
Wages	12,500	14,900	14,400
Salaries	3,000	3,000	3,200
Overheads	13,000	11,000	10,500
Materials	25,000	20,000	21,000
Dividends	—	—	10,000
Total	£53,500	£48,900	£59,100
Balance c/d	£(2,600)	£6,700	£8,840

There is expected to be a cash shortage in April, so presumably the bank manager would be asked to arrange for an overdraft to cover that month.

10.

	Cash budget		
	Jan	*Feb*	*Mar*
Balance	£(11,000)	£(11,900)	£(24,900)
Sales	55,000	45,000	45,000
Total	£44,000	£33,100	£20,100
Payments:			
Purchases	48,000	50,000	50,000
Wages and expenses	7,900	8,000	8,000
Total	£55,900	£58,000	£58,000
Balance c/d	£(11,900)	£(24,900)	£(27,900)

	July	*Aug*	*Sept*	*Oct*	*Nov*	*Dec*
Balance b/d	£	£(3)	£(2)	£(1)	—	£1
Sales	35	40	40	40	£40	40
Total	£36	£37	£38	£39	£40	£41
Payments						
Purchases	32	32	32	32	32	36
Vehicle						20
Expenses	5	5	5	5	5	5
Drawings	2	2	2	2	2	2
Total	£39	£39	£39	£39	£39	£63
Balance c/d	£(3)	£(2)	£(1)	—	£1	£(22)

11.

	Jan	*Feb*	*Mar*	*Apr*	*May*	*June*
Balance b/d	£(21)	£(25)	£(23)	£(21)	£(19)	£(17)
Sales	40	45	45	45	45	45
Total	£18	£20	£22	£24	£26	£28
Payments						
Purchases	36	36	36	36	36	40
Vehicle						
Expenses	5	5	5	5	5	5
Drawings	2	2	2	2	2	2
Total	£43	£43	£43	£43	£43	£47
Balance c/d	£(25)	£(23)	£(21)	£(19)	£(17)	£(19)

Forecast profit and loss 19–3

Sales		£510,000
Purchases		408,000
Gross profit		102,000
Expenses	£60,000	
Depreciation	12,000	72,000
Profit		£30,000

Balance sheet 19–3

Capital		£126,000	Fixed assets	£58,000	
Profit	£30,000		*Less* Depreciation	12,000	
Less Drawings	24,000	6,000			
		132,000		46,000	
Current liabilities		40,000	*Plus* Vehicle	20,000	£66,000
Bank overdraft		19,000	Current assets		
			Stock	80,000	
			Debtors	45,000	125,000
		£191,000			£191,000

12.

Production budget 19–2

	Closing stock £	Sales £	Sub-total £	Opening stock £	Production £
Jan	300	2,200	2,500	500	2,000
Feb	500	2,200	2,700	300	2,400
Mar	700	3,300	4,000	500	3,500
Apr	900	4,400	5,300	700	4,600
May	1,500	7,200	8,700	900	7,800
June	1,700	9,600	11,300	1,500	9,800
July	1,500	9,600	11,100	1,700	9,400
Aug	1,700	9,600	11,300	1,500	9,800
Sept	500	6,600	7,100	1,700	5,400
Oct	900	4,400	5,300	500	4,800
Nov	100	3,300	3,400	900	2,500
Dec	700	2,200	2,900	100	2,800

Purchases budget 19-2
'000 lb

	Closing stock	Production	Sub-total	Opening stock	Purchases	Purchases value = purchases × £200
Jan	2	20	22	4	18	3,600
Feb	6	24	30	2	28	5,600
Mar	6	35	41	6	35	7,000
Apr	8	46	54	6	48	9,600
May	18	78	96	8	88	17,600

	Closing stock	Production	Sub-total	Opening stock	Purchases	Purchases value = purchases × £200
June	14	98	112	18	94	18,800
July	16	94	110	14	96	19,200
Aug	16	98	114	16	98	19,600
Sept	8	54	62	16	46	9,200
Oct	12	48	60	8	52	10,400
Nov	4	25	29	12	17	3,400
Dec	6	28	34	4	30	6,000
						£130,000

13. (a)   *Production budget—units*

Product X:

	Jan	Feb	Mar
Sales	900	1,100	1,200
Closing stock	550	600	650
	1,450	1,700	1,850
Opening stock	450	550	600
	1,000	1,150	1,250

Product Y:

Sales	1,400	1,600	1,800
Closing stock	800	900	750
	2,200	2,500	2,550
Opening stock	700	800	900
	1,500	1,700	1,650

(b)   *Variable production cost budget*

Product X:

	Jan	Feb	Mar	Total
Direct materials	£18,000	£20,700	£22,500	£61,200
Direct wages	6,000	6,900	7,500	20,400
Variable production overhead	6,000	6,900	7,500	20,400
	£30,000	£34,500	£37,500	£102,000

Product Y:

Direct materials	£22,500	£25,500	£24,750	£72,750
Direct wages	6,000	6,800	6,600	19,400
Variable production overhead	7,500	8,500	8,250	24,250
	£36,000	£40,800	£39,600	£116,400

(c)   *Budgeted statement 1st quarter*

	X	Y	Total
Sales	£160,000	£216,000	£376,000
Direct materials	57,600	72,000	129,600
Direct wages	19,200	19,200	38,400
Overhead	19,200	24,000	43,200
	96,000	115,200	£211,200
	£64,000	£100,800	£164,800
Contribution			

Fixed overhead:

Production	£45,000	
Administration	15,000	
Selling	18,000	78,000
Profit		£86,800

(d) Factors which will influence stock policy.

(i) Minimising stock-holding costs
(ii) Utilisation of storage space
(iii) Facility to meet customers' requirements, thus avoiding cost of 'stock-outs'
(iv) Incidence of the time lag cycle of production.

(e) "Period costs" refer to the fixed costs to be incurred during an accounting period, e.g. depreciation of fixed assets. Two ways of accounting for the budgeted fixed overheads would be to absorb them by charging a cost per unit, or as a percentage of direct materials.

Chapter 21

17. (a) Standard cost:

	Product C	Product D
Material E	£3·20	£2·40
Material F	2·50	3·00
Total per unit (1)	£5·70	£5·40
Output (2)	12,000	900
(1) multiplied by (2)	£6,840	£4,860

(b) Material cost variance   SC − AC:

C	6,840 − 6,216	£624F
D	4,860 − 5,586	726A
		£102A

(c) (i) Material price variance AQ(SP − AP):

E	7,400 (0·80 − 0·84)	£296A
F	11,400 (0·50 − 0·49)	114F
		£182A

(ii) Material usage variance SP(SQ − AQ):

E	0·80 (7,500 − 7,400)	£80F
F (	0·50 (11,400 − 11,400)	—
		£80F

NOTE:

SQ for E	1,200 × 4	4,800
	900 × 3	2,700
		7,500
SQ for F	1,200 × 5	6,000
	900 × 6	5,400
		11,400

(d) The comment "material losses in production were less than had been allowed for in the standard" could be consistent with the variance analysis. This shows that for E, 100 units of material were saved, either because of the production loss being less than expected, or because production was efficient and so saved 100 units of the material input.

18. (a) Cost of each component:

	A	B	C
Direct materials	£12·00	£8·00	£10·00
Direct wages	12·00	6·00	9·00
Overhead	10·00	5·00	7·50
	£34·00	£19·00	£26·50

(b) Cost per lawn mower:

Direct materials		
Component A	£34·00	
Component B	36·00	
Component C	26·50	£98.50
Purchases		30·00
Direct wages		22·40
Overhead		11·20
Total		£162·10

19. (*a*)
  (*i*) Direct labour total variance:

$$SC - AC$$
£316,000 - £321,000   £15,000A

NOTE:

$$SC = AQ \times SC \text{ per unit}$$
158,000 × £2

(*ii*) Direct labour rate variance:

AH (SR - AR)
2,400 (£4·00 - £4·50)   £1,200A
800 (£4·00 - £3·75)   200F   £1,000A

(*iii*) Direct labour efficiency variance:
SR (SH - AH)
£4·00 (79,000 - 78,000)   £4,000F

(*iv*) Direct labour idle time variance:
A hours idle × SR per hour
2,000 × £4   £8,000A

20.
Direct materials:
  X 10 kg at £1   £10·00
  Y 5 kg at £5   25·00
Direct wages
  5 hours at £3   15·00
Production overhead   30·00
                                  ────────
                                  80·00
Profit   20·00
                                  ────────
Sales price   £100·00
                                  ────────

Direct materials total variance:
SC - AC
£332,500 - £340,800   £8,300A

Direct materials price variance:
AQ (SP - AP)
X   96,000 (£1·00 - £1·20)   £19,200A
Y   48,000 (£5·00 - £4·70)   £14,400F   £4,800A

Direct materials usage variance:
SP (SQ - AQ)
X   £1 (95,000 - 96,000)   £1,000A
Y   £5 (47,500 - 48,000)   £2,500A   £3,500A
                             £8,300A

Direct labour total variance:
SC - AC
£142,500 - £147,200   £4,700A

Direct labour rate variance:

$$AH(SR - AR)$$
$$46,000(£3\cdot00 - £3\cdot20) \qquad £9,200A$$

Direct labour efficiency variance:

$$SR(SH - AH)$$
$$£3(47,500 - 46,000) \qquad £4,500F \qquad £4,700A$$

Overhead total variance:

$$SC - AC$$
$$£285,000 - £290,000 \qquad £5,000A$$

Overhead expenditure variance:

$$BC - AC$$
$$£300,000 - £290,000 \qquad £10,000F$$

Overhead volume variance:

$$SC - BC$$
$$£285,000 - £300,000 \qquad £15,000A \qquad £5,000A$$

Overhead efficiency variance:

$$SC(AQ - SQ)$$
$$£30(9,500 - 9,200) \qquad £9,000F$$

Overhead capacity variance:

$$SC(SQ - BQ)$$
$$£30(9,200 - 10,000) \qquad £24,000A$$
$$= \text{Volume variance (as above)} \qquad £15,000A$$

Sales total variance:

$$BP - AP$$
$$£200,000 - £285,000 \qquad £85,000F$$

Sales price variance:

$$AQ(SP - AP)$$
$$9,500(£20 - £30) \qquad £95,000F$$

Sales volume variance:

$$SP(AQ - BQ)$$
$$£20(9,500 - 10,000) \qquad £10,000A \qquad £85,000F$$

Actual profit

Actual sales		£1,045,000
Direct materials	£340,800	
Direct wages	147,200	
Overhead	290,000	778,000
		£267,000

Profit and loss statement

		31st October
Budgeted sales		£1,000,000
Less Standard cost	10,000 × £80	800,000
Budgeted profit		200,000

Variances:
  Sales:

Price	£95,000F	
Volume	10,000A	£85,000F

  Materials:

Price	4,800A	
Usage	3,500A	8,300A

  Labour:

Rate	9,200A	
Efficiency	4,500F	4,700A

  Overhead:

Expenditure	10,000F		
Efficiency	9,000F		
Capacity	24,000A	5,000A	67,000F

Actual profit		£267,000

NOTE:

In calculating the total variances:

$$SC = AQ \times SC \text{ per unit}$$

9,500 × £35	Direct materials
9,500 × £15	Direct wages
9,500 × £30	Overhead

Index